# MODERN ASIAN PERFORMANCE 1

**Kevin J. Wetmore, Jr** is professor and chair of Theatre Arts at Loyola Marymount University, Los Angeles, USA. He is the co-editor with Siyuan Liu of *The Methuen Drama Anthology of Modern Asian Plays* (Bloomsbury Methuen Drama, 2013) and the author of *Athenian Sun in an African Sky: Modern African Adaptation of Classical Greek Tragedy* (2001), *Black Dionysus: Greek Tragedy and African American Theatre* (2003), *Shakespeare and Youth Culture* (2006) and *Post-9/11 Horror in American Cinema* (Bloomsbury Academic, 2012).

**Siyuan Liu** is assistant professor of Theatre at the University of British Columbia, Vancouver, Canada, and is currently the president of the Association for Asian Performance. He is the co-editor with Kevin J. Wetmore, Jr of *The Methuen Drama Anthology of Modern Asian Plays* (Bloomsbury Methuen Drama, 2014) and the author of *Performing Hybridity in Colonial-Modern China* (Palgrave Macmillan, 2013).

**Erin B. Mee** is assistant professor and faculty fellow of English, Drama, at New York University, USA. She is the author of *The Theatre of Roots: Redirecting the Modern Indian Stage* (2008), co-editor with Helene Foley of *Antigone on the Contemporary World Stage* (2011) and the editor of *Drama Contemporary: India* (2001).

# MODERN ASIAN THEATRE AND PERFORMANCE 1900-2000

*Kevin J. Wetmore, Jr, Siyuan Liu and Erin B. Mee*

*Series Editors: Patrick Lonergan and Erin Hurley*

B L O O M S B U R Y

LONDON • NEW DELHI • NEW YORK • SYDNEY

**Bloomsbury Methuen Drama**

An imprint of Bloomsbury Publishing Plc

| | |
|---|---|
| 50 Bedford Square | 1385 Broadway |
| London | New York |
| WC1B 3DP | NY 10018 |
| UK | USA |

**www.bloomsbury.com**

**Bloomsbury is a registered trademark of Bloomsbury Publishing Plc**

First published 2014

**British Library Cataloguing-in-Publication Data**
A catalogue record for this book is available from the British Library.

ISBN: HB: 978-1-4081-7719-8
PB: 978-1-4081-7718-1
ePub: 978-1-4081-7720-4
ePDF: 978-1-4081-7721-1

**Library of Congress Cataloging-in-Publication Data**
A catalog record for this book is available from the Library of Congress.

Typeset by Deanta Global Publishing Services, Chennai, India
Printed and bound in India

*Dedicated to J. Thomas Rimer*
*Sensei, arigato gozaimashita. Shīfu, xiexie*

# CONTENTS

# ACKNOWLEDGEMENTS

Thanks to Mark Dudgeon, Emily Hockley and the editorial and production teams at Bloomsbury Methuen Drama. Thanks to the series editors and the readers, Patrick Lonergan and Erin Hurley. Thanks to the Hannon Library at Loyola Marymount University, the College of Communication and Fine Arts and the Department of Theatre Arts and Dance.

Thanks to the Association for Asian Performance. We are duly grateful to Girish Karnad, Claire Conceison, Meng Jinghui, the Tsubouchi Shoyo Theatre Museum and Library at Waseda University. Thanks to Kim Tran and Khai Thu Nguyen for their help on Vietnamese theatre. Thanks to our colleagues, friends and teachers in the Association for Asian Performance, and the many fine scholars whose work paved the way: J. Thomas Rimer, Richard Nichols, Samuel Leiter, Donald Keene, Colin Mackerras, M. Cody Poulon, David G. Goodman, Evan Darwin Winet, Kathy Foley, Carol Fisher Sorgenfrei, Brian Powell, Jonah Salz, Ah-jeong Kim, Mariko Boyd, Catharine Diamond and Laurence Kominz.

Thanks to our spouses and families for the support, encouragement and understanding – Guoping Ma, Lacy Wetmore and Shanker Satyanath.

# INTRODUCTION: HYBRIDITY, MODERNITY AND THEATRE

'Asian theatre' in Western theatre histories and scholarship often, if not always, refers to the traditional theatres of Asia: nō, kabuki, jingju (Beijing Opera), kathakali or the shadow puppets of Southeast Asia. Yet for over a century, every nation in Asia has had a vibrant, modern, contemporary theatre developed and shaped by internal and external forces of modernity and culture. Most westerners remain unaware of the modern theatres of Asia due to the dominance of traditional theatres in many theatre histories. These forms are well represented in Western literature, and we hope that the present volume will allow the modern theatres of Asia to be equally appreciated.

The purpose of this book is threefold: to introduce to the English reader the modern theatres of Asia; to present a synoptic history of those theatres, in which parallel developments may be seen and traced; and to contextualise those theatres in the larger intercultural world in which pluralistic theatres develop as a result of cultural exchange in all directions. We seek to avoid simple binaries (East/West, traditional/ modern, etc.) and instead explore theatre history in its complexities and hybridities. We recognise that hybridity can be both intentional and unintentional, conscious or unconscious, the product of an individual or of a society. We also note that all theatre is hybrid and no theatre is pure; thus we simply focus on the hybrid drama that developed after contact with the West in the nineteenth century.[1] It should also be noted that Western drama at the time was also a larger group of interactive hybrids that was further shaped and hybridised by contact with the East (e.g. the theatres of Brecht, Artaud and Yeats).

While chapters proceed chronologically, we do not privilege chronology nor posit a simple, direct and unavoidable teleological journey from pre-modern, pre-colonial Asia to postmodern, present Asia. We invite the reader to think critically about the many modern theatres of Asia as well as to appreciate them. We invite understanding within the context of these theatres on their terms, not on the readers' or on Western ones.

In order to begin, we want to define our terms for clarity. 'Theatre' refers to performance on the stage, as opposed to 'drama' which refers to literature on the page. Modern Asian theatre saw both develop simultaneously, but in many cases the two also developed separately. For example, in Japan in the 1920s, often plays would be published as drama long before they were performed as theatre. Osanai Kaoru, at the opening of the Tsukiji Little Theatre (Tsukiji Shōgekijō) in 1924, controversially announced that it would only perform Western plays in translation, and no work by Japanese playwrights would be presented, as he believed acting evolved separately from playwriting and the modern actors needed to use more sophisticated European texts. Thus, while drama and theatre are intimately intertwined, they sometimes need be separated out in order to understand the theatre and drama of the periods covered in this volume. Likewise, traditional scholarship of Asian theatre tended to privilege the drama (as it was not necessary to journey to Asia to read its plays) and focused on the exotic and the different in performance. More recent scholarship has been much more sophisticated and comprehensive.

Modern drama and theatre are the result of specific cultural forces at work, both individually and collectively, consciously and unconsciously. Modern Asian theatre and drama developed as a result of contact with the West during the early modern period (1500–1900). Put simplistically, foreign drama, especially spoken realistic and naturalistic plays from Europe and America, profoundly shaped modern Asian drama. Contact with the West – either through colonisation or as voluntary modernisation under the threat of colonialism – resulted in theatrical exchanges that resulted in new ways of conceptualising theatre, new ways of doing theatre and new ways of understanding how theatre might work within society for both East and West. We wish to move beyond the simple 'impact-response' model and the tendency to perceive the development of modern Asian drama as a teleological journey from first encounters with European drama to arrive at today's plurality of forms.

Theatre is created and developed on the micro- and macroscales by internal and external cultural forces. It is the product of individual artists and collectives, yet is also the product of sociocultural, religious and political forces. Theatre always occurs within a specific context, created for a specific audience. Drama contains both historicity (the moment in time and place in which it is created) and transhistoricity (how it is read and performed in other, later contexts). For example, the conditions which created *The Recognition of Shakuntala* (Abhijñānaśākuntalam) in late-fourth-century CE India, *The Orphan of Zhao* (Zhaoshi gu'er) in thirteenth-century China, *The Treasury of Loyal Retainers* (Kanadehon Chūshingura) in eighteenth-century Japan, or, for that matter, *Medea* in fifth-century BCE Athens or *Hamlet* in Renaissance England no longer exist, but these plays are still performed in a variety of new contexts and cultures. Something about these dramas still resonates, but resonates differently from the original productions.

Modern drama is the product of the development of modernity. Echoing cultural, scientific, political and technological developments in the early modern period, culminating in the nineteenth century with the works of Darwin, Freud, Marx and Nietzsche, among others, the theatre began to develop the idea of realism, that the stage should reflect the day-to-day reality of human (read: middle and lower classes) existence. Émile Zola (1840–1902), already an advocate for naturalism in literature, in 1880 wrote the influential essay 'Naturalism in the Theatre', endorsing the idea that theatre should prioritise psychology over metaphysics and poetry and that it should present social reality on stage. As part of the larger cultural context, naturalism is also emblematic of the political movements of the time, seeking solidarity with the working classes. As Christopher Innes observes, the naturalistic theatre movement of the nineteenth century combined 'moral experiment and scientific analysis' in order to provide 'a coherent form of stage production' that would transform both theatre and society. Zola's theories from his manifesto were made manifest by André Antoine's Théâtre Libre, founded in Paris in 1887. Antoine created a forum in which naturalistic (as well as other developing dramatic movements such as symbolism and expressionism) might be presented on stage. The first production was an adaptation of a short story by Zola.

Antoine developed a realistic style of staging that would influence the development of modern theatre around the world, just as Antoine's Théâtre Libre would find its imitators (and even namesakes) in the Free Stage (Freie Bühne) of Berlin and the Independent Theatre of London, and the Free Theatre (Jiyū Gekijō) of Tokyo.

While Paris saw the development of the new naturalistic style of acting, dramatist Henrik Ibsen begins his naturalistic period with *Pillars of Society* in 1877, contributing to the development of naturalistic and realistic dramaturgy. Ibsen in many ways represented the dramatist for which Zola was searching. His plays, many of which are still mounted regularly all over the world, followed in rapid succession: *A Doll's House*, containing the so-called 'door slam heard around the world', premiered in 1879, *Hedda Gabler* in 1890 and *John Gabriel Borkman* in 1896, only 13 years before it was produced in Tokyo. *A Doll's House* in particular would prove profoundly influential in Asia, with numerous productions in the first few decades of the twentieth century in Japan and China (indeed, the future Madame Mao Jiang Qing played Nora in Shanghai in 1935 and Ayako Kano argues that Matsui Sumako's performance of Nora in Tokyo literally taught women how to act 'modern').[2]

The Moscow Art Theatre (MAT) was founded by Konstantin Stanislavski and Vladimir Nemirovich-Danchenko in 1898. Anton Chekhov's major plays were all initially produced at the MAT until his death in 1904.[3] The MAT was significant for its contributions to both the dramaturgy and performance. Chekhov's plays (which he considered comedies) are models of realistic drama, brimming with subtext and psychological insight. Stanislavski developed a system of acting that focused initially on the actor's own memory and imagination to craft as realistic a performance as possible. Chekhov, Stanislavski and Ibsen provided a series of models for the development of modern drama all over the world.

In Asia, modernity is made more complex by the fact that it was often imposed from without as part of colonisation, globalisation and contact with the West. Colonial nations such as Vietnam and India and semicolonial nations such as China (which was never fully colonised, but a series of military defeats at the end of the nineteenth century resulted in both foreign-controlled areas in coastal cities, including Shanghai, and trade concessions made by China to the nations of the West and Japan) experienced colonial modernity, which might be seen, as noted above, as 'a complex field of relations as opposed to positively defined elements'.[4] Asian modernity is not monolithic, nor is the modern experience of the nation states of Asia. Japan itself was a coloniser, not colonised (although it also found itself interacting with the nations of the West in an unequal fashion), and imposed its own modern culture on Korea and Taiwan for much of the first half of the twentieth century and on Manchuria and China during the Second World War. Despite resistance from culturally conservative elements in Japanese society and government, Japan's modernity was sought by the nation, not imposed from without, with individuals and organisations embracing Western technology, culture, social values and political structures. This embracing of modernity was echoed to some degree in every Asian nation, in some cases resulting in a comprador class of nationals who exploited their fellow citizens to enrich themselves and the colonisers, and in other cases resulting in artists embracing modernity as a means to change the society progressively.

The modern theatre movement in the nations of Asia thus had two purposes originally: to modernise drama and theatre themselves (often times also creating a new artistic space for individuals shut out of a traditional theatre-making system which relied upon patrilineal succession) and to modernise society by providing new models of behaviour and a means by which to critique perceived negative aspects of traditional culture. To modernise the nation, we must modernise the theatre was the rallying cry of these young, emerging artists. The theatre, which does not mean in and of itself but generates meaning when encountered by an audience, responds to events and movements within the society and culture producing it. Modern Asian drama and theatre thus was used as a tool to transform society but can also be read and studied now as a means of understanding modern Asian history in a different way through those same models for behaviour.

Although each nation of Asia has developed its own modern drama and each of those dramas has its own unique history and characteristics, there are several commonalities that we can outline. Modern theatre in

Asia often was distinguished as a spoken drama, developed as a hybrid of foreign and domestic sources, was initially a theatre by amateurs, was a theatre of the intellectual elite, and was one of the first areas of culture to promote equality for women.

## 'Spoken Drama'

Most, if not all, traditional Asian theatre employs all the elements of performance: music (both instrumental and sung), dance, acting and a prescribed *mise-en-scene*. Performances tend to be stylised and presentational. For example, one might look at jingju (Beijing Opera), kabuki, nō, p'ansori or kathakali to see highly stylised traditional theatres from China, Japan, Korea and India, respectively. Modern theatre from the West provided a radically different conceptualisation of performance that can be understood through the language to describe it. In China, modern drama was called Huaju ('spoken drama'); in Vietnam, the modern theatre is kịch nói ('spoken plays'), and the term 'spoken drama' is used in many cultures in Asia to differentiate the modern theatre from traditional plays in which dialogue was mostly sung or chanted. Modern theatre in Asia is *spoken* theatre.

The Japanese, however, began to refer to the first modern theatre that developed based on Western models as 'shimpa' or 'shinpa', meaning 'new school' of drama, in contrast to kabuki, which was seen as 'old school'. The second theatre that developed was dubbed 'shingeki', which means 'new theatre'. When Western plays were first performed by Europeans in the late nineteenth century, they were often described as 'seiyō kabuki' – Western kabuki. Whereas shinpa was also seen as a variant on kabuki, by the twentieth century, spoken drama in Japan was recognised as an entirely different kind of theatre – a new theatre. This inclination to distinguish between new and old theatre was also true in China in the first two decades of spoken theatre, where it was called 'xinju' (new drama) – as opposed to 'jiuju' (old drama) – or 'wenmingxi' (civilised drama). The term 'huaju' was adopted in the 1920s to emphasise the spoken words, in reaction to wenmingxi's insufficient attention to dramaturgy. Korea, colonised by Japan, was given the Japanese loan word 'shingūk', a Koreanised version of shingeki to describe its modern drama. Korea also inherited shinpa.

## Hybrid Theatres

As Siyuan Liu argues of modern Chinese theatre, we might argue of all modern Asian drama: initial attempts at developing a modern drama follow the same paradigm and results in hybrid drama. All drama is hybrid, from the ancient Greeks on, but in particular, modern Asian drama fuses the traditional performing culture with Western models and practices as well as other intercultural influences. The result is a series of hybrids within modern drama: literary hybrids, translative hybrids and performance hybrids.

Literary hybrids result when playwrights in the target culture employ the dramaturgies of both traditional dramas and European models. Translative hybrids result from translators moving plays from one culture to another, particularly when many of the markers from the source culture need to be changed in order to be understood by audiences in the target culture. For example, Kawakami Otojirō (1864–1911) directed an adaptation of Shakespeare's *Othello* in 1903. The play was not just a translation but an adaptation, as Venice and Cyprus (and their attendant cultural, ethnic and social markers) would not be known to Japanese audiences. So Kawakami set the play in Taiwan (an island nation far enough away to be exotic but close enough to be familiar). Similarly, when the Chinese wenmingxi director Lu Jingruo (1885–1915) adapted Kawakami's version in 1915, at the height of a national crisis prompted by Japan's territorial demand for China's Shandong's Province, Lu made Othello a Chinese general in defence of Manchuria, which Japan would eventually invade. Plays were not merely translated from European languages, they were significantly adapted to be comprehensible to indigenous audiences, to meet local performance tropes and conventions, and even to be reset in local contexts.

Performance hybrids also result from the meetings of two cultures. The aforementioned shinpa is a hybrid of kabuki, keeping the male actor of female roles, the onnagata, and Western drama, also employing

7

women to play some of the female parts. It was often performed in kabuki theatres but with attempts at realistic sets (Kawakami, for example, travelled to Taiwan for research in order to better represent Taiwanese customs and behaviours and the overall scenery in which the play would take place.). Wenmingxi included songs from jingju and local Shanghai performance forms, both actors and actresses performed female roles and most of its productions were based on scenarios and improvisation instead of complete scripts. The writers, actors, directors and producers of modern drama used the drama to educate their audiences about how to watch these new, different plays. Thus the development of modern drama always involves a series of transitions from traditional practices to imported ones. The transformation is never instant, or total, and thus the result is a series of performance (and even theatre-going convention) hybrids.

## A Theatre of Amateurs and Academics

Modern Asian drama develops in each nation with individuals making theatre. Those individuals, as often as not, are attached to particular universities or even secondary schools. Indeed, much modern drama evolves out of both foreign language programmes at Asian secondary schools and institutions of higher learning, especially English and French, as the foreign plays must be translated into the local language by individuals who understand both languages. Universities also tend to be centres of progressive thought and social change, and the impulse to transform society through drama finds root in them. Universities also often have the means of production – buildings, people and resources needed to develop plays. Lastly, universities have always regarded theatre and drama as didactic tools, whether Jesuit schools using theatre as a form of evangelisation or the schools of the European Renaissance encouraging students to perform plays in Greek and Latin in order to learn those languages. Theatre is a tool of education, and modern theatre is a tool of modern education. Many of the modern drama pioneers that you will find in this book are affiliated (at least initially) with these institutions.

Osanai Kaoru, co-founder of both the Jiyū Gekijō (the Free Theatre) in 1909 and the Tsukiji Shōgekijō (Tsukiji Little Theatre) in 1923, took as a slogan, 'We will turn professional actors into amateurs,' by which he meant that for a new theatre to emerge in Japan, Kabuki actors would have to learn a whole new form of theatre and acting.[5] Although Osanai was criticised for this attitude (as Maki Isaka Morinnga notes, why did Osanai want to collaborate with kabuki actors in the first place when he defined shingeki as 'that which is not kabuki'?),[6] it is important to note that Osanai saw the role of the new theatre to be performed by amateurs, in this case, professional actors working in a radically new style. In Japan at the time, professional actors meant kabuki actors, so early experiments in shinpa and shingeki featured kabuki actors.

Conversely, we might also note that the makers of almost all early modern Asian dramas were amateurs working at becoming professionals. Shingeki, huaju and other theatres were professional theatre by amateurs. In the cultures we explore in this book, the inventors of modern Asian theatre were amateurs in the sense that they did something for the love of it, but from the beginning they were also moving towards professionalism, although not commercialism. In Japan, for example, kabuki was seen by shingeki artists as the commercial theatre which they were rebelling against. In China, disillusionment of wenmingxi's overt commercialism led to the rise of an explicit amateur theatre movement known as 'aimeiju' (a transliteration of amateur that also means 'aesthetic drama') in the 1920s.

As a result of both their academic and amateur status, many early theatre artists might also be termed men (and women) of the theatre. These individuals are involved in theatre in multiple capacities: writing, directing, acting, designing, administering their own companies and/or theatres and, if academics, also teaching and writing about theatre and drama (among other things). For modern drama, this means that many early playwrights are not solely playwrights. They also write a wide variety of genres, styles, formats and media, as their dramatic output is part of a larger canon of modernisation. For example, Rabindranath Tagore, Kikuchi Kan and Hu Shi, all seminal figures in the development of modern Indian, Japanese and Chinese theatres, respectively, wrote all matter of materials: poetry, novels, literary studies, essays, short stories. They were teachers, politicians, public intellectuals and philosophers, each in his or her own way.

We might note that amateurism by professionals also indicates other forms of hybridity: the old and the new combined, the amateur and the professional combined, and the indigenous and the Western combined. This hybrid pattern emerges twice in modern Asian drama: once at the origins of modern theatre during the colonial period and then again in the 1960s, when post-colonial, culturalist and leftist-Nationalist movements in the wake of the Second World War and at the height of the Cold War emerge and demand new forms of theatre and drama. Just as the first wave of modern theatre was related to each country's status in global colonialism, the second wave was also tied to specific geographical, political and ideological concern, as evidenced in the independence of former colonies in south and southeastern Asia, Japan's Anti US-Japanese Mutual Security Treaty movement of the 1960s, Korea's democratic demonstrations of the 1970s and 1980s, China's post-Cultural Revolution reawakening in the 1980s and Hong Kong's anxiety over its return to mainland China in 1997. Unlike the first wave of modern theatre that sought to replace indigenous performance with Western theatre, the second wave hybridised indigenous performance traditions with contemporary Euro-American theatre.

## A Theatre of the Educated Elite

One of the ironies of modern drama around the world is that it championed the rights of the working class, purported to depict the reality of working-class life, and was made by artists claiming solidarity with the working class, but the audience was almost always an educated elite. In almost every Asian nation, the emerging modern drama was not a drama by, for and of the people, but a theatre by and for (and ultimately about) the educated middle class who could afford tickets, were interested in modern drama and were educated to understand Ibsen, Chekhov, Strindberg and others.

Eventually, in some nations, a modern drama for the masses would emerge (most notably in China), but even today, the number of people who attend modern, spoken plays is, as it is today in the West, a rather small percentage of the overall population. This is not to suggest that theatre does not have social, political or cultural power, and indeed many of the theatres discussed in this book were at the forefront of movements for social change, whose practitioners were arrested or imprisoned and whose work profoundly shaped their cultures. Overall, however, much of modern Asian theatre history is a history of drama written and theatre produced for an educated elite. At the same time, we also strive to shed light on popular forms of spoken theatre that have been largely ignored by traditional scholarship. The key to understanding this dynamic is to differentiate between plays being read and taught as exemplary literature versus popular theatre enjoyed by the masses. For example, shinpa and wenmingxi were commercial theatres that relied on melodrama and hybrid performance, which shingeki and huaju practitioners and critics have denounced as lesser forms of modern theatre. However, many of their hybrid performance strategies remerged in the post-colonial era. Therefore, studying these popular forms will lead to a more nuanced understanding of modern theatre in Asia.

## New Roles for the 'New Women'

Most traditional theatres of Asia are gender-exclusive. Men and women may not share the stage (India is a notable exception here). In Japan, women were banned from the stage by law in the seventeenth century, even though it was a woman, Okuni no Ise, who developed the form of theatre that became kabuki. There were companies of actresses in China, but for the most part, stages were single-gender and actresses disappeared from the stage for the most part of the Qing Dynasty (1644–1911). In all nations where women appeared on stage, they were associated with prostitution and being sexually available.

Part of the modern theatre movement is also a women's rights movement. Modern drama was seen in many nations as a means to promote women's rights, to interrogate longstanding assumptions and cultural practices rooted in gender and to increase the visibility of women in public. Kawakami Saddayakko (1872–1946) and Matsui Sumako (1886–1919) were hailed as pioneers in Japan for the roles they played. Women's organisations would hire theatres to perform Ibsen's *A Doll's House*, as it was seen to promote women's emancipation from traditional gender roles. In 1914 the all-female Takarazuka Theatre was formed as a wholesome alternative to the all-male kabuki. While claiming to be a finishing school, preparing women for marriage, the Takarazuka school and Theatre Company actually offered acting as a new profession for young women who could take control over their own lives and careers while portraying strong women on stage for mostly female audiences.[7] Obviously, many of the pioneering actresses encountered gender bias. The earliest wenmingxi actresses were at times depicted as seductresses and the genre's first mixed-gender company prompted heated debate of the moral and artistic merits of their performance.

Similarly, female playwrights appeared almost as early as their male counterparts and contributed significant perspectives to modern Asian drama, especially on – but certainly not limited to – the issue of women's fate in the patriarchal family. Okada Yachiyo (1883–1962), Osanai Kaoru's sister, was already an established playwright and novelist by 1909 when Osanai directed *John Gabriel Borkman* at the Free Theatre. Bai Wei's *Dachu youling ta* (Breaking Out of the Ghost Pagada, 1928) was one of the most powerful Chinese plays on women's rebellion against feudal oppression. Women directors emerged in the post-war period, in some cases making theatre by, for and about women and in some cases simply making theatre regardless of gender. Modern theatre created a career path previously unavailable to women in most of Asia.

## Process of Development

The modern theatres of Asia tend to move through the same four phases. The first is of intercultural adaptation, appropriation and hybridisation. This was the period of shinpa and wenmingxi. The second is a rejection of the first model after it became a new, modernist orthodoxy, the period of shingeki and huaju. The third phase is an emergence of nationalistic culture and identity from the 1960s to the 1980s, incorporating a repudiation of the West, which occurs in Japan, Korea and India, as well as China after the Cultural Revolution and a rejection of realism and naturalism by embracing Beckett and theatre of the absurd. The fourth phase (in which we find ourselves now) is one of contemporary pluralism and theatrical globalism. Late modern capitalism and commercialism, combined with postmodern interculturalism, results in a theatrical landscape across Asia that includes traditional theatres, hybrids (including adaptations of Shakespeare too numerous to count), contemporary, youth-oriented plays and the latest Broadway blockbusters translated into the local language. Conversely, globalisation has also made more and more modern Asian theatre available outside of Asia – tours of productions, translations of plays, collaborations with companies and artists in the West mean that those outside of Asia have more access to contemporary Asian theatre than ever before. Likewise, international festivals and regional festivals, such as the BeSeTo Festival (for Beijing, Seoul and Tokyo), which encourage theatrical exchange both within Asia and between Asia and the rest of the world, means that the modern Asian theatre is widely seen all over the world and is mutually influential with the dramas and theatres of many, many nations.

The overall structure of this volume has been determined by Asia's geographic divisions and by the mutually influential theatres that evolved within those areas. We begin with East Asia: Japan, China and Korea. South Asia consists of India, Pakistan, Bhutan, Nepal and Bangladesh. We focus on India, not only because it has, arguably, the largest and most vibrant modern theatre but also because it is the theatre that dominates and influences its geographic region. Southeast Asia is further subdivided into the mainland nations (consisting of Vietnam, Laos, Cambodia, Thailand and Myanmar), and the Maritime nations of the islands and peninsulas (consisting of Malaysia, Indonesia, The Philippines, East Timor, Brunei and Singapore). Even though we have divided the nations geographically, there is a large amount of pan-Asian influence and overlap of languages and ethnicities. Malaysia and

Singapore have large Chinese-language populations and thus large Chinese-language theatre. Singapore also has a significant modern English-language theatre, for example.

Our focus is, as the title suggests, 1900–2000, but these are arbitrary dates in the grand scheme of history. Modern theatre in Japan begins three decades before then, and practices and people did not stop with the turn of the millennium. Nor did traditional theatres stop because modern theatre developed, and likewise the modern and traditional theatres often interacted and developed hybrid forms throughout their respective histories. Thus, we caution the reader against removing modern drama and performance from the cultural contexts in which they originated and against seeing the journey as a simple teleology from traditional to modern, as if a switch had been thrown. It is our hope that the reader will see the rich, interactive panoply of modern theatre across Asia, with all its similarities and differences.

We begin in East Asia, with Japan, as modern Asian theatre in East Asia began in Japan and spread to China and Korea, specifically through students studying in Japan and returning to their home countries, bringing the model of modern, Western-influenced drama with them. Chapter 1 covers Japan from the Meiji Restoration in 1868 through the defeat of Japan in the Second World War, the occupation by the United States and its allies and ending with the rise of the post-occupation realistic theatre. Chapter 2 surveys Japanese theatre beginning with the radical changes in the 1960s moving through the apolitical 1980s to the millennium, with a quick glance at contemporary theatre in the wake of the twentieth century. Chapters 3, 4 and 5 present a survey of modern Chinese drama. Chapter 3 covers the development of huaju from the turn of the century to 1949, while Chapter 4 considers drama and theatre in the People's Republic of China, which was founded in 1949. Chapter 5 considers modern Chinese drama outside the mainland, with a particular focus on Taiwan and pre-handover Hong Kong. The sixth chapter canvasses the history of modern Korean theatre and performance from 1910 to the end of the century, through Japanese occupation, the split of the peninsula into two nations and the development of the respective post-war theatres in the Republic of Korea (South Korea) and the

Democratic People's Republic of Korea (North Korea). Two chapters on India follow. The first examines the history and development of many different modern Indian dramas and the influence of colonialism on modern Indian theatre, while the second is an analysis of the work of two particular individuals who transformed modern Indian theatre: Kavalam Narayana Panikkar and Girish Karnad. Lastly, Chapter 9 surveys the modern theatres of the eleven nations of mainland and maritime Southeast Asia.

The volume is intended to be a critical companion – not merely listing historical events and the players in chronological order but also providing analysis, interpretation, historical context, cultural context and a bigger picture. The larger purpose of the volume is to introduce modern Asian theatre and performance of the twentieth century within its context and provide the reader with avenues to explore and plays to read (in translation), and allow the reader to see the larger map of modern Asia, rather than focus on a single nation or culture.

We also believe that the study of modern theatre involves much more than the subject matter. To study modern Asian theatre and performance is to encounter and explore colonialism, feminism, economics, religion, politics and culture far beyond the theatre. As a social art form that engages the issues of concern to the society that produces it, the theatre reflects the people, their fears, their controversies, their conflicts and their concerns. The artists discussed in this volume frame every aspect of the culture in which they work. To understand modern Asian theatre is to understand modern Asian society. Likewise, in studying the modern Asian theatre, we can begin to examine how Asian nations responded to the pressures of modernity and even how the various cultures conceive of the idea of 'nation'.

Siyuan Liu wrote the chapters on China and the Chinese diaspora; Erin B. Mee was responsible for the chapters on India and Kevin J. Wetmore, Jr was the primary author on Japan, Korea and Southeast Asia. The volume, however, represents our collective work as Asian theatre scholars and artists in our own right, sharing a love of modern Asian drama and theatre. We hope our efforts inspire appreciation, interest and perhaps even love on the part of the reader as well.

## A Note on Names

In writing the names of individuals in this volume, we have followed the culture under discussion to determine the format. Thus, Western names are written with given name first, followed by surname, as are many Indian names (although some ethnic groups in India have different traditions and some groups, such as the Tamil, do not have a history of using family or surnames, or in Kerala, where people have the initials of their mother, followed by a first name – except in families where people have become Westernised and have a first and last name). Chinese, Japanese and Korean names are written surname first, then given name, as in keeping with the practices in those cultures. In Vietnamese, however, name order is family name, middle name and then given name. Like India, Indonesia has multiple practices, although in many cases there is no family name (such as with Suharto and Sukarno), or two personal names, or given name first, followed by either family name or names of parents. In any case, we follow the practice of the culture under discussion.

# CHAPTER 1
## MODERN JAPANESE THEATRE THROUGH THE OCCUPATION

Modern spoken drama in Japan, as in the rest of Asia, was ultimately built on Western models in response to social, artistic and cultural pressures, but also often reacted against Western influence during its century-long existence. Furthermore, Japan did not develop a single new drama in response to modernity, but rather several different forms emerged in response to modernity, some concurrently and some consecutively. As J. Thomas Rimer formulates, in the scramble to modernise after opening up to the world following two centuries of self-imposed exile, Japanese theatre artists and cultural reformers were confronted with the choice of 'modernisation' versus 'westernisation'.[1] Either the kabuki as the contemporary theatre of the masses could be modernised or a theatre based on Western models could be created. First, the former was tried, perceived to have failed and rejected, so then the latter occurred. 'Shin-kabuki' (new kabuki) represented an attempt to modernise theatre as it was. 'Shinpa' (new school drama) represented a hybrid, an attempt to build a theatre on Western models employing elements of the kabuki as well. 'Shingeki' (new drama) represented a theatre wholly based on Western models. All three will be explored in depth, below.

Ayako Kano describes the difference between the two hybrid forms as that shinpa entailed 'borrowing useful plots from Western plays and adapting them into Japanese theatre', whereas shingeki involved 'making Japanese theatre as western as possible'.[2] In other words, shinpa makes Western drama Japanese; shingeki makes Japanese theatre Western. Shingeki ultimately emerges triumphant and becomes the heart of modern theatre in Japan, although both shin-kabuki and shinpa will continue to be performed to the present day.

This chapter will also consider changes over time. The original shingeki sought to reproduce European theatre as exactly as possible, down to blonde wigs and fake noses for the actors so they would look 'European'. Later generations sought to assimilate shingeki, making it 'Japanese', no longer seeking to play westerners *qua* westerners on stage but to mount social realism and psychological realism for the purposes of transforming society. Both in this initial form and in the changes over time, we might also perceive a tension over Japanese identity, as well as a tension in its relationship to the West. Beginning in the 1930s, shingeki might be seen as part of the larger national conversation on Japanese identity, alternately looking to the West for models and rejecting the West as fundamentally un-Japanese.

David G. Goodman, one of the leading scholars on modern Japanese drama, provides a useful schema for thinking about the history of modern Japanese theatre, which he divides into five periods.[3] First is the establishment of the modern theatre, from 1887 to 1928, followed by the politicisation of that theatre from 1928 to 1945. Goodman also refers to these two periods together as 'the exile of the gods', as Japanese popular theatre, which had always featured the supernatural, the divine and the fantastic, saw a commitment to realism that entailed banishing those elements from the stage. From 1945 to 1960, realism modelled after Western drama became the dominant form of modern drama. Modernist realism was the heart of modern Japanese theatre. In the wake of the war, the occupation and the crisis sparked by the renewal of the mutual security treaty *Anpo jōyaku* (AMPO), the younger generation of theatre artists rejected this orthodox realism. Thus Goodman terms the period from 1960 to 1973 'the return of the gods', in which experimental theatre attempted to reconnect with pre-modern and pre-Western Japanese culture, developing a variety of hybrid forms. The mid-1970s to the present is a period of theatrical diversity, marked by continuity and discontinuity and continued tensions with the past, with the West and with competing (and ever-shifting) ideas of Japanese identity.

In this chapter we will first consider the historical and theatrical context of modernity as well as the traditional theatre. We shall then consider the attempts to reform kabuki and some of the early hybrids. Shinpa and shingeki will then each be considered in turn, alongside other forms that develop, such as the Takarazuka or the New National Theatre (*shinkokugeki*) of the 1920s. The bulk of the chapter will be on the history of shingeki: its origins, internal splits, wartime and occupation activities and its development as a form. As readers engage this history, they should remember that modern Japanese theatre, regardless of form and genre, is always an intercultural, international hybrid, in tension with the West and the Japanese past, always moving towards assimilation into Japanese culture. Shingeki audiences in the 1920s thought they were watching a foreign form; shingeki audiences of the 1950s thought they were watching Japanese theatre that had Western origins. Lastly, we should also consider Japan as site of modernity disseminated. Students from China and Korea experienced modern, spoken drama for the first time in Japan and brought it back to their home nations with them. The first modern plays in Chinese and Korean were performed first in Japan. Thus, in a genuine sense, Japan is the origin point for modern theatre and drama in all of East Asia.

## Traditional Theatre and the Historical Context of Modernity

In 1600, Tokugawa Ieyasu defeated his rivals at the Battle of Sekigahara, resulting in the emperor designating him Shogūn, the supreme military ruler of Japan. As a result, Japan was finally unified under a single government which Tokugawa then located in Edo, modern-day Tokyo. By this point there had been a European presence in Japan for almost six decades. In 1542 three Portuguese sailors landed in Japan, followed by Portuguese Jesuits (including the famous St Francis Xavier), Dutch traders and still others seeking trade, conquest and conversion.

Although initially welcomed, these *gaijin* (literally 'outside person' in Japanese, meaning foreigner) soon fell under suspicion. Toyotomi Hideyoshi, the previous ruler of Japan, ordered all Christian missionaries to leave the country in 1587, although the edict was not strictly enforced until a decade or so later. Finally, in 1639, Tokugawa Iemitsu, Ieyasu's grandson and successor, decided to close the country to foreigners entirely, with the exception of the Dutch and the Chinese, who were allowed limited trade on a man-made island in Nagasaki harbour, and the Koreans, who were allowed limited trade on Iki Island off the coast of Honshu. In short, Japan closed its doors to any outside influence for over two centuries.

The theatre during this time consisted primarily of four types of what we now think of as the traditional theatres of Japan. Nō developed in the fourteenth century at the court of the Ashikaga Shogunate (1336–1573). Zeami Motokiyo and his father Kan'ami, dancers of a form of court dance called *Sarugaku* that emerged out of Chinese court dance, further shaped it into a narrative dance form designed to have an emotional impact on the audience. Alongside nō, a comic theatre called kyogen also developed. Kyogen was shorter, spoken comic dialogues that alternated with the more serious nō plays. The culture of nō was profoundly influenced by Zen Buddhist aesthetics and was patronised by the Shogūn and the emperor, thus making it the theatre of the aristocracy.

The primary theatres of the masses developed in the seventeenth century, sharing a common dramatic repertory. Kabuki began at the start of the seventeenth century when a shrine priestess named Okuni no Izu began dancing in the dry Kamo River bed in Kyoto. Government censorship led to women being banned from the stage, followed by boys being banned from the stage when they took up the mantle of this new theatre called kabuki, literally meaning 'a little strange'. By mid-century, the kabuki was an all-male theatre aimed at spectacle and entertainment. It was the theatre of the merchant classes. Simultaneously, bunraku, a puppet theatre involving three puppeteers for each puppet, evolved by combining a more simple one-man street puppetry form with the music of the biwa, a four- or five-stringed lute-like instrument, and a form of narrative storytelling called jōruri. The original name for this art was *ningyōjōruri*, literally 'doll story-telling songs'. Bunraku grew sophisticated, and by the early seventeenth century, kabuki actors complained that the puppets were more popular than they were.

Kabuki and bunraku share a common dramatic repertory. Playwrights wrote primarily for one or the other, and the other form would perform the plays as well. Some of the most famous dramas in Japanese history such as *The Story of the Loyal 47 Rōnin* (*Kanadehon Chūshingura*), *The Love Suicides at Sonezaki* (*Sonazaki Shinjū*) and *The Love Suicides at Amijima* (*Shinjū ten no Amijima*) were written for the puppet theatre and rapidly adapted for kabuki. Other plays were written specifically for the kabuki, based on nō and kyogen originals, such as *The Subscription Scroll* (*Kanjinchō*), *The Maiden at Dojoji* (*Musume Dōjōji*) and *Mirror Lion* (*Kagami Jishi*). Many plays written for *both* kabuki and bunraku were inspired by true stories. The Bakufu (Shogun's government), however, wary of the power of theatre to rally the masses, banned true stories from the stage, so playwrights developed a practice called *mitate* (disguise), whereby stories based on real events were set in the distant past and linked to a different set of circumstances. For example, *Kanadehon Chūshingura* was based on a series of events which took place between 1701 and 1703. The playwrights set the play in the Muromachi period, four hundred years earlier, and changed the names slightly: Kuranosuke became Yuranosuke and Kira became Ko no Moronao, for example. This practice of using contemporary events to speak to the merchant and working classes of urban Japan made kabuki and bunraku the contemporary theatres of Japan until the late nineteenth century.

In July 1853, Commodore Matthew Perry sailed into Edo Bay with fifty-four ships, demanding to present a letter from President Millard Fillmore requesting a trade treaty with the government of Japan. He returned in February of 1854 and on 31 March 1854 the Treaty of Kanagawa was signed, supposedly maintaining the closed-door policy, but allowing American ships to dock at the harbours of Nagasaki, Shimoda and Hakodate. In February 1855, Russia and Japan signed the Treaty of Shimoda, granting them access to treaty ports. Other European powers rapidly followed with similar treaty demands.

The reaction in Japan was one of a nation divided. Conservative faction resisted the opening of the nation, and competing interests resulted in the weakening of the shogunate, an unstable economy and attacks on foreigners. This period (1853–67) is referred to as the *bakumatsu* (literally 'end of the curtain'). The slogan 'Sonnōjōi' ('Revere the emperor! Expel the barbarians!') became popular. Unrest and resistance to the bakufu grew, until the final crisis of 1867. Crown Prince Meiji (then fifteen years old) ascended the throne. Later that year, Yoshinobu, the last Tokugawa shogun, stepped down as leader of the government, and power was placed in a bicameral legislature with the emperor as the titular head of the nation. This became known as the Meiji Restoration (1868). Emperor Meiji (1852–1912) became an active participant, both in politics and in the reform and modernisation of Japan.

The Meiji era (1868–1912) became one of rapid modernisation across all aspects of Japanese society and culture. During this period, Japan transformed from a pre-industrial, feudal society with limited contact with the outside world to a highly industrialised, highly modernised world power with imperial ambitions of its own. Japan built huge industries in a matter of years, engaging in a rapid industrial revolution, which also brought about substantial urbanisation. The military was also modernised, the samurai abolished, universal conscription instituted and Japan proved itself a modern power by winning the Sino-Japanese War (1894–5) and the Russo-Japanese War (1904–5). Having seen the colonisation of the rest of Asia, Japan was determined not only to avoid that fate but also to be a power equal to that of the United States and European nations.

It is in this context in which modern drama developed. The theatre was seen as part and parcel of the modernisation project of the Meiji era. The theatre artists themselves responded to events and movements of their time. The rapid urbanisation of Japan also produced large audience bases for theatre makers, although Tokyo was and is the heart of the modern theatre of Japan. As Mari Boyd observes: 'Although modern Japanese theatre is commonly treated as a monolithic whole, the term in practice refers mainly to the theatre generated and consumed in the Kantō area, i.e. Tokyo, Kawasaki, Yokohama, Saitama, and Chiba. A center versus periphery dichotomy underlies this phenomenon, in which the dominance of the former practically guarantees the erasure of the latter.'[4] Studies in both Japanese and English privilege the greater Tokyo area theatre history and performance culture, although in fairness, the greater share of modern theatre practice is in Tokyo. Whenever possible, this chapter will consider modern drama from outside the centre as well.

Lastly, it is also important to remember that just nine years after the Meiji Restoration, Henrik Ibsen wrote *Pillars of Society* (1877), considered his first 'contemporary' play, followed two years later by *A Doll's House* (1879). In other words, contemporaneous with Japanese modernisation is the advent and evolution of the naturalism movement in Europe. Realism was being invented at the same time that modern Japan was, and the latter looked to the former as a model for its own modern theatre. Ibsen would serve as a significant model for Japan (and China and Korea). The modern theatre in Japan was developing simultaneously with the modern theatre of the West.

## A Desire to Change the Nation and the Theatre

As part of the drive to modernise the nation, the arts were also called to transform, or, more accurately, 'reform' (*kairyō*). The government's official program was 'civilisation and enlightenment' (*bunmeikaika*), designed to modernise all aspects of Japanese culture, including the theatre. The purpose was twofold: first, to modernise the theatre itself so it would be the equivalent of the 'civilised' theatres of Europe, and second, to use the theatre to promote social and cultural reforms. Kabuki was seen as 'lewd', and reformers wished to purge it of the sexual content, prostitution, excessive violence and unsavoury characters that dominated late Meiji kabuki. Once these negative characteristics were eliminated, the reformers argued, the theatre could be used positively. Donald Keene reports a newspaper editorial arguing for the use of theatre to present models of modernity for popular audiences: 'If we borrow the actors' mouths, what will the public not obey?'[5] The theatre was perceived as a pedagogical institution to promote modernisation.

Reform also helped the theatre makers. Actors were freed from pre-Meiji social status as outcasts and *hinin* (non-human); now actors are considered *heimin* (common people), and were seen as beneficial to society. In 1872 actors were placed under the control of the Ministry of Religious Education (*Kyōbushō*). In 1882 actors were required to be licensed by the government and pay taxes. These changes to the profession legitimised actors and the theatre, but did not go far enough.

The Theatre Reform Movement (*Engeki Kairyō Undō*) began in the 1880s with the founding of the Society for Theatre Reform (*Engeki Kairyōkai*). Suematsue Kencho (1855–1920), son-in-law of Prime Minister Itō Hirobumi and a journalist and law student who studied at Cambridge University from 1881 to 1886, returned to Japan as one of the founders of Engeki Kairyōka. Some members of the group wanted to superficially change the offensive content of kabuki without eliminating its fundamental qualities. Others wanted to eliminate every defining characteristic: the onnagata, the hanamichi, the music, the make-up and so forth. Under Suematsue, Engeki Kairyōka had three major goals: first, to eliminate vice and promote virtue on stage, second, to promote new drama, and third, to build modern theatre buildings.

Other members advocated further reforms. Tsubouchi Shōyō (1858–1935), who had begun translating Shakespeare into Japanese in 1884 and who would play a major role in the development of shingeki, wanted to reform playwriting. Mori Ōgai (1862–1922) wanted drama separated into musical and non-musical categories. Then, in 1887, something happened that further legitimised theatre: the imperial spectatorship of kabuki (*tenran kabuki*), meaning the emperor Meiji attended a kabuki show. In that same year, Engeki Kairyōkai disbanded in 1887, but in 1888 the Japan Entertainment Moral Reform Society (*Nihon Engei Kyōfydai*) was formed. Popular and academic organisations continued to push for the 'reform' of theatre.

## Reform Kabuki and Shin-kabuki

In 1872, at the opening of the Shintomi-za, in front of several thousand guests, including prime minister Sanjō Saneyoshi, kabuki actor Ichikawa Danjūrō IX (1838–1903), in tails, read a speech in which he announced:

When one thinks back upon it, the theatre of recent years has drunk up filth and has smelled of the coarse and the mean.

It has discarded the beautiful principle of rewarding good and chastising evil, it has fallen into mannerisms and distortions, it has been flowing steadily downhill. Perhaps at no time has this tendency been more marked than now. I, Danjūrō, am deeply grieved by this fact, and in consultation with my colleagues, I have resolved to clean away the decay.[6]

In the previous year, 1871, Danjūrō performed 'realistically' in the kabuki play *Sanada Komura*, serving as the beginning of his attempt to modernise the kabuki and perform plays centred on historical accuracy and realism.

Partnering with Morita Kan'ya XII (1846–97), producer, theatrical impresario and builder of the Shintomi-za, Danjūrō sought to simultaneously reform the kabuki and modernise it. He turned to playwright Kawatake Mokuami (1816–93) for dramas that would reflect the new modern Japan to be performed by the kabuki. Mokuami began to write 'living history' plays (*katsurekimono*). As per Danjūrō's promise, these plays rejected the salaciousness of late Tokugawa kabuki and offered greater verisimilitude and topicality. The 1878 play *Two Bows and the Multifaceted Shigeto* (*Nichō no Yumi Chigusa no Shidedō*) by Kawatake Mokuami was the first to be called katsureki by critic Kanagaki Rōbun (1829–94), who did not intend it as a compliment.[7] Other representative katsureki mono include Mokuami's *Peony Tales of the Heike* (*Natori Gusa Heike Monogatari*, 1876) and *Takatoki* (*Takatoki*, 1884). Katsurekimono were supported by scholars and reformers but never caught on with the general public and were abandoned by 1886.

Similarly, Danjūrō's rival Onoe Kikugorō V (1844–1903) asked Mokuami to write modern kabuki plays for him to perform in. The result was 'crop-hair plays' (*zangirimono*). As the reforms of the Meiji period took hold, an obsession with the surface elements of Western culture and modernity took hold over the middle and upper classes. Kimonos were discarded in favour of Western suits, bowler hats and pocket watches became the rage, and topknots (*chonmage,* the hairstyle of the samurai) were cut off, resulting in 'crop hair plays': plays that featured modern men without topknots. Twenty-four plays and fourteen dances were produced in the style, most written by Mokuami and performed by Onoe Kikugorō V. These plays, however, merely replicated the external aspects of modern life within traditional kabuki dramatic structures and performance conventions, and the genre was abandoned in 1882.

The next attempt to modernise the kabuki came in the form of shin-kabuki (new kabuki). Rather than a new dramatic genre, as zangiri and katsureki mono were, shin-kabuki developed its own performance conventions. Developing later than the reform kabuki and occurring simultaneously as shinpa and shingeki, shin-kabuki should not just be seen as a step in the evolution of modern drama, especially because it continued to exist after the other forms developed and some of its plays are in the repertory of the traditional kabuki. Similarly, some artists worked in more than one form. Playwrights especially would write for shin-kabuki, shinpa and shingeki.

'Shin-kabuki' was coined in 1919 by Kusuyama Masao (1884–1950) to refer to kabuki plays written under Western influence. Since then the term has been employed to refer to kabuki from late Meiji on that was written by playwrights not formally attached to the kabuki (often scholars and novelists), influenced by Western dramaturgy while still employing the apparatus of kabuki. Music is employed only when the context justifies it. Plays feature greater stage realism and focus on character psychology. Traditional acting, dramatic poses (*mie*), special effects (*keren*), acrobatics, stylised stage fights (*tachimawari*) and stylised make-up (*kumadori*) are all eschewed in favour of a more realistic approach. Tsubouchi Shōyō's *Paulownia Leaf* (*Kiri Hitoha* published 1894, staged 1904) is considered the first shin-kabuki play. Certain kabuki actors were drawn to the new form, pioneers including Onoe Kikugorō VI (1885–1949) and Ichikawa Sadanji II (1880–1940), who went to Europe in 1906 to study theatre and returned the following year embracing modern theatre and driving him to be one of the pioneers of shingeki as well, co-founding the Jiyū Gekijō in 1909.

As noted above, the dramatic repertory of shin-kabuki was different from that of traditional kabuki in that the playwrights were not attached to the kabuki or from the kabuki world. Instead, writers outside the theatre began writing for the theatre. Okamoto Kidō (1872–1939), for example, was a student of Chinese and English literature who began writing published but unperformed plays in 1896. Ultimately he wrote 196 plays, mostly for the kabuki. His plays were actor driven, eliminating music and dance and instead offering realistic treatments of historic subjects. He began writing plays for Ichikawa Sadanji II, including *The American Envoy* (*Amerika no Tsukai*, 1909), about Townsend Harris, the first American ambassador to Japan, in honour of the fiftieth anniversary of the opening of the port of Yokohama; *The Tale of Shūzen Temple* (*Shūzenji Monogatari*, 1911) concerning a mask maker and his daughter, which is considered his first great work; and *Banchō Sarayashiki* (1916), a modern interpretation of a popular bunraku play. He was well known for presenting traditional subject matter in modern terms, such as in *Onoe and Idahachi* (*Onoe Idahachi*, 1915), which portrays the repercussions of a botched love-suicide on the participants and their families.

Similarly, Mayama Seika (1879–1948) was first and foremost a novelist who also wrote a few early shingeki plays, notably *The First Man* (*Daiichininsha*, 1907) and *If He Had Not Been Born* (*Umarezarishi Naraba*, 1908), and shinpa dramas, including the popular historical drama *Gembokuand Chōei* (*Gembokuto Chōei*, 1924). Altogether he wrote sixty plays; after 1928, his focus was on shin-kabuki, writing a ten-play cycle based on Japan's national epic *Kanadehon Chūshingura* called *Genroku Chūshingura* (1934–41), a realistic retelling of the story of the puppet play infused with psychology and a more naturalistic presentation. Other shin-kabuki playwrights include Mori Ōgai, Matsui Shyō (1870–1933), Oka Onitarō (1872–1943) and Takayasu Gekkō (1869–1944), all of whom both built on tradition within the kabuki and brought modern ideas and dramaturgy to the form.

While shin-kabuki plays continue to be performed to this day, it is no longer a modernising force transforming the kabuki, but fully incorporated into the kabuki world. Kabuki crystallises in one sense – the actors and artists of kabuki continue to perform in the style of late Meiji kabuki to the present day. Until the moment of shin-kabuki, kabuki itself was the contemporary theatre of Japan, with new scripts being constantly written and actors continually developing their art through experiment. While kabuki remains a living form, the popular presentation of kabuki today is Meiji kabuki.

## Shinpa

If kabuki reforms represented an attempt to modernise the indigenous Japanese theatre by making a hybrid of kabuki with Western dramaturgy, then the next step in the evolution of modern drama represented an attempt to create a hybrid based on Western models incorporating elements of the kabuki. Shinpa, 'new school', was a fusion form that also blended indigenous and foreign, traditional and modern. M. Cody Poulton states 'shinpa melodrama provided the theatrical bridge between tradition and modernity in Japan'.[8]

Kabuki had held a virtual monopoly on Japanese theatre, and only a rare few who were not born into the kabuki world would be allowed to participate. Japanese government until the Meiji Restoration had also been a closed world, run by the Bakufu and the shogun. The Meiji Restoration suddenly opened up both worlds, the theatrical and the political, to new participation. Shinpa ('new school drama'), in fact, was the direct result of those openings. Political opposition parties formed in the 1880s and employed popular culture as a means to get their messages to the public, and so theatre was also used.

In Osaka, Sudo Sadanori (1867–1907), a former journalist, policeman and leader of the Liberal Party, began to stage agitprop dramas in 1887. These amateur productions mark the beginning of shinpa. Known as 'hooligan plays' (sōshishibai), the dramas were political in nature, designed to push a progressive agenda and open politics to those from outside the samurai caste. The plays were more realistic than the kabuki, and, as the name suggests, were performed by young political activists.

Shinpa continued to develop with Kawakami Otojirō (1864–1911), a failed politician turned theatrical impresario. Kawakami initially became famous singing 'Oppekepe', a vulgar, topical, satirical nonsense song during an interlude in his 1891 production of *Itagaki-jun Sōnan*

*Jikki* (*Disaster Strikes Itagaki: A True Story*), a *sōshishibai* about the 1882 assassination attempt on liberal politician Itagaki Taisuke (1837–1919). Both the play and the song were commercial successes, driving Kawakami to develop additional documentary dramas. He produced a series of sensational dramas based on true crime stories entitled *Strange!* (*Igai*), *Strange Again!* (*Mata Igai*) and *Strange Yet Again!* (*Mata Mata Igai*). Proving himself to be a shrewd self-promoter despite a lack of theatrical training, Kawakami claimed he took his company to the front in Korea during the Sino-Japanese War (1894–5), returning to Japan to stage elaborate recreations of the battles in plays like *The Sublime, the Delightful Sino-Japanese War* (*Sōzetsu Kaizetsu Nisshin Sensō*) and *Kawakami Otojirō's Battlefield Report* (*Kawakami Otojirō Senchi Kembunki*), in which he played himself at the front.

Tsubouchi Shōyō referred to Kawakami as 'the Osaka clown', but Kawakami proved an ability to pander to audience's taste for novelty, as well as a genuine desire to create new forms of theatre. Marrying the former geisha Sadayakko (1872–1946), Kawakami set out in April 1899 with eighteen company members and his wife, returning to Japan in 1901, touring the United States and Europe again from 1902 to 1903 and again from 1907 to 1908, making them the first Japanese theatre company to perform in the West. They performed in Honolulu, San Francisco, Seattle, New York, Washington, D.C., London, Paris, Moscow and Stockholm. They performed a play entitled *Bushi to Geisha* (translated as *The Knight and the Geisha*), playing in front of presidents and monarchs and crowds all over Europe, calling themselves 'The Imperial Court Theatre of Japan'.

Having watched Henry Irving and Ellen Terry perform *The Merchant of Venice*, Kawakami announced his company would perform the trial scene in Japanese, marking the beginning of a long career as one of the first Shakespearean performers in Japan. Returning to Tokyo after the first tour, Kawakami called his style 'true drama' (*seigeki*), to distinguish it from kabuki. Kawakami meant 'true' in the sense of 'straight' theatre – pure drama without singing and dancing, modelled after Western naturalism. He proceeded to present productions of *Hamlet* (famous for including a bicycle in the production, on which Hamlet entered, riding down the hanamichi of the rented kabuki theatre), *Othello* (which Kawakami reset from Cyprus to Taiwan) and, of course, *The Merchant of Venice*.

While his contemporaries disparaged him as a low-class showman, Kawakami was an intercultural pioneer who contributed a number of innovations to the modern Japanese theatre, not the least of which was his promotion of the use of actresses. Shinpa initially relied upon onnagata, as it modelled itself in part on kabuki. Kawakami Sadayakko, however, performed on stage with the Kawakami company, despite it being illegal for her to do so, as mixed gender companies were not allowed. The Kawakamis also opened the first school for actresses in 1908, the Imperial Actress School, paving the way for women to be on stage for the first time since the beginning of the seventeenth century. The ban was finally lifted by law in 1891 but it was not until fifteen years later that it became socially acceptable.

After Kawakami Otojirō's death in 1911, Sadayakko continued to perform in plays such as Oscar Wilde's *Salome*, but she was increasingly criticised for her melodramatic performances and mannered style, which could not compete with the younger actresses emerging in shingeki, and so she retired in 1917. The work of the Kawakamis, however, paved the way for actresses such as Mizutani Yaeko (1905–79), who debuted on stage in 1913 at age eight and went on to perform in shinpa, shingeki and eventually film. Her work on stage in the 1920s led to a shinpa revival, although she was also famous for her shingeki roles, including Nora in *A Doll's House* and even Hamlet in *Hamlet* in 1933. Shinpa's great contribution to modern Japanese theatre was the introduction of actresses, both for the social progress they represented along with the theatrical progress they represented: true naturalism was now possible.

The shinpa of the Kawakamis, however, was superseded by another kind that also developed in the last decade of the nineteenth century, pioneered by actor Ii Yōhō (1871–1932), emphasising shinpa's artistic potential rather than its novelty. Actors Takada Minoru (1899–1977), Kawai Takeo (1877–1942) and Kitamura Rokurō (1871–1961), the last two being onnagata, all managed shinpa theatres with large audiences, presenting popular plays. Source material for drama came from newspaper serials, novels or kabuki plays. Following Kawakami's model from the Sino-Japanese War, numerous shinpa companies presented documentary dramas about the Russo-Japanese War of 1904–5 with titles such as *The Imperial Army Vanquishes the Russians* (*Seiro no Kōgun*), *The Fall of Port Arthur* (*Ryojun-kō Kanraku*) and *Battle Report Drama* (*Senkyō Hōkoku Engeki*), the last featuring Kawakami as himself once again, attempting to recapture his former glory.

One popular shinpa playwright was Izumi Kyōka (1873–1939), who began writing melodramatic fiction in the late nineteenth century. Shinpa artists adapted his stories for the stage, including *Loyal Blood, Valliant Blood* (*Giketsukyōketsu*), adapted for the stage by Kawakami in 1894. Izumi, however, took exception to the changes made in adaptation and began writing his own plays in 1900, moving away from melodrama and into mythology and the supernatural. His shinpa dramas were more gothic than sentimental, and in plays such as *Demon Pond* (*Yashagaike*, 1913), *The Sea God's Villa* (*Kaijinbessō*, 1913) and *Tale of the Castle Tower* (*Tenshu Monogatari*), strange creatures, surrealistic plots and mythic subject matter resulted in a different kind of shinpa, one that moved away from realism and back towards the fantastic of late Tokugawa kabuki.

By the end of the first decade of the twentieth century, shinpa had stagnated. The rise of shingeki combined with the advent of cinema, which was first shown commercially in Japan in 1903, created greater competition for audiences at a time when shinpa began to run out of novelties. The nationalistic fervour possible in wartime dramatisations ended with the signing of the Treaty of Portsmouth in September 1905, and audience taste for sentimentality and melodrama began to wane. Shinpa experienced revivals in 1917, in the mid-1920s, thanks to Mizutani Yaeko and in the early 1930s, but declined after the war. Although there was a brief shinpa revival in the 1950s, lack of new actors, an aging audience and changes in popular taste caused a rapid wane in the 1960s. While shinpa is important both as a hybrid mode of performance and as the theatre form that first presented Western dramas on the stages of Japan, and while it is still performed sporadically today in small theatres to self-selecting audiences, it was eventually eclipsed by shingeki, and the form proved to be an evolutionary dead end for modern theatre.

## Shingeki

The word 'shingeki' was first used in 1913 in reference to a production by Shimamura Hōgetsu (1871–1918) and Matsui Sumako (1886–1919), but historians retroactively apply it to the 1909 production of Ibsen's *John Gabriel Borkman* at the Jiyū Gekijō (Free Stage) under the direction of Osanai Kaoru (1881–1928). It is now often employed as an umbrella term for modern theatre based on Western models – so Stanislavskian realism, German expressionism and Brechtian drama are all 'shingeki'. It is seen as a 'translated form' – the style, conventions and conceptualisation of theatre, not to mention the primary dramatic texts are all translated from European and American theatre. According to M. Cody Poulton, 'shingeki' should not be considered as synonymous with 'modern drama', and the preferred terms are *kindaigikyoku* and *kindaigeki* (both mean 'modern drama' and indicate something larger than shingeki).[9] Poulton even sees an 'anti-theatrical' element in shingeki, as is existed primarily as a literary form for so long, with an emphasis on text over spectacle.[10]

The makers of shingeki had two objectives, according to Mariko Boyd: first, to elevate modern drama into true art, and second, to develop realism for the people.[11] Shingeki began with small, university-affiliated companies that sought to develop a modern theatre based on Western models. The two early groups and their leaders that initiated shingeki were the Bungei Kyokai (Literary Arts Society), founded at Waseda University in 1906 by Tsubouchi Shōyō, a professor of English who sought to develop a new theatre through dramatic literature, and the Jiyū Gekijō (Free Stage), founded by Osanai Kaoru and kabuki actor Ichikawa Sadanji II (1880–1940), and loosely connected to Keio University, and which sought to develop a new theatre through performance. Previously, Osanai founded *New Tides of Thought Magazine* (*Shinshichō*, 1907) to introduce Western dramatic theory to Japanese literati.

Osanai, Shimamura and Sadanji all went to Europe individually in order to study the theatre as it happened there, returning to Japan to implement the techniques acquired. Tsubouchi, who began translating Shakespeare into Japanese in 1884 and finished the complete works forty-four years later, never travelled to Europe again. Instead, he focused on translating Western plays into Japanese and writing plays based on Western models. As noted above, he was part of the kabuki reform movement, wrote shin-kabuki plays and was highly critical of Kawakami Otojirō. Tsubouchi initially attempted to work with kabuki actors to stage Shakespeare, but realised that classical Japanese actors were not equipped to perform modern Western drama. He thus founded the Bungei Kyokai as an amateur dramatic organisation, training students to develop this new theatre. He translated and directed productions of *Merchant of Venice* (1906) and *Hamlet* (1907) and, arguably most important, he produced Shimamura's translation (which Shimamura also directed) of Ibsen's *A Doll's House* in 1911, the first production of Ibsen in Japan, with Matsui Sumako as Nora. This production was of great significance, as it proved that modern European plays could be translated and performed effectively on Japanese stages, that actresses were an effective and viable alternative to onnagata and that drama could be used to promote women's rights.[12]

The shaping influence of Ibsen in the development of shingeki cannot be overestimated. Takayasu Gekkō (1869–1944) published partial translations (from the English) of *An Enemy of the People* in 1893 and *A Doll's House* in 1901. The Jiyū Gekijō's inaugural production was 1909's *John Gabriel Borkman*. Several modern playwrights were profoundly influenced by Ibsen, including Mayama Seika (whose *Umarezarishi Naraba* seems to have been modelled after *Ghosts*), Satō Kōroko (1874–1949), Nagata Hideo (1885–1949) and Nakamura Kichizō (1877–1941), the last of whom was so identified with Ibsen that he was nicknamed 'Henrik Nakamura', and his play *A Vicarage* (*Bokashi no Ie*, 1911), which he called the first 'war cry' of the shingeki movement, replicated plot elements from several major Ibsen plays.[13]

## Shingeki's First Split: Literary versus Performative

From its very inception, shingeki fell into two camps. The Jiyū Gekijō, named after the Théâtre Libre, André Antoine's theatre in Paris, was founded by Osanai and Ichikawa who had been inspired by the little theatre movement in Europe. They presented intimate, non-commercial, socially progressive dramas in a naturalistic mode. The actors were professionals from Ichikawa's kabuki company, with the female roles played by onnagata. Osanai sought to transform their acting process and performances to suit Western plays, believing he could retrain professional actors. The Bungei Kyokai, however, attached to a university, employed students as performers, with females in the women's roles. It sought to train amateurs through great dramatic Western texts. The Jiyū Gekijō focused on contemporary European playwrights, whereas Bungei Kyokai's primary focus was on Shakespeare. Neither approach worked.

Osanai disbanded the Jiyū Gekijō in order to travel to Europe, but scandal ended the Bungei Kyokai. Shimamura, who was married, carried on an affair with Matsui. The resulting tension disbanded the company. Shimamura and Matsui then founded the Geijutsu-za (Art Theatre), which first performed the plays of Maurice Maeterlinck and Nakamura Kichizō. Shimamura, however, died in the 1918 influenza epidemic and the public blamed Matsui, who committed suicide backstage during a 1919 production of *Carmen*. Still, during her brief career she played roles that served as models for Japanese women to act 'modern' and paved the way for Japanese feminism.[14]

With the disbanding of the two companies, shingeki was much more of a literary activity than a performative one. Many plays were written and published, but few were staged and fewer still were staged well. Writers, however, began driving the development of new theatre. Writers better known for other forms – novelists, essayists and poets – began to craft plays. Among the better known were Tanizaki Jun'ichirō (1886–1965), Yamamoto Yūzō (1887–1974) and Kikuchi Kan (1888–1948). The last wrote a number of rather significant plays: *The Father Returns* (*Chichi Kaeru*, published 1916, performed 1920), considered a model one-act play for its structure, dialogue and characterisation, telling the story of a prodigal father being rejected by his eldest son in a remarkable blow against filial piety; *The Madman on the Roof* (*Okujō no Kyōjin*, 1916), which demonstrated that a madman capable of enjoying the beauty of a sunset is better off than a sane man immersed in the 'real world'; and *Tōjūrō's Love* (*Tōjūrō no Koi*,

1919), which is about famous Kabuki actor Sakata Tōjūrō, although it is really an advocacy piece for Stanislvskian-based realism, as Kikuchi seemingly argues Tōjūrō must first experience things in real life in order to replicate them on stage. Such modernist experiments as these were often published before being performed.

Other theatrical movements and companies emerged during the decade. Sawada Shōjirō (1892–1929) was a Waseda University student who became an actor in Tsubouchi's Bungei Kyōkai, later achieving popularity in performances with the Geijutsu-za appearing opposite Matsui Sumako and in the Modern Drama Society (*Kindaigeki Kyōkai*). He believed that shingeki was too elite a form and other theatres too commercial and lowbrow. Sawada wanted to create theatre that would appeal to the urban masses but which was also not crassly commercialised. In 1917 he developed and began performing what he called 'new national theatre'(*shinkokugeki*). It failed initially in Tokyo, but he took his company first to Kyoto, then to Osaka, where, in desperation, they added a swordfight scene to a play about samurai. Unlike the kabuki, whose *tachimawari* combat scenes are a highly stylised dance, this fight was energetic, fast and violent. The novelty appealed to audiences and shinkokugeki began to grow in popularity.

Sawada formulated his *hanpozenshinshugi* (sometimes called *hanposhugi* – the 'half-step principle'). If modern theatre takes a full step forward, he theorised, the mass audience will not follow. If theatre stays where it is right now, there is no progress in the art. Thus, a half-step is necessary to lead the audience forward without leaving them behind, guiding the audience to better theatre. From 1919 to the early 1920s he appeared in a number of popular plays about Edo era samurai and thieves, while also playing in translated shingeki plays, such as an adaptation of Dostoevsky's *Crime and Punishment*, in which he played Raskolnikov. His sword-fighting plays, however, remained his most popular and influenced period films (*jidaigeki*) and sword fighting films (*chambara*). Sawada performed in 169 plays in his nineteen-year career, but shinkokugeki began to fade with his death in 1929 and finally ended due to austerity during the war years. Although the patriotism of his plays appealed to the wartime government, the company was simply too expensive to maintain, especially when audiences could not afford tickets.

The next major advance in Japanese theatre history came about as a result of a terrible natural disaster. Municipal codes prevented the building of new theatres in Tokyo. In 1923 the Great Kantō Earthquake, the deadliest earthquake in Japanese history, measuring 7.9 on the moment magnitude scale, struck right before noon on 1 September. Tokyo was devastated and hundreds of thousands died. As a result, new buildings of all kinds were allowed. Hijikata Yoshi (1898–1959), a wealthy aristocrat and theatre devotee, rushed back to Japan from his studies in Europe. Hijikata partnered with Osanai, with the former financing the project and the latter designing it, resulting in the building of a state-of-the-art theatre in Tokyo, near the fish market, which gave the theatre its name: Tsukiji Little Theatre. It had a Gothic-Romanesque exterior, and a plain grey flexible interior with benches that could seat no more than five hundred. It also had the latest lighting equipment.

Just before the Tsukiji opened, Osanai announced that no Japanese plays would be performed there, only Western plays in translation. This decision was highly controversial. In response, Osanai published an essay entitled 'What is the Reason for the Existence of the Tsukiji Little Theatre?' In it he argued that the Tsukiji must privilege theatre over drama – the value is in the performance, not the literature. Thus, the Tsukiji was a venue to present plays of established value, not to introduce untested new plays. His argument was that Japanese dramaturgy was not as advanced as Western dramaturgy, and if actors were to learn their craft, they would be better served by performing Western plays. Second, the Japanese modern theatre must develop directors, designers and technicians, who only learn by working on the best. Lastly, he argued that the intended audience was the masses and their needs superseded the egos of the writers; theatre existed for the people, not for the playwrights.

The Tsukiji's opening season consisted of Reinhard Goering's *Sea Battle*, Chekhov's *Swan Song* and Emile Mazaud's *Holiday*. More European plays followed in the second season. Finally, in 1926, the Tsukiji started presenting Japanese plays, beginning with Tsubouchi's

*En the Ascetic* (*En no gyōja*, written in 1916) and a modernist version of Chikamatsu's *The Battles of Coxinga* (*Kokusen'ya Kassen*, 1715) in the style of Russian director Vsevolod Meyerhold, directed by Hijikata. As per Osanai's argument, many actors, designers, directors and eventually writers trained at and performed in the Tsukiji Little Theatre. The genealogy of almost all shingeki from the 1930s to the present can be traced back to this one institution. Yet Osanai's contentious banning of Japanese playwrights for the first two years of the Tsukiji's existence and the large number of published but never produced plays demonstrate a serious split in the efforts to develop a modern theatre in Japan.

## Takarazuka: Another Modern Theatre

To draw passengers to Hankyu's Takarazuka Line, a railway to a town outside of Osaka famed for its hot springs, Kobayashi Ichizō (1873–1957) built a resort and in 1913 founded the Takarazuka Singing Troupe (*Takarazuka Shōkatai*), an all-girls chorus. A year later the group began staging all-female musical plays. For Kobayashi, the idea was to provide wholesome, family popular entertainment with an all-female company. He coined the motto 'Purely, Beautifully, Correctly' and began penning scripts.

In 1919 the company became known as the Takarazuka Music Opera School (*Takarazuka Ongaku Kageki Gakkō*). In 1924, the Takarazuka Grand Theatre opened and in 1934 the Tokyo Takarazuka Theatre also opened, seating four thousand, having begun offering performances in Tokyo as well in 1918. Strongly influenced by French theatre, the school began performing revues, including the landmark 1927 show *Mon Paris*. This revue established the skill of the actresses as well as established the model for Takarazuka performances. Performers began calling themselves 'Takarasiennes'.

Once accepted into the school, the student would be assigned a role type based on talent, body type and personality. Otokoyaku are performers who play male roles. These actresses are often fan favourites and will often dress masculine offstage as well. Musumeyaku are performers of female roles. Each role type learns its own music, acting, dancing, make-up, hairstyle, signing and speaking.

During the war the Takarazuka were conscripted to entertain the troops and cross-dressing was forbidden. After the war, the Americans took over the Tokyo Takarazuka and renamed it the Ernie Pyle Theatre, after a soldier killed in the South Pacific. After the Occupation, the Takarazuka flourished again, offering popular Western-style musicals in addition to their revues. Based on a popular graphic novel and set in eighteenth-century France, *Berusaiyu no bara* (*The Rose of Versailles*) became a blockbuster hit in 1974, frequently revived and always popular. More popular musicals followed, including 1977's *Gone with the Wind* (*Kaze to tomonisarinu*, based on the Margaret Mitchell's novel) and a series of Broadway musicals in the eighties: *Guys and Dolls* (1984), *Me and My Girl* (1987) and *Kiss Me Kate* (1988).

Currently the Takarazuka is celebrating a century of performing. The company consists of the Takarazuka Music School, at which all performers train for years, the theatres in Takarazuka and Tokyo, and approximately four hundred actresses in five troupes: Flower Troupe (*Hanagumi*), Moon Troupe (*Tsukigumi*), Snow Troupe (*Yukigumi*), Star Troupe (*Hoshigumi*) and Cosmos Troupe (*Soragumi*). As with role types, actresses are assigned a troupe at graduation to which they will belong until they retire. Upon retirement, Takarasiennes go on to careers in other parts of show business: film, television, legitimate stage and even musical performing for Tōhō or other production companies.

Some scholars regard the Takarazuka as a site to explore Japanese ideas about gender, politics and identity, observing that even though the all-female company empowers women on stage, off stage the company is predominantly run by men and that the otokoyaku are valued and privileged above the musumeyake, thus preserving gender bias within the company. Still, for a hundred years the Takarazuka has been a fan favourite, generating huge audiences for their productions. Inaugurated in the second decade of the twentieth century as a wholesome, all-female alternative to the all-male kabuki, it has developed into a huge entertainment conglomerate with a huge influence on Japanese popular culture and its own unique form of modern theatre.

## Shingeki's Second Split: Psychological versus Political

Osanai Kaoru died on 25 December 1928 at the age of 47. With his death, the Tsukiji company split into two factions, although the theatre itself continued to function as a home for performance for both, echoing the larger emerging split within shingeki culture itself. On the one side were the politically committed artists who wanted to use the theatre to advance a progressive, and for some a socialist, agenda and thus embraced social realism. On the other side were those who were apolitical and wanted to focus on developing shingeki through psychological realism.

The leftists saw theatre as a means to address social issues, to raise consciousness and to promote Japanese socialism. Their leader, Kubo Sakae (1900–58), was a student of German and an aficionado of German drama, writing his thesis at Tokyo Imperial University on German expressionist dramatist Georg Kaiser. In 1926 he joined the literary department at the Tsukiji Shōgekijō, already a committed Marxist. When the company split two years later, Kubo led the leftist faction and in 1934 co-founded the New Cooperative Company (*Shinkyō*). Kubo's masterpiece, *Land of Volcanic Ash* (*Kazanbaichi*, 1938), which sought to demonstrate Marxist theory, both politically and artistically, was first published in the magazine *Shinchō* in 1937–8 and then performed by Shinkyō at the Tsukiji Shōgekijō in June and July of 1938.[15] The play, which is set in Hokkaido (the 'land of volcanic ash' of the title) and features a cast of over fifty characters in a story that takes place over the course of a year, demonstrates the failure of both small, independent farming families and larger capitalist agricultural concerns, and its Marxist hero fights for the only possibility of success: collectivisation.

Kubo was arrested in 1940 for his refusal to cooperate with the war efforts and spent the war in prison. After the war he was initially regarded as a hero for his resistance to the military government, but during the occupation, as an avowed Marxist, he fell into struggles within both the shingeki and socialist movements and grew less relevant a figure in both movements. He published and directed a few more plays, but took his own life in 1958. His reputation remains cemented by *Land of Volcanic Ash*, which many critics perceive as the finest pre-war realistic shingeki play. Ironically, even for leftist artists, the audience for shingeki was an educated, intellectually elite one, spurned by the working class which preferred kabuki, shinpa and especially cinema.

Those who favoured a literary approach to shingeki, embracing an apolitical psychological realism are represented by Kishida Kunio (1890–1954). Kishida studied French at Tokyo University and then travelled to Paris to study under Jacques Copeau. Kishida wrote his first play in French, returning to Japan in 1923 to begin promoting dramatic literature and dialogue-based psychological realism. Initially influenced by Copeau to write on acts that blended realism and symbolism, Kishida eventually developed as a writer and began writing complex, multi-act dramas, including his masterpiece, *The Two Daughters of Mr. Sawa* (*Sawa-shi no futarimusume*, 1935). In 1937 playwrights Kishida, Kubota Mantarō (1889–1963) and Iwata Toyō (1893–1969) founded the Literary Theatre (*Bungaku-za*), which became the only shingeki company that was able to perform continuously during the war and subsequently be one of the three most important post-war companies. Although his wartime role resulted in his being accused of collaboration with the military, occasioning his purging from most theatrical circles, his reputation as one of the most significant playwrights of the twentieth century and his influence on modern theatre's development resulted in the Kishida Kunio Drama Prize (*Kishida Kunio Gikyoku-shō*) being established in 1956 after his death, awarded to the best new Japanese play of the year.

## Modern Drama during the War: Censorship and Service

Shingeki slowed down productions during the Second World War and like all theatre in Japan was pressed into service of the nation and the military government. Shingeki companies were drafted into providing entertainment for troops at home and abroad, especially in Korea, Manchuria and China. The military government dictated content and heavily censored production. Plays were required to have patriotic content (or at least apolitical entertainment with a dose of nationalism), although 'national drama' (*kokuminengeki*) was heavily promoted, and government approval was required for all public performances. Leftist artists were arrested and imprisoned and left wing companies were forcibly disbanded. On 1 August 1940 alone, over one hundred left-leaning actors, writers and directors were arrested and their companies banned.

Kishida Kunio became the head of the Cultural Department of the Imperial Rule Assistance Association in 1940, charged with coordinating all aspects of culture to support the war effort. After the war the American occupation forces accused him of wartime collaboration and he was dismissed from all posts and his work could not be performed in public. From 1924 to 1935 he wrote fifty plays; during and after the war he wrote only five. Still, the company he co-founded, the Bungaku-za, was the only theatre group allowed to perform uninterrupted during the war.

The second major shingeki company of the era, the Actors Theatre (*Haiyū-za*), was founded in 1944 by Senda Koreya (1904–94) and others. The Haiyū-za stated three main purposes for the company: first, to educate audiences; second, to promote amateur theatrics; and third, to develop a professional theatre company. Senda began his career with the Tsukiji Little Theatre and became a committed socialist after studying under director Erwin Piscator in Germany for four years in the late 1920s. He spent much of the war in prison, arrested by the military government for his politics and was banned from directing when released in 1942. The Haiyū-za survived the war to become one of the most important companies of the second half of the twentieth century. Senda also became the foremost interpreter of Brecht in Japan, translating and directing most of Brecht's plays for the first time in Japan after the war. Senda also directed acclaimed productions of Shakespeare and Chekhov, as well as most of Abe Kōbō's early plays.

## Drama under the Occupation

In December 1945, less than four months after the Occupation began, modern theatre began to be performed again. Three separate companies, the Tokyo Arts Theatre (*Tokyo Geijutsu Gekijō*), the Bungaku-za and the Haiyū-za, gathered together and performed Chekhov's *The Cherry Orchard*, starring Senda Koreya and Sugimura Haruko (1909–97), among others. Sugimura had begun acting with the Tsukiji Shōgekijō in 1927 and rose to prominence and influence over the course of a seventy-year career that included shinpa, shingeki, film and television. She was a founding member of the Bungaku-za and was Japan's first Blanche DuBois in a 1953 production of *A Streetcar Named Desire*. Her most popular role was Nunobiki Kei in *A Woman's Life* (*Onna no Isshō*), written in 1945 by Morimoto Kaoru (1912–46), a playwright with the Bungaku-za. Sugimura toured with the production and frequently revived the play.

David Jortner asserts that the Supreme Commander of the Allied Powers (SCAP, the occupation bureaucracy headed by General Douglas MacArthur), Civil Information and Education Division (CI&E, charged with promoting democratic values through education and the media) and the Civilian Censorship Detachment (CCD, charged by SCAP with approving plays and performances, among other duties) actively attempted to assert an American realist mode for shingeki, which a 1946 memo characterised as the 'problem child' of Japanese theatre.[16] CI&E officials and CCD censors encouraged playwrights, directors, actors and even theatre critics to embrace American aesthetics and artistic ideas, publishing the quarterly journal *American Theatre* (*Amerikan Engeki*), beginning in 1948, and encouraging the production of American realist plays. SCAP also strongly promoted an American model of production. Whereas Japanese theatre was organised along company lines, in which the same group of artists produced and performed plays by a resident playwright, SCAP wanted companies disbanded and producers to organise individual productions, hiring actors, designers and directors on a play-by-play basis. Eventually, growing concerns over communism in the Cold War led to a so-called 'Red Purge' in the early 1950s which restricted leftist shingeki groups and sought to eliminate amateur shingeki organised in the workplace. American dramas such as Thornton Wilder's *The Skin of Our Teeth* continued to be heavily promoted and encouraged. Whereas the first coming of Western drama in Japan had European theatre as a model, the post-war emergence of shingeki was rooted in American drama.

Methods of show business were changing, as were relationships with audiences. Rōen, the abbreviated title of Workers Theatre Association (*Kinrōsha Engeki Kyōkai*), was founded in Osaka in 1949, and soon all major cities had one. Rōen was an audience association organisation, meaning its members would buy a membership and then would receive tickets to local productions. Rōen grew very powerful very quickly by means of its control of audiences. Productions would only be able to break even, let alone show a profit, if Rōen supported it by purchasing tickets.[17]

In 1947 another major company was founded that quickly became a powerhouse of shingeki. People's Art Theatre (*Mingei*) was founded by, among others, actor Takizawa Osamu (1906–2000), who had trained at the Tsukiji Shōgekijō and who was known for his Stanislavskian psychological realism. Takizawa played Willy Loman in the first Japanese production of *Death of a Salesman*. Mingei, Bungaku-za and Haiyū-za, were the dominant shingeki companies during the occupation and throughout the 1950s and 1960s. All three companies were dedicated to actor training, realism and presenting both the major plays from the West and new realistic Japanese plays.

## Japan Looks West Again: Post-Occupation Theatre to 1960

The occupation ended in 1952. Shingeki had become the dominant form of modern drama, and psychological realism was the heart of shingeki. In the immediate post-occupation period, Japan looked to the West again, this time to American models Arthur Miller and Tennessee Williams, as well as shingeki staples Ibsen and Chekhov. In 1953 Bungaku-za presented an acclaimed production of *A Streetcar Named Desire*. The following year a major translation of Stanislavski's *An Actor Prepares* appeared, foregrounding Western-style method acting. The year after that, Mingei's *Death of a Salesman* achieved great success.

In Goodman's terms, shingeki had become orthodoxy. Its practitioners and audiences for the most part were conservative, traditional and nervous about communism and the dangers posed by the Soviet Union and China. Realism dominated the theatre, as did the written text. The post-occupation playwright was king of the theatre, actors were in the service of the text.

Shingeki became a victim of its own success and its own increasing conservatism. By playing it safe to ensure Rōen would continue to support the major companies, by repeating the same realistic narratives and theatrical conventions over and over, and by failing to address changing social concerns, shingeki was in danger of becoming irrelevant to the younger generations and in danger of becoming crystalised itself.

Shingeki had radically changed in the first half of the twentieth century, as had Japan. The opening of Japan in the latter half of the nineteenth century was followed by rapid modernisation, including the cultural challenge of developing a modern theatre for Japan. Although initially attempts had been made to modernise the kabuki, a series of modern forms based on Western models ultimately triumphed as the form modern theatre would take. Following the examples of Ibsen and Chekhov especially, Japanese playwrights and actors first developed shinpa, a melodramatic hybrid form, followed by shingeki, a modern, naturalistic theatre. In 1850, Japan had been relatively the same as it had been in 1650. By 1950, Japan was one of the most advanced nations on the planet. It had fought and lost a world war, but for the decades before defeat had dominated Asia as a colonial power and served to spread modern drama (as will be discussed in Chapters 3 and 6).

Changes were on the horizon by the late 1950s. The introduction and growing influence of Samuel Beckett's plays contributed to the rise of Japanese absurdism, which would bloom in the 1960s. The rise of post-war youth culture and the rise of anti-realism, both at home and in the world, would eventually result in a theatrical revolution in the modern theatre. Just as shingeki once rejected kabuki and shinpa in favour of a new model, the theatre artists of the 1960s would reject shingeki in favour of something new as well.

# CHAPTER 2
## MODERN JAPANESE THEATRE: 1960 THROUGH THE MILLENNIUM

While realism had become orthodoxy by the 1950s, a new paradigm began to emerge in the late 1950s that solidified in 1960 because of the so-called AMPO incident (the renewal of the Treaty of Mutual Cooperation and Security between the United States and Japan, the Japanese acronym of which is AMPO). The organisation of this volume and the chapter dates are thus somewhat arbitrary and not indicative of immediate change, but rather an evolution with an immediate cause. Shingeki continues throughout the 1960s, through the rest of the twentieth century, but 'shingeki' has become something of a pejorative term now. The preferred terms are 'current theatre' (*gendaigeki*) and 'modern drama' (*kindaigeki*).

This is the period of 'little theatre', underground theatre, quiet theatre and contemporary plurality and multiculturalism. As noted in the previous chapter, David Goodman refers to this era as 'the return of the gods', as the modern theatre broke away from a slavish devotion to realism on stage and once again presented gods, demons, monsters, ghosts and the fantastic.[1] As with previous generations, the theatre of the 1960s was company-organised and driven, usually with one or two leaders (frequently but not always a playwright, director or playwright/director) driving a group of actors, creating a distinctive product. It is also the period of the internationalisation of modern Japanese theatre, with figures like Mishima Yukio, Suzuki Tadashi and Ninagawa Yukio seeing their work performed in the West regularly.

Major themes in the drama of the second half of the twentieth century include the search for Japanese identity, especially one perceived to be lost or corrupted during the war and through Western influence. Conversely, another significant purpose of the theatre of this period was to give voice to the underrepresented: women, Koreans in Japan and other disenfranchised groups. Lastly, as always, the theatre responded to, represented, resisted and sometimes reinforced social, political and cultural contexts. What follows is a survey of major artists and their work from the past half century.

## Transitional Figures: Mishima, Abe and Others

Mishima Yukio (pen name of Hiraoka Kimitake, 1925–70), although a conservative nationalist himself, shared many of the concerns of the younger, more left-leaning playwrights. Though Mishima disagreed politically and aesthetically with many of his contemporaries in the Japanese theatre world, he sought what they sought: a post-war Japanese identity connected in some way to the pre-modern past. His spectacular suicide in 1970, combined with his body of non-dramatic literature, has ensured that Mishima received the lion's share of attention paid to modern Japanese drama in English in the 1960s, 1970s and 1980s, although he was also a prolific playwright, whose dramas were regarded very highly by critics, audiences and fellow artists. In 1955, nine Mishima plays were staged in Tokyo alone. A 1995 survey of Japanese theatre critics selected Mishima as the greatest of the post-war playwrights and his play *Madame de Sade* (*Sado Kōshaku Fujin*, 1965) the finest Japanese play of the twentieth century.[2] In short, Mishima was a major figure in post-war theatre, despite being an iconoclast and the ideological opposite of much of the theatre movement of the period.

He wrote shingeki, kabuki and hybrid drama in the form of his modern nō plays. Mishima wrote nine 'modern nō' plays, which were not performed in a nō style by nō actors. Rather, they were shingeki dramas, based on nō plays (except for *Steeplechase* (*Daishōgai*, 1956), an 'original modern nō play'). The other eight plays based on nō dramas include *Magic Pillow* (*Kantan*, 1950), which was staged by Bungaku-za, *The Damask Drum* (*Aya no tsuzumi*, 1951), *Sotoba Komachi* (*Sotoba Komachi*, 1952), *Lady Aoi* (*Aoi no Ue*, 1954), *Hanjo* (*Hanjo*, 1955),

*Dōjōji Temple* (*Dōjōji*, 1957), *Yuya* (*Yuya*, 1959) and *Yoroboshi* (*Yoroboshi*, 1960). Mishima focused on the psychology of the characters, their sense of obsession, loss and desire, transforming Buddhist-infused classical dramas into contemporary psychological realism. Mishima also wrote six kabuki plays, which he argued were not shin-kabuki but real kabuki, written in the classical language of kabuki. These fifteen plays earned critical acclaim and saw Mishima proclaimed as the finest post-war kabuki playwright.

His shingeki plays also received a good deal of attention and acclaim. He became the resident playwright of the Bungaku-za from 1957 to 1964, providing that group with at least one new multiact play each year, starting with *Deer Cry Hall* (*Rokumeikan*, 1956). He adapted plays from multiple sources, including the story of Sleeping Beauty, set in Japan as *The Pirate and the Rose* (*Bara to Kaizoku*, 1958), his own version of *The Oresteia*, called *The Tropical Tree* (*Nettaiju*, 1959), and an Edogawa Rampo detective novel, *Black Lizard* (Kuro Tokage, 1961). Conflicts over Mishima's controversial, conservative play *The Harp of Joy* (*Yorokobi no Koto*, 1963) led to a bitter split with the Bungaku-za and a very public ending of the friendship between Mishima and Sugimura Haruko, lead actress and one of the leaders of Bungaku-za. Mishima and thirteen other company members left to start the New Literary Theatre (NLT) in 1964, which is where *Madame de Sade* premiered in 1965. When NLT turned to predominantly producing comedy in 1968, Mishima left that group to found Gekidan Roman Gekijō (*Romantic Theatre Company*). That company debuted with Mishima's next play, *My Friend Hitler* (*Waga Tomo Hittorā*, 1968), which presents Hitler in 1934 in a series of conversations with underlings in which he must assassinate extremists at either end of the political spectrum in order to preserve, unify and raise the nation. Romantic Theatre Company followed *Hitler* with a revival of *Madame de Sade*.

With a small group of followers from the Shield Society (*Tatenokai*), a private paramilitary group he founded in 1968, Mishima occupied the commandant's office of the headquarters of Japan's self-defence forces in Tokyo, gave a speech designed to rally the soldiers to the emperor, then killed himself by *harakiri* (cutting his own abdomen open with a samurai sword). The plays he had completed before his death were staged and his past plays revived regularly. His work has since been performed all over the world.

Like Mishima, Abe Kōbō (1924–93) is first and foremost a novelist whose plays were equally significant and groundbreaking. Initially, Abe worked with Senda Koreya, who directed all of Abe's early plays at the Haiyū-za between 1955 and 1965. Abe's play *The Ghost is Here* (*Yūrei koko ni iru*, 1958) won the Kishida Prize. Abe combined traditional shingeki dramaturgy with the emergent absurdism to comment on social norms. While he presented seemingly natural scenes, the content, situations and characters were absurd or surreal. For example, among his more inventive plays was the trilogy *The Man Who Turned into a Stick* (*Bō ni natte otoko*, 1969), consisting of 'The Suitcase' in which two women worry over the contents and noise coming from a suitcase, played by another actor; 'The Cliff of Time', in which a boxer reflects upon his life; and 'The Man Who Turned into a Stick', in which two hippies ignore a stick until agents from hell arrive to purchase it. *Friends* (*Tomodachi*, 1967) is arguably his best known play, in which a family of strangers invite themselves into a man's apartment and then every aspect of his life in a critique of Japanese society. Similar to Ionesco's *Rhinoceros*, realistic dialogue was undercut by the unreal absurdity of the situation. In 1973, Abe and his wife Yamada Machiko (1926–93) opened Abe Studio to train actors to perform in avant-garde productions. After 1979, however, he focused mainly on fiction.

Mishima and Abe are the playwrights whose work has been seen most outside of Japan in the 1960s, 1970s and 1980s, with performances in New York, London and other cities. They became the face of modern Japanese theatre outside of Japan, replaced perhaps in the late 1980s by Suzuki Tadashi and Ninagawa Yukio.

Playwrights who remained active throughout the shōgekijō period include Tanaka Chikao (1905–95), Yashiro Seiichi (1927–98), Hotta Kiyomi (b. 1922–), Fukuda Tsuneari (1912–94) and Kinoshita Junji (1914–2006). Tanaka Chikao saw his first play, *Mother* (*Ofukuro*), performed in 1933, and joined Kishida Kunio's Bungaku-za where he studied French dramas as well as O'Neill, Lorca and Pirandello and directed a few productions. After the war, however, he matured as a dramatist, moving away from realism and embracing existentialism. An unbaptised Roman Catholic, his own religion also shaped his writing. In 1951 he joined the Haiyū-za as director, dramaturg, playwright and acting teacher. His play *Education* (*Kyōiku*, 1957) was written for the students there, won the Yomiuri Prize and marks the beginning of what Tanaka called his 'misogynistic plays' – dramas in which belief in God is challenged by women. The best example of this genre is his play *The Head of Mary* (*Maria no kubi*, 1959), in which a group of cryptic Christians led by a nurse and a prostitute conspire to steal the title statue in Nagasaki after the bombing. Although initially realistic in style, the head of Mary comes to life in the play and speaks to the gathered faithful, a miraculous occurrence that demonstrated the coming shift away from realism. Tanaka remained an ardent shingeki artist, however, penning the critical work *Introduction to an Appreciation of Shingeki* (*Shingeki kanshō nyūmon*) in 1981.

Yashiro Seiichi studied French at Waseda University and began writing plays for the Haiyū-za and the Bungaku-za in the late 1940s. A Catholic, Yashiro wrote in a variety of styles and on a variety of subject matters. He won the Kishida Prize for his 1953 play *The Mural* (*Hekiga*). Yashiro was active in shingeki for several decades, with some of his best plays being written in the 1960s and 1970s, including *They Vanished at Dawn* (*Yoake ni kieta*, 1968), concerning first-century martyrs in Palestine, and his *ukiyo-e* trilogy, three plays about woodblock print artists: *Sharaku* (*Sharaku-ko*, 1971), *Hokusai Sketchbook* (Hokusai Manga, 1973) and *Lewd Eisen* (*Inrasai Eisen*, 1975).

Hotta Kiyomi is best known for *The Island* (*Shima*, 1955), the first play about the atomic bombing of Hiroshima, where he was from (although not present at the time the bomb was dropped). He began writing in 1947 with *Son of a Driver* (*Untenko no musuko*), first in a long line of plays about the working class. His leftist politics led to his purging in 1950, but after the occupation he joined Mingei in 1955. *Shima* was written for that company and won the Kishida Prize. Hotta worked as an assistant director and playwright for Mingei for several years, but departed the company in the early 1960s and ceased writing plays.

Fukuda Tsuneari, playwright, scholar, director and translator of Shakespeare, rose to prominence with *Typhoon Kitty* (*Kitii taifu*, 1950), a satire of Japanese intellectuals through a parody of Chekhov's *Cherry Orchard*. Although the bulk of his work was criticism, including many important essays on Shakespeare, he wrote several plays in the 1950s and 1960s, including *Damned if I Know It* (*Wakatte tamaruku*, 1968). He spent the 1950s as a director and writer for Bungaku-za, most notably translating and directing a production of *Hamlet* in 1955 that was praised for its naturalistic language. He departed that company, however, to co-found the Cloud Company (*Kumo*) in 1963. Unlike many of the artists of this period, Fukuda was a social conservative.

Kinoshita Junji studied English Renaissance literature at Tokyo University and by the 1970s had translated the complete works of Shakespeare. A director and prolific playwright in his own right, his first play *Turbulent Waves* (*Fūrō*) was produced in 1939. He wrote dozens of plays since that fall into two categories: folk plays (*minwa geki*) that were modern adaptions of traditional tales, such as his classic *Twilight Crane* (*Yūruza*, 1949), and historical plays (*gendai gekki*). The latter category dominated his work during this period in plays such as *A Japanese Named Otto* (*Otto to yobareru Nihonjin*, 1963) about the Japanese counterpart to Soviet spy Richard Sorge and *Between God and Man* (*Kami to hito to no aida*, 1970), a documentary drama based on the Tokyo war crimes trials. Kinoshita was highly influential on later generations of shingeki artists, not least of which because he thought modern Japanese was insufficient as a stage language and sought to develop an idiom that worked effectively in the theatre. He also shared angura's concern with the Japan's past.

## The New Paradigm: Post-Shingeki

The five decades of post-shingeki theatre can be divided roughly into five periods. Presented here is a modified version of Japanese theatre critic Senda Akihiko's perceived four generations (as of 1997) of post-AMPO theatre.[3] After the millennium there is clearly a fifth if not a sixth generation. Senda constructs theatre history as a journey, arguing that the playwrights, actors and directors since the 1960s were 'setting out on a voyage of theatrical discovery' that has changed practices and intentions, but never ceases seeking a new theatre.[4] The first generation came of age in the 1960s, their work growing out of a frustration with the AMPO crisis, with shingeki, with everything in their lives. The second generation, rising in the 1970s replaced the frustration of the 1960s with a sense of loss, impotence and misery. This period is also regarded as transitional between the experiments of the 1960s and the commercialism of the 1980s. The third generation, inventive, playful and postmodern, transformed the 1980s into the decade of metatheatre, apocalypse and apolitical commercial theatre. The fourth generation, centred mostly in the 1990s, returned to psychological portraits of life, the so-called 'quiet theatre' movement showing the lives of soft desperation and loneliness while others raised social issues through a newly emerging political theatre. Lastly, the fifth generation began creating theatre around the millennium and their concerns reflect the challenges of living in contemporary Japan. We should note that artists can work in more than one generation. Suzuki Tadashi and Ninagawa Yukio are active in all five, and their styles, concerns and theatres have transformed over time. Noda Hideki has been active in the third, fourth and fifth generation, his theatre also changing over time, as has several of the artists whose work is surveyed here, although artists tend to remain identified with the generation during which they emerged.

## First Generation: The Rise of Angura and Shōgekijō

Just as the first shingeki production after the war was Chekhov's *The Cherry Orchard*, the first shingeki production of the 1960s was Haiyū-za's January 1960 mounting of the same play, celebrating the company's mastery of Russian realism. It would later be read, however, as a symbol of how out of touch the older generation of theatre artists had become. The Treaty of Mutual Cooperation and Security between the United States and Japan, known in Japan by its acronym AMPO, was renewed by the government despite widespread opposition, and signed on 19 January 1960, going into effect on 19 May 1960. Young people held numerous protests leading up to and after the signing, lasting from March 1959 to

June 1960. The unrest caused President Eisenhower to cancel his state visit to Japan in 1960, which was seen as a victory, but otherwise none of the protests effected any change. The failure of the older generation to prevent the renewal, which meant nuclear weapons and American military hardware and personnel would remain on Japanese soil, was condemned by the younger generation, which also saw the embrace of Western realism as another failure of the older generation, effectively disconnecting them from their Japanese roots.

The terminology to describe the theatre that emerged in the 1960s has varied and been used interchangeably. Scholars and artists from the time and from subsequent eras have called it 'angura' and 'shōgekijō' or 'shōgekijō undō'. Some use the phrase 'post-shingeki', although shingeki continued throughout the 1960s into the present, the 'big three' (Bungaku-za, Mingei and Haiyū-za) and dozens of minor companies continuing to perform the types of play identified as shingeki throughout the period. Angura and shōgekijō are often used interchangeably as synonyms, and the terms are related, but should not be conflated, as they ultimately refer to variations on a theme.

Angura is a corruption of the word 'underground'. The angura artists were anti-establishment, anti-realist postmodern playwrights, directors and actors. They reconceived every aspect of theatre, including theatrical space, the nature and purpose of the actor and the relationship between performer and audience. Street performances, tent theatres and small storefront performance spaces were the stages of the angura companies, which eschewed traditional dramaturgy and psychological realism. Each company also had its own unique vision and style, so no two angura companies were exactly alike. While many companies were led by director/playwrights, all, even those with strong leaders, at least gave lip service to the collective and sought to eliminate traditional hierarchies within the theatre, allowing for group-created performances.

Shōgekijō undo, which means 'little theatre movement', refers to the same movement, which moved away from traditional theatre spaces and towards a more integrated relationship with the audience. Perhaps the key difference is that 'angura' died out in the 1970s, replaced by a new avant-garde, while shōgekijō continues to the present. Alternative theatre is no longer the underground theatre, but part of the mainstream. The counterculture has become the culture.

Regardless of nomenclature, angura was an 'angry young man' theatre, much like the emerging alternative theatres of Europe and the United States in the early 1960s. Playwriting was seen as an integral part of the production process, not carried out separately by an isolated individual. Dramaturgical structure changed radically, no longer linear or logical. The plays were both dark and accusatory, yet also playful, with a wicked sense of humour. The plays were experimental, actor-centred and eclectic, disdaining realism (whether psychological or social) in favour of mythic narrative, metamorphosis (both metaphoric and literal) and an embrace of the pre-modern past. Subject matter often involved the marginalised others within Japan's rather homogenous society: Zainichi Koreans (ethnic Koreans who are permanent residents of Japan), women and disaffected youth. Other major themes include epiphanies, transformations and the idea that salvation is indistinguishable from damnation.[5] The angura artists also looked to the traditional theatres, once again developing hybrid forms and embracing elements of and actors from nō, bunraku and kabuki. Dramas from those traditions were also adapted with modern sensibilities, frequently to critique nationalism, the government and the Second World War.

Emphasis was placed on the physicality of the actor, especially because realistic dialogue was also avoided, except ironically. Emphasis was also placed on transforming theatrical space, employing found spaces, alternate spaces or even no specific space. Terayama Shuji's *Knock: Street Theatre*, for example, co-written with Kishida Rio, was designed to be performed around Tokyo in thirty-three locations over thirty hours on 19–20 April 1975. The intention was to reconfigure performer/audience relations, call into question the ideas of authorship, performance and theatre, and explore language. Interesting though it was, many 'audience' members were unaware they were watching drama, and spontaneous participation by passers-by was minor at best.

Many of the companies were affiliated in some way with universities. The Waseda Little Theatre (Waseda Shōgekijō, 1966–84) founded by Suzuki Tadashi and Betsuyaku Minoru, among others, developed at and by students of Waseda University. The audience for angura was young: college students and college-educated twenty-somethings living in Tokyo. Artists in fact sought out small audiences and in some cases actively worked to offend the audience (and in some cases, literally assault the audience during productions). In *Heretics* (*Jashūmon*, 1971), Terayama Shūji's black-robed, *kurogo*-like (the black-garbed stage hands of kabuki) characters threatened audience members, 'prevented some people from getting to their seats and literally carried others away' at the start of the play. At the conclusion of the play, the company destroys the set, turning on the audience and haranguing them. 'The play only ends when the last audience member leaves.'[6]

Unlike shingeki, which from its inception was intended as a theatre of politics, in a real sense angura artists were no longer interested in the masses or class issues. The plays ignore the daily concerns of both the working and middle classes. At heart, the angura theatre was a middle-class countercultural movement, driven by young, college-age intellectuals rejecting the previous generations' values, with much in common with youth theatre in the West that was emerging at the same time (The Living Theatre, *Dionysus in 69*, etc.), although shingeki companies and some of the angura groups at least paid lip service to socialism.

One of the first companies that transitioned into post-shingeki style theatre was the Youth Art Theatre (Seinen Geijutsu Gekijō), founded in 1959 by actors trained in Mingei's training program who were offered no place in the shingeki company upon completion of their training. The group was also driven by the intensity and passion developed during the initial student protests against AMPO. Fukuda Yoshiyuki (b. 1931), a committed socialist, joined Seinen as the resident playwright and is best known for his work *Find Hakamadare!* (*Hakamadare wa doko da*, 1964), in which a group of peasants search for a legendary hero to lead them. When he is revealed to be a self-serving opportunist and tells them a secret police is necessary for his rule, they kill him and set up their own government. Fukuda influenced Kara Jūrō, Betsuyaku Minoru and Satoh Makoto, all important angura playwrights who worked with Seinen. Although Fukuda's work moved from socialist realism to a much more experimental style employing

Brechtian techniques, he was frequently regarded by critics as a lightweight playwright whose work was not particularly significant.

Four major angura figures who would continue to develop and create theatre for the rest of the century emerged out of the angura environment surrounding Waseda University in the early 1960s: Suzuki Tadashi (b. 1939), arguably the best-known Japanese theatre artist in the world today, playwright Betsuyaku Minoru (b. 1937), the 'Japanese Beckett,' playwright Shimizu Kunio (b. 1936) and director Ninagwa Yukio (b. 1935). Betsuyaku and Suzuki founded the Free Stage (*Jiyū Butai*) in 1962 with a production of Betsuyaku's *Elephant* (*Zō*), a play about atomic bomb victims. In 1966, the company reorganised as the Waseda Little Theatre (*Waseda Shōgekijō*), performing above a café near the university. Its first production was Betsuyaku's *The Gate* (*Mon*), directed by Suzuki. Suzuki began to emphasise acting over playwriting, and Betsuyaku left the company in 1968.

Suzuki then began devising his own texts and developed a system of actor training focusing on exploring the body and especially the 'grammar of the feet' in a search for a genuine Japanese performance style. In 1967 actress Shiraishi Kayoko (b. 1941) joined the company and became Suzuki's muse. He developed his system around her, and he wrote a series of theatrical experiments, such as *On the Dramatic Passions II* (*Gekiteki naru mono o megutte II*, 1970), which featured Shiraishi as a madwoman. She also rose to international acclaim in Suzuki's adaptations of Greek tragedies, including *The Trojan Women* (*Toroia no onna*, 1974), *The Bacchae* (*Bakkosu no shinjo*, 1978) and *Clytemnestra* (*Ohi Kuritemunesutora*, 1983). Shiraishi left the company in 1989 and continues to act on stage, screen and television in a variety of projects.

Suzuki left Tokyo in 1976 to move to the small village of Toga in Toyama prefecture to continue his theatrical experiments without the distractions of the big city. He also began writing theoretical texts about his theatre which were published in Japan and rapidly translated into many other languages. In 1982 he began an annual summer theatre in Toga and officially changed the name of the Waseda Shōgekijō to Suzuki Company of Toga (SCOT). Suzuki became internationally famous for his signature style, particularly when applied to adaptations of Shakespeare and Greek tragedy.

Betsuyaku Minoru was one of the first playwrights to latch onto the absurdist theatre emerging from Europe. His plays featured minimalist set and props, with broken characters failing to communicate, speaking at or past, not to, each other. Winning the Kishida Prize, *The Little Match Girl* (*Machi-uri no shōjo*, 1966) became an exemplary work. Based on the Hans Christian Anderson short story, a pair of children arrive to accuse an elderly couple of forgetting them, a stunning indictment of wartime deprivation and refusal of the older generation to take responsibility for, or even acknowledge any culpability for, the actions of the nation in the 1930s and 1940s.

By the mid-1960s, Betsuyaku was not affiliated with any single company or troupe but wrote for several. His style also became less bleak and more comic. In the 1970s and 1980s his work became more fixated on the physical and on the actors' bodies, resulting in his 'corpse plays' (*shitai geki*), in which a couple is confronted with the reality of a physical dead body. By the end of the century, Betsuyaku had written over one hundred plays.

Ninagawa Yukio began as an actor in 1955, but switched to directing, partnering with Waseda-educated playwright Shimizu Kunio. In 1969, Shimizu and Ninagawa launched Modern Man's Theatre (*Gendaijin Gekijō*) with *Such a Serious Frivolity* (*Shinjō afururu keihakusa*) as its inaugural production. The two staged a series of edgy 'struggle plays' (*tōsō geki*) that depicted conflicts rooted in a repressive society. In 1974, however, Ninagawa was hired by Tōhō, an entertainment conglomerate that produced commercial theatre and cinema, to direct mainstream productions for them, beginning with Shakespeare's *Romeo and Juliet*. While some in the angura community saw this as selling out, Ninagawa continued to work with Shimizu on smaller productions while staging large commercial events that rapidly grew in popularity.

Like Suzuki, Ninagawa became known as an international success for his stagings of Greek tragedy and Shakespeare, including *Medea* (1983, 1987), *Macbeth* (1985), *The Tempest* (1988), *Hamlet* (1998) and *King Lear* (1999), all in elaborate productions infused with Japanese culture. He began directing regularly in the United Kingdom and some of his plays toured the world and were performed on

Broadway. 'Ninagawa' might even be termed a style, as remountings of his productions featured titles preceded by his name: *Ninagawa Macbeth, Ninagawa Medea* and 2005's *NINAGAWA Twelfth Night*. He also directed updated, spectacular versions of traditional plays, such as *Tales from Chikamatsu* (*Chikamatsu Monogatari*) and Mishima's modern nō plays, making Ninagawa arguably Japan's most successful and well-known commercial director.

His partner Shimizu continued to write angura plays with existential themes, continuing his collaborations with Ninagawa. Later plays in the 1970s began to explore the nature of theatre, the lost sense of Japanese identity and the search for home, such as in *The Dressing Room* (*Gayuka*, 1977), concerning four actresses, two alive, two ghosts, seeking roles that feel like home. The full title of the play is *The Dressing Room, or That Which Flow Away Ultimately Becomes Nostalgia*. Other plays from this period also present actors in search of a home: *An Older Sister, Burning Like a Flame* (*Hi ni yō ni samishii ane ga ite*, 1978) and *Tango at the End of Winter* (*Tango fuyu no owari ni*, 1984).

In the wake of Seinen's founding and the AMPO crisis, numerous angura groups formed, often organising around the vision of a playwright/director who developed the style of the group. Kara Jūrō (1940–) founded the Situation Theatre (*Jōkyō Gekijō*, 1962–88), using a signature red tent to stage plays anywhere in Tokyo and Japan, not being limited to actual theatres. He appropriated kabuki techniques and referred to actors as 'riverbed beggars,' referencing the founding of kabuki. Many of his plays have at the heart the search for a true Japanese identity. His play *The Virgin Mask* (*Shōjo kamen*, 1969), which won the 1970 Kishida Prize, concerned characters in an underground coffee shop named 'The Body' in which the Japanese tendency to bury historical memory was critiqued. *John Silver, The Beggar of Love* (*Jon Shiburaa, ai no kojiki*, 1970) featured young characters searching for physical love, spiritual meaning, lost selves and even a messiah. *Two Women* (*Futari no Onna*, 1979), based on an episode from the *Tale of Genji*, was set in a mental hospital and demonstrated the loss of self that comes with the loss of connection to tradition and history. Kara's theatre privileged the body and focused on physicality and movement over dialogue.

Like Kara, Satoh Makoto (1943–) also staged plays in a tent. Beginning as Theatre Center 68/71 (*Engeki Sentā*), Satoh then founded the Black Tent Theatre (*Kokushoku Tento*), which is still active today, touring to indoor theatre spaces now, however. Satoh attended Waseda University, but dropped out and began being active in the angura theatre. His first play, *Ismene* (1966), an adaptation of the Antigone story which examines inaction in the face of tragedy, was staged by the Jiyū Gekijō, an angura company begun by Satoh that took the name of Osanai Kaoru's original shingeki company. *My Beatles or, The Funeral* (*Atashi no biitoruzu aruiwa sōshiki*, 1967) was directed by Suzuki Tadashi for the Waseda Shōgekijō, based on a true incident in which a Korean man killed a Japanese woman. Satoh used the play and the incident to interrogate Japan's imperialist past and colonisation of Korea, while including the Beatles as spirit figures (*marebito*). *Nezumi Kozō: The Rat* (*Nezumi Kozō Jirokichi*, 1968) is a retelling of a Japanese Robin Hood-type myth. In the first play written for the Black Tent Theatre and directed by Satoh, *The Dance of Angels Who Burn Their Own Wings* (*Tsubasa o moyasu tenshi-tachi no butō*, 1970), loosely based on Peter Weiss's drama *Marat/Sade*, freedom and revolution are interrogated and found lacking. Satoh returned to Japanese imperialism as subject matter in the trilogy *Comic World of Shōwa* (*Kigeki shōwa no sekai*, 1975–6, 1979).

In the late 1970s, Satoh's interest in pan-Asianism and exploring cultural history resulted in *Journey to the West* (*Saiyūki*, 1980), an inventive staging of the Chinese classic Ming Dynasty epic novel, which toured Asia. Throughout the 1980s, Satoh remounted plays and directed significant productions of Dario Fo, Georg Büchner and Bertolt Brecht. In 1993, the Black Tent Theatre opened an acting school, but Satoh returned to playwriting at the end of the twentieth century. His play *The Last Airplane* (*Zettai hikōki*, 2003) is an imaginative exploration of the thoughts in Mohammed Atta's mind as his plane strikes the World Trade Center during the terror attacks of 11 September 2001.

Arguably one of the dominant and emblematic figures of the late angura period was the iconoclastic, provocative, countercultural and confrontational Terayama Shūji (1935–83). Founding Peanut Gallery

(*Tenjō Sajiki*) in 1967, Terayama embraced outsiders and the strange. Terayama's plays honoured alternative and taboo sexualities, sideshow freaks, Oedipal desires, violent confrontations between characters (and sometimes the audience!), and folklore and shamanism. Terayama was a believer in both big spectacle and in confounding audience expectations. In plays such as *The Hunchback of Aomori* (*Aomori-ken no semushi otoko*, 1967), *The Dog God* (*Inugami*, 1967), *Maria in Furs* (*Kegawa no Marii*, 1967), *Heretics* (*Jashūmon*, 1971) and *Bluebeard's Castle* (*Aoigeko no shiro*, 1979), Terayama sought to celebrate outcasts, such as hunchback dwarves, transvestites and the damned. Metatheatre frequently figured in his plays, which were always acknowledged in performance as performances. His politics were never overt. Terayama was haunted by the quest for a true Japanese identity, but his work was also suffused with a playful refusal to take anything seriously, heralding the apolitical playfulness that would dominate the 1980s.

## Angura and Butō

Another development in the 1960s was the rise of *butō*, created by Hijikata Tatsumi (1928–86), a dance/performance art, sometimes called '*ankoku butō*' (dance of utter darkness), although the name literally means 'dance stomp'. Hijikata, trained as a modern dancer, first premiered his new form in 1959 in a production called *Forbidden Colors* (*Kinjiki*), inspired by the 1953 Mishima Yukio novel of the same name, itself a euphemism for homosexuality. His style, like that of the angura movement, was a rebellion against Western cultural influence in modern dance and seeking a form that suited the Japanese body and spoke to Japanese cultural heritage.

Other butō performers followed in Hijikata's footsteps. Ōno Kazuo (1906–2010) developed a different form of butō, much lighter and more playful. His best known piece was *Admiring La Argentina* (*La Argentina Shō*, 1977), a tribute to the Spanish dancer, whom Ōno saw perform in Tokyo in 1929. He was seventy-one when he first performed the piece, touring the world with it for the next decade. Great Camel Battleship (*Dairakudan*) was a butō dance group founded in 1972 by

Maro Akaji (b. 1943), a student of Hijikata's. Dairakudan, still active as of this writing, is known for its highly dramatic spectacles, with whitewashed bodies performing fragmented and broken movements, over-emotional expressions and emphasising the grotesque. Sankai Juku, also still active, an all-male butō company formed in 1975, prefers evocative pictorial composition to erotic grotesque. Butō has grown in popularity internationally, and its practitioners perform all over the world, although it still plays to an elite, self-selecting audience in Japan.

Ironically, even as the 1960s saw the rise of a counterculture that rejected commercialism and capitalism, the theatre also witnessed a rise of a new commercialism in the form of musicals and other larger-scale popular entertainments. Writer/director/producer Kikuta Kazuo (1909–73) began developing first small-scale, then increasingly bigger musicals for Tōhō, which subsequently produced *My Fair Lady* in 1963, Japan's first all-Japanese cast musical, demonstrating audiences would accept Japanese casts singing in Japanese in musicals set in foreign lands. The floodgates opened. Within the decade, Tōhō had seven theatres for staging Western-style musicals and large-scale straight plays, including its flagship two thousand-seat Tokyo Imperial Theatre, which was inaugurated with *Scaretto*, a musical adaptation of *Gone with the Wind* (the only musical adaptation authorised by Margaret Mitchell's estate). Tōhō productions of *Fiddler on the Roof, The Man of La Mancha* and *The King and I* rapidly followed. Tōhō continues to revive shows regularly every few years, keeping their musicals in regular rotation.

Four Seasons Theatre Company (Gekidan Shiki, known popularly as 'Shiki') was founded in 1953 by Asari Keita (b. 1933) as a shingeki company staging Western dramas in translation, including plays of Chekhov, Anouilh and Giraudoux. Inspired by the touring American production of *West Side Story* in 1964, however, Shiki began mounting original musicals, such as *The Emperor's New Clothes* (1964). In 1973, Asari directed a production of *Jesus Christ Superstar* that employed kabuki make-up. By the end of the 1970s, Shiki had grown into a massive company of over one thousand members with nine home theatres in Tokyo, Nagoya, Osaka, Sapporo and Fukuoka, which collectively staged over 3,000 performances a year, for an average of eight hundred per show of up to twelve current productions. Subsequent productions include *Cats* (1983 premiere), *Phantom of the Opera* (1988 premiere) and *The Lion King* (1998). Shiki also produced original musicals, such as 1987's *A Dream within a Dream* (*Yume kara sameta yume*), 1989's *Yuta and Enchanting Friends* (*Yuta to fushigi na nakama tachi*) and 1991's *Ri Kōran*, the former two based on popular novels of the same names, while the latter is named after and based on the life story of a famous singer during the Sino-Japanese War. Japanese musicals have proven to be a one-way street: Western musicals will often premiere in Japan soon after their debuts in New York or London, but Japanese musicals cannot find audiences outside of Japan.

## Second and Third Generations

In hindsight, the 1970s were a period of transition. Many angura artists continue to work and evolve, but the radicalism and socialism of the 1960s began to wane with the end of the decade. In 1972 the United Red Army Incident, in which the revolutionary left wing of the Japanese Communist Party was discovered to have killed fourteen of its own members for not being ideologically pure or revolutionary enough, calling the executions 'death by defeatism' ('haiboku shi'). The nation was shocked and the political left lost a great deal of credibility. That scandal, combined with a recession that began in 1973 at the same time as the Organization of the Petroleum Exporting Countries (OPEC) oil embargo, signalled the beginning of a cultural shift to the right.

Figures like Yamazaki Tetsu (b. 1947) arose out of the 1960s and moved theatre into a new direction during this period. Yamazaki joined Kara Jūrō's Jōkyō Gekijō as an assistant director after dropping out of Hiroshima University in 1970. He also became the leader of Deaf Gallery Theatre (*Tsunbo Sajiki*) with the intention of developing new audiences. Disbanding that group in 1979, he founded Transposition 21 Company (*ShinTen-i-21*) in 1980 for the purpose of developing what he called 'life-size' theatre. Yamazaki believed that the 1960s were larger than life and looked to find a theatre that would preserve human possibility while not expanding into the realm of the mythopoetic. He wrote plays with contemporary dialogue that were also presentational, featuring simultaneous action. Rather than a retreat back to naturalism and realism, Yamazaki sought a theatre that would avoid the excesses of angura and speak to the audiences of the 1980s.

Tsuka Kohei (b. 1948) was a second-generation resident Korean without Japanese citizenship who attended Keio University. Writing under a pen name, his *The Atami Murder Case* (*Atami satsujin jiken*, 1973) was a huge success and marked Tsuka as the first playwright born after the war to win the Kishida Prize. The drama censured police for caring more about public perception than actually solving crimes. The play resulted in a 'Tsuka Boom', attracting a younger audience to his plays. His company, Tsuka Kohei Company (*Tsuka Kohei Jimusho*), was established in 1974. Tsuka's plays also marked the first major departure in style from angura. They were intensely funny, apolitical and ironic comedies dealing mostly with loss and emptiness. While Tsuka was arguably the most popular playwright of the 1970s, from 1982 to 1987 he stopped his involvement in theatre to focus on novels.

Another playwright who began in the 1960s but rose to prominence in the 1970s was Ōta Shogo (b. 1939), who was born in Jinan, China, and repatriated to Japan at the end of war. His childhood experiences of privation, travel and loss shaped his dramaturgy. In 1968 he co-founded Theatre of Transformation (Tenkei) with Hodojima Takeo and Shinagawa Tōru. In 1970 he became the resident playwright and director of Tenkei. His masterpiece from this period was 1977's *The Tale of Komachi Told by the Wind* (*Komachi Fuden*), based on the nō play *Sotoba Komachi*, which subsequently won the Kishida Prize.

Ōta's dramaturgy eschews spoken language and realistic movement. His cycle of 'station plays' is wordless, instead presenting a series of actions and images proceeding with nō-like slowness to create feelings of dislocation and unease in the audience that they then carry out into the street after the performance. Ōta's plays from the 1980s portrayed scenes of devastation and collapse, demonstrating the apocalyptic mode, discussed below. *The Water Station* (*Mizu no eki*, 1981) featured eighteen characters slowly moving past a dripping water faucet, while a man sitting in trash observes them. *The Earth Station* (*Chi no eki*, 1985), *The Wind Station* (*Kaze no eki*, 1986) and *The Sand Station* (*Suna no eki*, 1993) followed, although Tenki disbanded in 1988. The next two decades saw more experimental drama from Ōta, who also began teaching, first at Kinki University, then at Kyoto University of Art and Design.

The 1980s saw Japan develop the so-called 'bubble economy'. It was a decade of wealth and economic expansion and excess that saw Japan ascendant on the world stage. Conspicuous consumption was a large part of 1980s culture in Japan, as in the West, as was conspicuous construction. Real estate and new buildings were a centre of the new economy, and with the new building boom came dozens of new theatres – in department stores, hotels, office buildings and schools. The 1980s also featured a media-saturated culture and postmodernism and poststructuralism in the academy. Scepticism towards the claims of modernism, rejection of humanism and a recognition of the inherent instability of texts, language and meaning led to greater play of language and rejection of the 'grand narratives' of history, such as Marxism and Christianity. Those who came of age in this period were the generation born after the occupation. Unlike the artists of the 1960s, who knew war in their childhood, privation and occupation in their early years and the disappointment of a failed political movement, 1980s artists grew up in a period of prosperity. If angura rebelled against shingeki, 1980s theatre in part was a rebellion against angura.

The theatre of the 1980s was postmodern, apolitical for the most part, commercial (or at least commercially oriented), playful, intertextual and influenced by popular culture, especially manga and anime. Uchino Tadashi argues that the two dominant modes of 1980s drama were neonationalism and apocalyptic.[7] Pride in ascendant Japan and its economic power and rising cultural power, combined with fear of nuclear weapons and threats from the Soviet Union, North Korea and the People's Republic of China, resulted in both a sense of Japanese superiority and a sense of the imminent end of the world. A third theme, however, was the opposite of the first. The empty promise of economic security and the lack of spiritual satisfaction conversely led to both 'the idealisation of a homogenous Japanese identity' and a refusal to resist power, but instead to illustrate the lives of quiet despair of contemporary middle-class Japanese.[8]

Kitamura Sō (b. 1952), for example, offered a new model with *Ode to Joy* (1979), set in a ruined city after a nuclear war. Comic dialogue called into question the reality of the situation, as characters compare the atomic detonations to fireworks, or the characters' plan to walk to Jerusalem from Japan. The title is both ironic and serious, as the characters are filled with joy at the end of the world, the extinction of Japan and humanity not spoiling their good moods.

Likewise, Kawamura Takeshi (b. 1959), founder, director and chief playwright of Daisan Erotica (est. 1980), co-founded with other students from Meiji University, presented an apocalyptic vision of the present and future. He separated himself from the angura generation by attacking their theatre. Kawamura also employed English-language titles and presented plays filled with political critiques and images of devastation. *Nippon Wars* (*Nippon wōzu*, 1984), The *Last Frankenstein* (*Rasuto Furankenshutain*, 1986) and *Tokyo Trauma* (*Tokyo torauma*, 1995) all explore traumatic national history during and after wars, display concern for technology as tool and danger, and are highly referential, citing other texts from *Blade Runner* to the plays of Shakespeare. Kawamura disbanded Daisan Erotica in 2000, but began working with a new company, T-factory, offering more mature, subtle plays.

Popular culture references and much more fun apocalypses can be found in the work of Noda Hideki (b. 1955), who was influenced by Kara Jūrō and who founded the Dream Wanderers (*Yume no Yūminsha*) in 1976 at the University of Tokyo. With Yume no Yūminsha, Noda created his signature style, combining angura physicality, with 1970s humorous wordplay and pop culture references. It very quickly became known as 'the body that won't stand still' style. Time travel, intermixing characters from different plays, and grandiose narratives were combined with a frenetic performance style that became very popular – apolitical youth theatre influenced by manga and anime. His plays might feature the end of the world or a post-apocalyptic landscape, but it was never presented in horror or despair. Rather, these setting merely allowed for greater play of the imagination. In Noda's theatre, the end of the world isn't necessarily a bad thing, and often is quite enjoyable. In 1992 Noda disbanded the company and studied in the United Kingdom for a year, returning to Tokyo to found NODA MAP in 1993. In the 1990s, Noda's work became more politically oriented, in plays like *Red Demon* (*Akaoni*, 1996), in which a man washes ashore and, not sharing a common language with the inhabitants, is treated as a monster. Noda also became interested in adaptations and hybrids of classical dramas, as will be discussed below.

Another playful playwright from the 1980s was Ōhashi Yasuhiko (b. 1956), who began his studies as an electrical engineering student, so his plays are effect driven, with elaborate visuals and special effects. In 1983, Ōhashi and Itō Yumiko (b. 1959) formed Freedom Boat Theatre Company (Gekidan Riburesen), whose name suggests both voyaging and artistic and political freedom. His Kishida Prize-winning play *Godzilla* (*Gōjira*, 1987) places the titular monster in a relationship with an eighteen-year-old girl whose family rejects him as a possible son-in-law. The play is a satire on materialism and status-conscious middle-class Japanese, but the play is also funny and ludicrous, verging on nonsense as other monsters such as Mothra, Gamera and Ultraman arrive to debate and the grandmother of the family reveals she used to date a tadpole.

Like Tsuka Kohei, Chong Wishin (b. 1957) was a Korean-Japanese playwright who wrote plays dealing with outsider identities. With other 'Special Permanent Resident Koreans', Chong was part of the Shinjuku Go-Getters' Club (*Shinjuku Ryōzanpaku*). His signature play was *A Legend of Mermaids* (*Ningyō densetsu*, 1989), which portrayed a nomadic family ejected from every town it approached, but never ending the quest for a home that would allow them to preserve their identity. While other 1980s playwrights tended to the comic, Chong tended to the physical and metaphorical. His plays explored movement while limiting verbal exchange, replacing linguistic play with physical action.

The 1980s also experienced an emergence of female playwrights, directors and collectives. Women had become more active in the

1960s, but it was in the 1980s when many individual and groups of women gained eminence. Kishida Rio (1950–2003) graduated from law school and joined Terayama's Tenjō Sajiki in 1974. She collaborated with Terayama on several plays, and with his encouragement founded With the Help of My Big Brother Theatre Company (*Ka-i Gekijō*) to focus on plays about women. After his death she founded The Kishida Office (*Kishida Jimushō*), her own theatre company. In 1984 she wrote her masterwork *Thread Hell* (*Ito Jikoku*, also sometimes translated as 'Woven Hell'), concerning the plight of Meiji-era female silk workers. In the late 1980s she became interested in collaboration between cultures and especially with Korea, identifying Japanese imperialism with the patriarchy and oppression of women with the emperor system. Her 1994 play *Bird! Bird! Blue Bird!* (*Tori yo, Tori yo, Aoi Tori yo*) was about Korean occupation and Japanese cultural colonialism. She later collaborated with Singaporean playwright Ong Keng Sen on multilanguage Shakespeare adaptation for multinational audiences and with Korean director Lee Yung-tek in the first Japanese-Korean collaborative production, *Happy Days* (*Sewoli-Chota*). In 2001 she took over as director of Asian Women's Theatre Conference.

Watanabe Eriko (1955–), another feminist playwright from the 1980s, founded Thirty Circles Company (*Sanjū-maru*, 1980–97), reflecting her concept of drama as a series of concentric circles that move past earthbound concepts. As with other 1980s playwrights, her work is playful and referential. Her Kishida Prize-winning play *Kitarō the Ghost Hunter* (*Gegege no ge*, 1982) features a bullied young boy haunted by his stillborn twin sister who copes through comic book fantasies. Kisaragi Koharu (1956–2000) founded the student group Freak (*Kiko*) in 1976 at Tokyo Woman's Christian University, and her own company, NOISE, in 1983. Her plays are non-realistic multimedia mashups, frequently compared to Noda Hideki's work due to similarities in playfulness, multimedia and popular culture references.

Collectives, both all-female and mixed gender, also emerged in the 1980s at a time of increased support for the arts and space in which to perform. Paradoxically, by the end of the decade, the 1960s concept of the collective ensemble would be vanishing, as economic realities made such style of production less feasible. The producer-based model the Americans attempted to institute during the occupation would begin to rise during the 1990s. Two significant collectives stood out: One was Blue Bird Company (*Gekidan Aoi Tori*, 1974–93), with six founding female members, all trained at Tokyo Theatre Ensemble (*Tokyo Engeki Ansamburu*) and whose plays are attributed to 'Ichidō Rei', the pen name of company that means 'all bow together'. The other was dumb type, founded in 1984 by graduates of the Kyoto Prefectural College of the Arts, whose signature works include *PLEASURE LIFE* (1988), *pH* (1991) and *S/N* (1994). The title of the last stands for 'signal to noise ratio' and was the last piece by founding member Furuhashi Teiji (1960–95) who died of AIDS the year after the production premiered. Dumb type continued to perform into the twenty-first century.

In 1989 Emperor Hirohito, the monarch during the Second World War, revered by Mishima and protested against by the angura playwrights, died. The Shōwa era ended; Heisei began. One year later, the economic bubble burst, the bubble economy collapsed and Japan went into recession. The year 1990 marked the end of an era in more ways than one and the theatre once again transformed in response to new cultural conditions.

## Fourth Generation

The term 'Quiet Theatre' (*shizuka na engeki*) was first used in the late 1980s but the movement came into its own in the 1990s. Quiet theatre marked a return of sorts to realism after the experiments of the 1960s through the 1980s. Similar to earlier literary shingeki, focusing on psychological realism, Quiet Theatre was a reaction to the larger spectacles of theatre makers like Noda Hideki and Kawamura Takeshi. It also focused on the urban middle class in a manner that earlier shingeki, with its preference for working-class subjects, did not. Quiet theatre also features a dedication to small details through a series of glimpses. For example, Iwamatsu Ryō's play *Futon and Daruma*, discussed below, is named after futons (traditional Japanese bedding) and daruma (hollow, round dolls given as good luck gifts). The play was inspired by a conversation Iwamatsu overheard in a café one day in which two elderly men spent over an hour discussing daruma. The conversation was solely about dolls, but Iwamatsu understood that a subtext could be easily discerned under the seemingly frivolous topic.

The main proponent of this type of theatre was Hirata Oriza (b. 1962). The Youth Group Theatre Company (*Seinen-dan*) was formed in 1982 by Hirata at International Christian University in Tokyo with his peers. In 1986 he graduated college, and began working in the 150-seat Komaba Agora Theatre. Writing plays in which large casts spoke overlapping dialogue, establishing a collective narrative greater than the sum of its parts, Hirata directs his own plays with an emphasis on the everyday reality of the situations. A year in Korea resulted in his play *Citizens of Seoul* (*Sōru shimin*, 1989), concerned with the lives of Koreans in Japan in 1909, the year before annexation. His signature work, however, *Tokyo Notes* (*Tokyo nōto*, 1994), a Kishida Prize winner, was set in a Tokyo art museum as patrons enter and discuss both the art and a war in Europe, leading to no conclusion but demonstrating the disconnect of the lives of the characters from events happening anywhere else in the world.

Another standard bearer for Quiet Theatre, Iwamatsu Ryō (b. 1951) was the leader of Tokyo Electric Battery Company (*Tokyo Kandenchi*), founded 1976. It was Iwamatsu's *Tea and a Lecture* (*Ocha to sekkyō*, 1986) that was regarded as the first quiet play. Iwamatsu wrote plays, frequently in trilogies, that dealt with the public and home lives of men in moments of quiet psychological crisis. For example, his play *Futon and Daruma* (*Futon to Daruma*, 1988), another Kishida Prize winner, dealt with the confusion of a father coming home the evening after his daughter's wedding. Nothing monumental or dramatic happens in the play, but his sense of loss and his inability to relate to his wife, the bride's stepmother and his friends show a middle-aged Japanese office worker with no sense of identity or self. Iwamatsu became more involved in film and television work as the decade went on, although he continued to write and direct for the theatre throughout the last decade of the twentieth century and the first decade of the twenty-first.

Often identified as a member of the Quiet Theatre movement, Miyazawa Akio (b. 1955) wrote more politically oriented works than Hirata or Iwamatsu, preferring to confront audiences with topical issues. He established the Amusement Park Operations Renewal Group (*Yūenchi Saisei Jigyōdan*) in 1985, but his best work, *Hinemi*, was first performed in 1992. In the play, the protagonist attempts to draw a map of Hinemi, his hometown, but unable to remember it. He moves back and forth through time, meeting his future children and dead brother. The play demonstrated both his concern for Japanese cultural memory and his dramaturgy of uncertainty and anxiety, shaped by the conditions and events of the 1990s.

By 1993, Japan's economy had sunk to its lowest point since the occupation. Then, two events in 1995 further filled the nation with uncertainty, anxiety and fear. On 17 January the Great Hanshin-Awaji Earthquake, also known as the Kobe Earthquake, struck creating a huge amount of damage and displacing tens of thousands of people. Then, on 20 March, the Aum Shinrikyō Tokyo subway sarin gas attacks, known in Japan as the *Chikatetsu Sarin Jiken*, occurred. A religious cult released a deadly nerve gas in the Tokyo subway system during rush hour, killing several and sickening thousands. The investigation led to a nationwide manhunt, the arrest of the perpetrators and the leader of the cult. A nation already concerned with economic disaster was suddenly coping with vast natural disaster and terrorism. The theatre immediately engaged these topics.

Emerging in the 1990s was a theatre of social critique. Not as confrontational as the theatre of the 1960s, the social theatre of the 1990s nevertheless offered a vision of a nation gone wrong and challenged the audiences of the time to recognise their own culpability in social injustices.

Nagai Ai (b. 1951) was active in theatre in the early 1980s as an actress, but lack of good roles and opportunities led her to Two Rabbits Company (*Nitosha*), founded in 1981 with Ōishi Shizuka (b. 1951). Her plays were naturalistic, influenced by Chekhov and her Stanislavski training, but she showed an early inventiveness in *Kazuo* (1984), in which two actresses play twelve roles, except the omnipresent (but not seen on stage) title character. In 1991 Nagai became artistic director of Nitosha and her plays became more political and socially aware. She wrote a trilogy about life in Japan after the war, including *Time's Storeroom* (*Toki no Moonoki*, 1994), a critique of the turbulent period after the AMPO crisis, and *Daddy's Democracy* (*Papa no demokurashii*, 1995), depicting the uncertainty in Japan during the transition from military government to democracy during the occupation. *Murderous Impulse without 'Ra'* (*'Ra' naki no satsui*, 1997) was a critique of masculine bias in Japanese language, while *The Three Hagi Sisters* (Hagi-ke no san shimai, 2000) was a playful riff on Chekhov to examine contemporary Japanese women's lives and gender stereotypes in contemporary Japan. *Hello, Mother* (*Konnichiwa, kāsan*, 2001) offered an analysis of corporate restructuring and its effects on the lives of women.

Another artist of social critique, Sakate Yōji (1962–) began studying literature at Keio University in 1981 and in the following year joined Transposition 21 Theatre Company, run by Yamazaki Tetsu. In 1983 he formed Theatre of Phosphorescence (*Rinkōgun*), which is still his production company three decades later. Sakate is known as a playwright concerned with social issues and responsive to events and movements within Japanese society. His plays comment on and critique what he perceives to be inequality, unethical or situations that he finds alarming. *Tokyo Trial* (*Tōkyō saiban*, 1988) was concerned with injustices within the legal system during the trial of a Korean Airlines bombing suspect. *Come Out* (*Kamu auto*, 1989) explored a lesbian discovering her sexual identity. *Breathless* (*Buresuresu*, 1991), initially concerned with garbage in Tokyo, was rewritten in 1995 to incorporate the Aum Shinrikyō Tokyo subway sarin gas attack. *Epitaph for the Whales* (*Kujira no Bohyō*, 1993) engaged the moral complexity and economic anxiety created for Japanese whalers after commercial whaling was banned. *Emperor and Kiss* (*Tennō to seppun*, 1999) was a critique of the Emperor system. *Hikkikomori*, the practice of young people becoming social shut-ins, unable to cope with the outside world, was the subject matter of the award-winning *Attic* (*Yaneura*, 2002). *Danger! Mines!* (*Daruma san ga koronda*, 2004) presented four stories dealing with the problems caused by landmines. Sakate remains a prolific playwright committed to exploring social issues in his plays.

The twentieth century has closed with continuity in Japanese theatre. Suzuki Tadashi, Satoh Makoto, Noda Hideki, Ōta Shogo, Kara Jūrō, Ninagawa Yukio and many others from the 1950s, 1960s, 1970s, 1980s and 1990s continue to develop new work, remount older pieces and present their theatre all over the world, including tours to Europe, Asia and the Americas. Genealogies can be traced; for example, Yamazaki Tetsu was a member of Kara Jūrō's company in the early 1970s. Sakate Yōji learnt from Yamazaki in the 1980s, as Kara had from Fukuda Yoshiyuki in the early 1960s. Each artist developed his or her own style, but was influenced by those who taught him and those who came before. The theatre may have significantly changed in the second half of the twentieth century, but those changes grew out of a theatre with a long history. Lastly, the advent of a new theatre form does not mean the end of the old. Shingeki, anugra, shinpa, musicals and other forms all continue to occupy the stages of Japan, ensuring continuity as well as variety, novelty and invention.


## Fifth Generation: Hybrids for a New Century

Just as the twentieth century began with hybrids of traditional and Western theatres, it ended with hybrid and fusion productions and non-Japanese working in traditional theatres. More recently, new playwright/directors, actors and designers are emerging as part of the next generation of theatre artists. Okada Toshiki (1973–) founded his own company chelfitsch (its name is a play on the English word 'selfish' and is never capitalised) in 1997 at the age of 24 and rapidly rose to international attention. Okada's work combines choreography, the use of images and a sophisticated, fragmented, abbreviated, idiosyncratic and hyper-colloquial language. His plays have been described as a fusion of drama and abstract dance. Major works include *Five Days in March* (*Sangatsu no Itsukakann*, 2004), which juxtaposes the beginning of the Iraq war with the brief affair of a couple and won the 2005 Kishida Kunio Prize, *We Are the Undamaged Others* (*Watashitachi wa mukizuna betsujin de aru*, 2010), *We Don't Understand Each Other the Way We Don't Understand Home Appliances* (*Kaden no yō ni wakariae nai*, 2011) and *The Sonic Life of a Giant Tortoise* (*Zougame no sonikku raifu*, 2011). His work is at the forefront of the next direction of Japanese theatre, the inheritors of shingeki, angura, shōgekijō and international theatre practice.

Traditional theatres in search of new, younger audiences have found advocates who have created new hybrids at the end of the twentieth century. These hybrids have replaced the slowness of the traditional form with a much more rapid performance style, replaced texts concerned with the ghosts of samurai or wandering priests with plays about contemporary concerns, and added a good deal of playful visual spectacle. Introduced by Shochiku in 1986, 'Super Kabuki' (*SupaaKabuki*) is a modernised style of kabuki developed by Ichikawa Ennosuke III (b. 1939) and designed to appeal to contemporary audiences more used to film and television than classical theatre. Ichikawa's motto is 'Story, Speed, Spectacle', which also highlights the specific emphases of SupaaKabuki. The first production was *Prince Yamato Takeru* (*Yamato Takeru*) by Umehara Takeshi (b. 1925), which has been followed by a dozen or so plays over the next three decades. Scripts are new, based on myths, legends and literature. Until recently, Ichikawa starred in all of them. In 2012, a new actor took the name Ichikawa Ennosuke IV and announced his intention to continue SupaaKabuki by remounting *Yamato Takeru* with a national tour that year.

In 1994, Theatre Cocoon artistic director Kishida Kazuyoshi collaborated with kabuki performers Nakamura Kankurō V and Nakamura Hashinosuke to develop 'Cocoon Kabuki', another modernist adaptation of kabuki. The first show, *Yotsuya Ghost Story* (*Tōkaidō Yotsuya Kaidan*, 1994), was a contemporary version of a classic nineteenth-century play, followed by *Summer Festival at Naniwa* (Natsumatsuri Naniwa kagami, 1996), originally written for the bunraku, appropriated by the kabuki and then further modernised for a Cocoon Kabuki production. Similarly, Noda Hideki has also collaborated with Nakamura Kankurō V to make contemporary kabuki informed by Noda's theatrical style and sense of playfulness.

Kabuki is not the only traditional theatre to inform a modern hybrid; philosopher Umehara Takeshi, who wrote the first SupaaKabuki play, also developed 'Super-kyogen' (*Supaakyōgen*) and has been working on

'Super-nō' (*SupaaNō*). Supaakyōgen has had several productions since its inception with the 2001 *Mudskippers* (*Mutsugorō*), an environmental comedy in which fish accuse humans of destroying habitats through development. *Human Clone Namashima* (*Kurōn ningen Namashima*, 2002) was a satire in which a plan to clone baseball players goes horribly awry. In *The King and the Dinosaur* (*Ōsama to kyōrū*, 2003), the target is George W. Bush and the Iraq War, as well as economic policies, as the king is taught to summon 'Mr. Money' with the magic word 'globalisation'.[9] While the plays themselves are hybrid new kyogen examining current concerns (environmentalism, cloning, business practices and the Iraq War), the plays espouse traditional values and at least some Japanese nationalism, although Umehara's ultimate targets appear to be short-sighted politicians, unscrupulous and self-serving businessmen, and individuals who refuse to combat destructive practices of all nationalities.

The end of the twentieth century and the beginning of the twenty-first has also seen even greater internationalisation of the Japanese theatre. The BeSeTo Festival, named after Beijing, Seoul and Tokyo, was founded, alternating between the named cities in a theatrical exchange between the nations of East Asia. Artists such as Suzuki, Ninagawa, Satoh, Sakate and, more recently, Okada and collectives like dumb type and Sankai Juku receive regular invitations to present their work all over the world. Numerous other artists engage in collaborations across Asia and around the world, working with theatre companies and individuals from other nations to create transcultural dramas. Miyamoto Amon (b. 1958), the Artistic Director of the Kanagawa Arts Theater, for example, whose original 1987 musical *I Got Merman* attracted a good deal of international attention, became the first Asian ever invited to direct on Broadway. His revival of *Pacific Overtures* by Stephen Sondheim and John Weidman in 2004 was nominated for four Tony Awards.

The beginning of the new millennium has marked a new chapter in modern Japanese theatre, one of hybrids, collaborations, new forms and commitments to continuing the work of the last century. Modern theatre and drama of Japan continues to present the now 'classic' works of shingeki and angura, some of which are also performed outside Japan as the shrinking globe allows for greater sharing of texts and performances. As with all theatres, modern Japanese theatre began as an intercultural form, shaped by forces outside Japan. It continues to be an intercultural, international theatre, demonstrating a fluidity between continuity, novelty and response to social and political contexts.

# CHAPTER 3
## MODERN CHINESE THEATRE TO 1949

Like many other Asian cultures, China has a long theatrical tradition that involves speech, songs, dance and acrobatic combat. Its modern theatre, known as huaju (spoken drama), started in the first decade of the twentieth century as China was forced to open up to the world as a result of global colonialism. This chapter discusses the rise of huaju and its maturity as a dramatic and theatrical form, running from the first half of the twentieth century to the formation of the People's Republic of China in 1949. It will be divided into four sections:

1. Emergence of the Spoken Theatre (1900s–1910s)
2. Social Functions and Formal Experiments (1920s)
3. Maturity of Huaju (1930s)
4. Huaju During and After the War of Resistance against Japan (1937–49)

### Emergence of the Spoken Theatre (1900s–1910s)

In the second half of the nineteenth century, starting from the Opium War (1839–42), China suffered a series of defeat in the hands of Western powers and Japan, which led to various attempts at technical, constitutional and cultural reforms. After the failed constitutional reform in 1898, which was thwarted by Qing Dynasty (1644–1911) Empress Dowager Cixi (1835–1908), a group of leading intellectuals were exiled in Japan where they witnessed, among other issues, Japan's success in reforming kabuki from entertainment of the pleasure district to respectable theatre fit for the emperor and Western dignitaries. They were also inspired by the formation of a new spoken theatre in Japan called shinpa (new school drama, see Chapter 1) that actively propagated Meiji reform ideals and Japanese nationalism. Consequently, one of the group's leaders and leading voice of late Qing reform Liang Qichao (1873–1929) identified, in 1902, the power of theatre, together with vernacular novels, as 'to permeate, immerse, shock, and transcend' (*xun, jin, ci, ti*) the masses in their nationalist conscience.[1] Other theatre reform advocates denounced Chinese theatre as indulging in obscenity, trivialising historical heroes, and incapable of inspiring nationalism.

One of the origins of spoken theatre came from student productions in China's port cities that were forced to open up to international settlement after the Opium War. This was especially true in Shanghai, where amateur theatre productions flourished in the international communities and in church and Chinese schools. These school plays fostered the first generation of new drama artists. Parallel to these locally educated activists, some Chinese students in Japan formed the Spring Willow Society (Chunliu She) at the end of 1906 and staged several plays in the following years, starting from an act of *La Dame aux Camélias* in February 1907 and, in June, a five-act adaptation of *Uncle Tom's Cabin* renamed as *Black Slave's Cry to Heaven* (*Heinu yutian lu*). This production is generally considered the beginning of modern Chinese theatre because of its nationalist message, its predominant reliance on speech rather than singing and dance, its five-act structure, its complete script rather than scenarios and improvisation (which was the case in most new theatre plays of the subsequent decade), the use of ensemble acting, as well as the use of (semi)realistic costumes, set design and make-up. By prioritising the defiant slave George Harris over the good and suffering Uncle Tom, the play, following the nationalist reading of the novel's Chinese translator Lin Shu (1852–1924), turned Harriet Beecher Stowe's anti-slavery novel into a rallying cry over possible racial demise during the height of U.S. discrimination against Chinese immigrants. The play's script was written by Zeng Xiaogu (1873–1936) and its set was designed by Li Shutong (1880–1942), both founders of the Spring Willow Society and art students at the Tokyo School of Fine Arts (Tokyo Bijutsu Gakkou). Before repatriating to Shanghai after the 1911 Revolution, the group, now under the leadership of Lu Jingruo (1885–1915) and Ouyang Yuqian (1889–1962), staged several other productions in Tokyo, including Victorien Sardou's *La Tosca*, by conscientiously imitating shinpa performance styles. In time, their shinpa-based style contested and hybridised with the performance style of locally trained artists in Shanghai to establish China's first form of spoken theatre known as wenmingxi (civilised drama).

The first large-scale new theatre production in Shanghai was another *Black Slave's Cry to Heaven* performance staged by Wang Zhongsheng (1884?–1911) and his Spring Sun Society (Chunyang She) in October 1907, which used a different script from the Spring Willow's. This production was important not for its script or performance, but for its introduction of lighting and proscenium stage to Shanghai's Chinese theatre community as it was staged in the Lyceum (Lanxin) Theatre that had been exclusively occupied by amateur Western settler performance and international touring shows. Wang's production showcased modern stage technology and architecture and led to a building boom of proscenium-stage theatres in Shanghai that eventually surpassed teahouse stages as the standard venue for wenmingxi, jingju (Beijing opera) and other theatrical forms. In the spring of 1908, Wang staged another new play *Joan Haste* (*Jiayin xiaozhuan*), from Lin Shu's translation of a novel by the Victorian adventure novelist Henry Rider Haggard (1856–1925). His collaborator was Ren Tianzhi (dates unknown), who had been living in Japan for several years and was heavily influenced by shinpa. While the production had a better-written script than their previous production and more cohesive acting, it failed to attract an audience and Wang disbanded the Spring Sun Society.

Ren returned to Shanghai in 1911 before the Revolution to form the Evolutionary Troupe (Jinhua Tuan), which staged shinpa-style nationalist plays, including direct depictions of the Revolution after its eruption in October. For a couple of years, Ren's company spread new theatre and its revolutionary message along the Yangtze River, although it failed to win a sustained spot in Shanghai where it lost a month-long competition with jingju in 1912. After the group disbanded, its actors became the core of other wenmingxi companies in Shanghai, making Ren's acting and production style the mainstream of wenmingxi artistry. Apart from its repertoire, the Evolutionary

Troupe's impact is evident in several ways: First, most of its plays used scenarios instead of complete scripts, which ushered in wenmingxi's predominant reliance on scenarios and improvisation. Second, the Evolutionary Troupe initiated a role category system following the jingju model, in part to facilitate improvisation. Finally, Ren initiated the use of out-of-curtain scenes (*muwaixi*) by performing transitional scenes in front of an inner curtain to hide set changes. In time, Ren's style became the dominant force in wenmingxi performance, largely because its hybrid Western, shinpa, and Chinese aesthetics was much closer to the abilities of wenmingxi actors and expectations of the Shanghai audience than Spring Willow's shinpa-inspired dramaturgy and performance that focused on the script and ensemble acting.

However, neither group (and its repertoire) was able to survive commercially in Shanghai until Zheng Zhengqiu (1888–1935), a former jingju critic and one of China's earliest film writers and directors, created a sensational melodramatic hit titled *An Evil Family* (*E jiating*) in 1913 with his New People Society (Xinmin She). Zheng's success ushered in the first boom of commercial success for spoken theatre, until wenmingxi faded by the end of the 1910s. *An Evil Family* tells a meandering story of Pu Jingcheng, a poor merchant who strikes a fortune through bribery, and his concubine abusing his family and acquaintances and the latter's fighting back and eventual triumph. Several reasons contributed to its success, including the play's focus on domestic melodrama, a topic familiar to the Shanghai theatre audience; its reliance on a meandering narrative structure with twists and turns similar to traditional theatre and popular novels; and a serialisation format that spread the production over five cliff-hanging nights and ensured returning spectatorship. Finally, wenmingxi was accessible to the audience and was able to compete with jingju for a brief period of time.

This focus on audience accessibility and acceptance also extended to translated shinpa and European (mostly through shinpa) plays as they were usually localised with Chinese names and environment, although a few plays retained Western *mise-en-scène*, most notably those from Spring Willow's Tokyo days – *La Dame aux Camélias*, *Black Slave's Cry to Heaven* and *La Tosca*. Wenmingxi's heavy emphasis on adaptation and localisation revealed an inherent need for audience reception as a commercial theatre, instead of a desire to maintain the original content through literary translation. While important for reading and literary studies, direct translation was considered unsuitable for the wenmingxi stage because of the foreign content still alien to the Shanghai audience and a lack of theatrical experience on the part of the translators, some of whom even used classical Chinese that was only suitable for reading. The inclination for mixing Western, shinpa, and Chinese elements in translation and script construction is also reflected in the hybridity of performance styles that prioritised audience accessibility and familiarity, including the addition of songs from jingju and popular tunes. Another feature of wenmingxi performance was the coexistence of male actors of female roles (*nandan*) and emerging actresses who often endured social bias in a still conservative society.

By the late 1910s, however, Wenmingxi's inclination for audience acceptance through localised content and performance received heavy criticism as being overly commercial and abandoning modern theatre's nationalist roots in pursuit of popular entertainment. Consequently, the following decade became an antithesis to *wenmingi* with its amateur theatres, vehement anti-feudal spirit and dazzling formal experimentations.

## Amateur Theatres, Social Functions and Formal Experiments (1920s)

One of the most important events in modern Chinese cultural history is the New Cultural Movement (*Xin wenhua yundong*) of the late 1910s that sought to upend traditional Chinese culture, including the form and efficacy of its theatre. For the two years between March of 1917 and 1919, the bastion of the movement, the *New Youth* (*Xin qingnian*) magazine published articles on the future of theatre in almost every issue, culminating in two special issues: the Ibsen issue in June 1918 and the dramatic reform issue in October of the same year. While the issues included essays that defended indigenous theatre's theatricality, conventionality and musicality, the majority of the articles, including those of the two most ardent proponents of the movement Chen Duxiu (1879–1942) and Hu Shi (1891–1962), denounced old theatre, especially jingju, as 'toys' and 'tricks' with no social efficacy or literary value, and could not be utilised for the sake of social enlightenment. For them, the only path to achieving this function was to remove the 'vestiges' of the old society and adopt new concepts, methodologies and forms from the West, particularly realistic theatre, as embodied by Henrik Ibsen. To this end, the Ibsen issue published three of his plays (first instalments of *A Doll's House*, *An Enemy of the People* and *Little Eyolf*) and two introductory articles: 'Ibsenism' and 'A Biography of Ibsen.'

One direct effect of the attention on theatre's social efficacy on plays of the following decade was their focus on the struggle between individual freedom by the young generation against feudal ethics represented by the tyranny of family patriarchs. One of the earliest plays of this genre is Hu Shi's *The Main Event in Life* (*Zhongshen dashi*), a one-act that was published in the March 1919 issue of *New Youth*. Originally written in English, the play is about the love between a young woman Tian Yamei and Mr Chen, which is disapproved by both her mother – based on the supposed incompatibility of their birthdays – and her father who, while objecting the mother's supposition, cites his clan's prohibition on marriage between those with the same family name, even though the Tians and Chens had diverged over 2000 years ago. In the end, Yamei leaves her home to join Mr Chen who is waiting outside in a car, leaving a note to her parents: 'This is the greatest event in your daughter's life. Your daughter ought to make a decision for herself. She has left in Mr. Chen's car. Goodbye for now.'[2]

The suffocating effect of arranged marriage was an acute and oftentimes personal issue for many of the emerging playwrights, including Hu Shi himself who remained with his wife through arranged marriage. In this play, Yamei and Mr Chen have been friends since their student days in Japan, but in the eyes of her parents, their love is insignificant compared to the blind fortunate-teller's words or her father's standing within the family clan. In the end, the only way left for Yamei is to leave her home, following Nora's footsteps. In many subsequent plays of the same theme, the family became a prison with its patriarchs as unbearably hypocritical tyrants, with whom there was no possibility of compromise; escape, either alive or through death, was the only way out. Another example was the play *Zhuo Wenjun* (1923) by Guo Moruo (1892–1978), who wrote the play in Japan while refusing to stay with his wife at home through arranged marriage. Based on a West Han Dynasty (206 BCE–9 CE) woman Zhuo Wenjun who, as a widow living in her father's home, elopes with the famous writer Sima Xiangru (179–127 BCE) when they fall in love through music. Here, the purity of their love is contrasted with her father's hypocritical distain for Sima's poverty and her father-in-law's lascivious desire for her body. Another important character in the play is Wenjun's maid Hongxiao who slays her lover, the servant Qin Er, for betraying Wenjun to her father, before taking her own life, a device obviously borrowed from Japanese kabuki and *bunraku* (puppet theatre) love-suicide plays to show the fiery and uncompromising nature of love and pursuit for freedom, as well as the price of such defiance.

Another important play on the clash between pursuit of love and feudal oppression was a one-act play titled *The Night the Tiger Was Caught* (*Huohu zhiye*) by Tian Han (1898–1968), which takes place in a village at night when the wealthy hunter Wei Fusheng and his helpers set up a trap to catch a tiger as dowry for his daughter Liangu's upcoming wedding to an important family. When a creature is trapped and brought on stage, everyone is surprised to find the assumed tiger, now mortally wounded, to be a young man called Huang Dasha. Huang is Liangu's lover from childhood, but their love became hopeless after his parents died and Liangu's father forbade their meeting. In his desperation to see Liangu before her wedding, Dasha has triggered the gun for the tiger and fallen into the trap. At the end of the play, the father drags away Liangu – who has been clinging to Dasha – to flog her. Left alone on stage, Dasha kills himself with a hunting knife. The play injected an important theme of class division into the clash of generations as well as a rural perspective into the mostly urban plays, with vibrant dialogues peppered with local colours. It was also a highly dramatic play with tight plot development.

This rural emphasis was further delineated in the full-length three-act *Breaking Out of Ghost Pagoda* (*Dachu youlingta*) by the female playwright Bai Wei (1894–1987), another victim of arranged marriage before her escape to Japan. The play depicts three women in varying stages of 'breaking out' of the 'ghost pagoda', the house of a country tyrant Hu Rongsheng. The oldest of them is Xiao Sen, who at one time had an illegitimate daughter with Hu, but is now the representative of the local women's federation. She comes to Hu's house to help his seventh concubine Zheng Shaomei, who loves Hu's son Qiaoming because of their similar interests but is determined to leave Hu and devote her life to serving the anti-warlord troops as a nurse, which she succeeds with the help of Xiao Sen and the peasants association. The youngest woman in the group is Xiao Yuelin, Hu's coveted maid and adopted daughter, as well as the object of love by his son Qiaoming. As it turns out, Yuelin is in fact the daughter of Hu and Xiao Sen from their erstwhile affair and has been secretly guarded by Hu's butler Gui Yi, who has long harboured affections for Xiao Sen. At the end of the play, Qiaoming is stabbed to death by his father when trying to save Yuelin from rape by the latter, Yuelin takes a bullet for her mother during a shootout between her parents, and Xiao kills the tyrant Hu with her pistol. It is a hauntingly powerful play that it both points towards viable paths of self-fulfilment for independent women and the still dominant feudal power that ruthlessly smothers the lives of two young lives. In terms of its dramaturgy, the play was a precursor to several plot devices that were popular in later plays, including the cyclical nature of affairs, incest and revenge, the inescapable web of blood relations, and the usage of ghost images for both atmospheric emphasis and plot advancement.

Of course, not all plays on the issue of family were against arranged marriages, as evidenced by Ouyang Yuqian's *After Returning Home* (*Huijia zhihou*, 1922), in which Lu Zhiping, who has studied in the U.S. and married Mary Liu, returns home to divorce his first wife Wu Zifang, only to find her imminently sensible, caring and modern in thought and behaviour. By contrast, Mary, who has followed Lu, turns out to be a tigress who pushes him for the divorce and storms away after witnessing his hesitation. The play may have been influenced by Ouyang's own happy marriage that, although arranged and was forced on him despite his protest, turned out to be a loving experience.

While the theme of individual freedom was indeed popular among plays of the 1920s, they were written in diverse styles that were far from being restricted to realism. In fact, this was a decade that witnessed a flourishing of modernist styles (known at the time as neoromanticism), especially aestheticism (as represented by Oscar Wilde and Gabriele D'Annunzio), symbolism (Maurice Maeterlinck and Gerhart Hauptmann) and expressionism (Georg Kaiser and Eugene O'Neill). One important expressionist play of this decade is Hong Shen's *Yama Zhao* (*Zhao Yanwang*, 1923), which borrowed from O'Neill's *The Emperor Jones* to stage the miserable life of soldiers during the endless civil wars between warlords. In this play, Zhao Da, a loyal orderly for a battalion commander, is driven to shoot the commander and runs away with the latter's embezzled money into a dark forest at night. In the last two acts, Zhao, just like Jones in O'Neill's play, becomes increasingly deranged and sees apparitions from his past filled with wartime cruelties, ending with a Western missionary who takes away Zhao's land and drives him to the war. Exhausted, Zhao eventually dies in the forest. While the play bewildered Hong's audience at the time, it was an important attempt to expose wartime crimes with expressionist technique.

Similarly, aestheticism's dogged pursuit for beauty and sensual pleasure against rigid moral codes provided another outlet for the irresistible creative energy of the decade. In this sense, Oscar Wilde became the perfect symbol of the age. The *New Youth* alone published translations of his *An Ideal Husband*, *A Florentine Tragedy* and *Lady Windermere's Fan*. Other magazines also published his *The Importance of Being Earnest* and *Salomé*, along with enthusiastic introductory articles that cast Wilde as a victim of Victorian morality that 'will not tolerate those who create castles in the air, who dream, and live for the sake of their imagination' and praised *Salomé* as a play about 'love to death and being loved to death', a sensual and imaginative play 'cloaked in exaggerated similes, exotically archaic words, and ancient rhythmical ballads'.[3] The productions of his *Lady Windermere's Fan* (1924) and *Salomé* (1929) were also important events in modern Chinese theatre. Apart from Wilde's works, D'Annunzio's *The Dead City*, Maeterlinck's *The Blue Bird*, Hauptmann's *The Sunken Bell*, Kaiser's *From Morn to*

*Midnight* and O'Neill's *The Emperor Jones* were some other Western works that greatly influenced the plays of the decade.

Among them, *Pan Jinlian* (1928) by the former Spring Willow actor Ouyang Yuqian transformed the play's eponymous heroine from a historically notorious woman of lust, who kills her husband out of love for his brother Wu Song, into an individualistic and modern woman. Before being killed by Wu Song in revenge for his dead brother, she unabashedly declares her love for him: 'Ah, you want my heart. That's very good. I've already given you my heart. It was here, but you didn't take it. Come and see—[*She tears open her clothing*] inside this snow white breast is a very red, very warm, very true heart. Take it!'[4] Here, Pan Jinlian was obviously created in Salomé's spirit as an individual willing to pursue her love interest regardless of death. While in Japan, Bai Wei, the author of *Breaking Out of Ghost Pagoda*, was especially fascinated by the symbolist plays *The Blue Bird* and *The Sunken Bell*. Her 1926 poetic and symbolic play *Linli* is a wildly imaginative play about the triangular love between a poet and two sisters. Two of the play's three acts take place within Linli's dreams in which her passion and her sister's youthfulness are so potent as to bring the demise of Death himself. Like Salomé, her love is all consuming and present: 'If only there's the most fervent, the most pure moment, then there'll be the future we long for/ Our tragedy is that you don't give me this most fervent, more pure moment!'[5] Her younger sister scolds the poet for separating flesh and soul: 'And you deserved to be an artist!/ Youth, beauty, evil, art . . ./. Without flesh, what is soul?'[6]

Another dramatic form that also flourished in the 1920s was comedy, largely propelled by those returning from Britain, as represented by Ding Xilin (1893–1974) and Yuan Changying (1894–1973). Yuan studied literature at the University of Edinburgh and the Sorbonne. Her *A Kiss before the Wedding* (*Jiehun qian de yiwen*, 1930) was in the same vein as *The Importance of Being Earnest*. Ding's one-act comedies *A Wasp* (*Yizhi mafeng*, 1923), *Oppression* (*Yapo*, 1925), *Three Dollars of National Currency* (*San kuai qian guobi*, 1939) and *Miaofeng Mountain* (*Miaofeng shan*, 1940) represent some of the best achievements of modern Chinese comedy that dramatised the same vexing social issues previously discussed with humour, wit and verbal elegance. His

*A Wasp*, for example, is another play on the choice between love and arranged marriage, but written as a stylistic union of Ibsen and Wilde. The play starts with Madame Ji who has been visiting his son Mr Ji and is about to return home in the South. Before leaving, though, she is worried about the marriages of her son and nephew, as the latter has asked her to act as a go-between for him and Miss Yu, a nurse, who is in fact in love with her son Mr Ji. While Miss Yu is disappointed to find out Madame Ji had someone other than Mr Ji in mind for her, she refrains from confrontation with the old lady by saying she will ask for her parents' consent. When Mr Ji arrives, the two have a chance to finally express their mutual love, ending with Ji excitedly giving Yu a hug. His sudden action leads Yu to scream, which brings in the old lady and a servant, leading the couple to act as if Miss Yu has been stung by a wasp. There is no shooting or storming out of the home, but an urbane elegance for the educated even as they are struggling with the same issues with their country counterparts.

In tandem with the theoretical and dramatic achievements of the decade was the theatrical rejection of wenmingxi's commercialism through the amateur theatre movement, known in Chinese as the *aimeiju* (a transliteration of amateur which means 'aesthetic') movement. Chen Dabei (1887–1944), a wenmingxi veteran, wrote a long article in 1922 titled *Amateur Theatre (Aimei de xiju)* as a guideline with chapters on the history and characteristics of amateur theatre, as well as instructive chapters on playwriting, directing, performance and design. While the movement was a direct response to wenmingxi, the concept of amateur spoken theatre was not new, as evidenced by turn-of-the-century school theatre in Shanghai. Even as wenmingxi was all the rage in Shanghai, the Nankai School New Drama Troupe in Tianjin, another port city about ninety miles south of Beijing, was staging quality original and translated plays under the direction of Zhang Pengchun (1892–1957), who had studied at Columbia University where he wrote scripts in English for student performance. The Nankai School New Drama Troupe trained a number of important figures in modern Chinese theatre, including Cao Yu (1910–96), huaju's best playwright.

Back in Shanghai, after wenmingxi's decline, a group of actors, led by the star Wang Youyou (1888–1937), staged George Bernard Shaw's

*Mrs. Warren's Profession* in 1920 with an all-male cast that included several jingju actors. Despite extensive preparation and advertisement, it was a box-office disaster and was met with strong resistance from the audience, many of whom left during the performance, some while cursing. Wang Youyou concluded that the failure of his *Mrs. Warren's Profession*, which at the time was still banned from public performance in Britain, resulted from a miscalculation of the dynamic between popularisation and elevation. It was also true that none of the practitioners in Shanghai at the time had first-hand knowledge of professional theatre in the West. This situation was changed in 1922 when Hong Shen, who had studied theatre at Harvard under George Pierce Baker and worked in professional theatres in New York, returned to Shanghai and became China's first professional director in his works with the Theatre Association (Xiju xieshe). Hong gradually built up a director-centred rehearsal system and cemented gender-appropriate casting. As Hong explained, 'having read too much of Professor Freud's book on "sexual perversity," I felt truly uneasy every time I saw a man dressed as a woman'.[7] His tactic to convince the actors still invested in female impersonation was to programme two one-acts in the same bill – *The Shrew* (*Pofu*) by Ouyang Yuqian and *The Main Event in Life* by Hu Shi – with actresses in female roles in the first play and an all-male cast in the second play. 'Sure enough, after watching gender-appropriate performance, which they felt very natural, the audience watched men performing women with shrill voices and affected gestures and found them utterly hilarious. As a result, they could not stop laughing, which greatly embarrassed the actors. Their laughter sounded the end of female impersonation at the Theatre Association.'[8] The emphasis on concrete physical characteristics as the winning argument for gender-appropriate casting is reminiscent of a similar battle in Japanese shingeki nearly a decade earlier. According to Ayako Kano, the definitive event took place in 1914 when the actress Matsui Sumako performed the dance of seven veils in Oscar Wilde's *Salomé* by showing the sensuality of her body. 'It was by showing their bodies that women proved they were better than onnagata [male specialists of female roles] in performing the role of women.'[9] Another contributing factor to Hong Shen's victory in the gender-appropriate casting was the changing social attitude in the 1920s when modern 'scientific' discourse in China emphasised the incompatibility of biological sexes. In 1924, Hong directed Oscar Wilde's *Lady Windermere's Fan*, which is generally considered the first 'authentic' huaju production that adhered to the modern Western production conventions of strict rehearsal under a coherent directorial vision, although it still presented a localised, Chinese *mise-en-scène*.

Another important theatre group of the 1920s was the Southern China Society (Nanguo She) led by Tian Han. Through several public performances and tours in the late 1920s that staged *Pan Jinlian*, *Salomé* and Tian Han's own plays, the society became a rallying point that brought together discrete huaju forces, especially Hong Shen and Ouyang Yuqian, to join forces with Tian Han as they prepared for the maturing of huaju in the following decade.

## Maturity of Huaju (1930–7)

After wenmingxi and the amateur theatre movement – after ideological and formal experiments in dramaturgy of the 1920s – huaju came of age in the 1930s, an era that witnessed the increasing threat of Japanese invasion, which loomed from its occupation of the Northeast (Manchuria) in September 1931 until the Marco Polo Bridge Incident on 7 July 1937, which signalled the full-scale war. For huaju, the previous decade's experimental exuberance – in forms and ardent pursuit of individual freedom against the oppressive feudal society – turned to realistic observation and depiction of social realities. In addition, the looming national crisis and international leftist theatre movement pushed many theatre practitioners to seek serving the masses and venture into agitprop theatre. Tian Han, for example, publicly 'turned left', in part forced by his radical students, and rejected his works of the 1920s as expressing 'a common sentiment, a tone of the "torment between the body and soul"' that was far from social realities.[10] In 1931, the Chinese League of Left-Wing Dramatists (Zuoyi Xijujia Lianmeng) was formed in Shanghai with Tian Han as its nominal head.

Another backdrop to this popular theatre movement was the natural progression of huaju's dramatic proficiency and theatrical professionalism. Dramatically, multiact plays replaced one-acts and a number of outstanding plays brought huaju dramaturgy to a new height, culminating in Cao Yu's four masterpieces between 1934 and 1941 that elevated modern Chinese dramatic literature to a peak rarely surpassed in the subsequent decades. Theatrically, the decade witnessed the return of professional theatres, as evidenced by the success of China Traveling Theatre Company (CTTC, Zhongguo Lüxing Jutuan, 1933–47) and the rise of quality productions as well as maturing actors and directors in Shanghai and elsewhere.

As previously mentioned, Cao Yu received his theatre education as a student in Nankai Middle School in Tianjin where the Columbia graduate Zhang Pengchun introduced him and a number of future huaju professionals to classical and contemporary Euro-American drama and modern production principles. Zhang also gave Cao Yu the *Complete Works of Henrik Ibsen* in English, which he read with the help of a dictionary. In 1934, he published *Thunderstorm (Leiyu)* before graduating from Tsinghua University in Beijing, which was quickly followed by *Sunrise* (*Richu*, 1936), *The Savage Land* (*Yuanye*, *The Wilderness*, 1937) and *Peking Man* (*Beijing ren*, 1941). *Thunderstorm* is a story of two families, the capitalist Zhous and the servant Lus. Zhou Puyuan is the owner of a mine. His present wife Fanyi, who is much younger than him, has been in love with his first son Zhou Ping, who is only several years younger than her. However, Zhou Ping is now in love with the maid Lu Sifeng, who is also the object of love by Fanyi's son Zhou Chong. Unknown to all of them, Sifeng's mother Shiping, who is now married to Zhou's head servant Lu Gui, is in fact Zhou Ping's mother and was exactly in Sifeng's situation 30 years ago. She had two sons with Zhou Puyuan but was later driven out of the Zhou house, bringing with her the second son Lu Dahai, who is now a miners' representative negotiating with Zhou Puyuan during a strike. At the end of the play, when the incestuous relationship between Zhou Ping and Sifeng is revealed, three of the young generation die: Sifeng, Zhou Chou and Zhou Ping, and the old generation is left to mourn and deal with the consequence of their actions. Taking place within a suffocating summer day, the play skilfully appropriates European dramatic techniques – from fate and retribution in Greek tragedy to neoclassic unities to Ibsen's *Ghosts* to John Galsworthy's *Strife* – to expand the popular theme of young individuals versus the feudal family with much more complicated characters and tighter plot constructions. Zhou Puyuan, for example, is a more sympathetic patriarch than his one-dimensional counterparts from the previous decade. Here, he is a European-educated industrialist who regrets abandoning his love three decades ago and tries to provide for her while still maintaining their class difference. The death of the three young characters is driven directly by forces outside his control even though he bears ultimate response. Similarly complicated are the three female characters: Shiping, who is in an almost Greek struggle to avoid her original 'sin' of loving her master's son only to see her own daughter falling in the same fate; Sifeng, her daughter, as the vibrant young woman being trapped in the intergenerational web of class and passion; and Fanyi, the most defiant female character in the play, yet also vulnerable and ultimately destructive to those she loves. In terms of structure, *Thunderstorm* follows the unity of time, place and action with an unbearably tight and inescapable rhythm that leads to physical and mental destruction of the major characters.

In 1936, Cao Yu published *Sunrise*, a story about the traps facing Chinese Noras after leaving home for independence. Set primarily in a hotel room in a big city in northern China (presumably Tianjin), the play portrays a kaleidoscope of characters around Chen Bailu, an educated young woman who once lived with a poet in the countryside, only to leave him and the boredom of the country for a life supported by bank manager Pan Yueting and surrounded by other high-society figures, such as a foreign-educated bureaucrat who complains about his wife and a rich widow in pursuit of a young gigolo. Chen also tries but fails to rescue from the claws of gangsters a girl Pipsqueak (Xiao Dongxi) who is sold to a low-class brothel and eventually hangs herself. We also meet Chen's former friend Fang Dasheng who attempts but fails to lead Chen to a new life. Completing this societal portraiture are Pan's secretary Li Shiqing who make ambitious gambles in his attempt to climb up the social ladder, only to pay with the life of his son; Huang Xingsan, a laid-off clerk in Pan's bank who is driven to kill his three children; Cuixi, a kind-hearted prostitute who shares a room with Pipsqueak; and such low-life characters as the hotel steward and a gangster. Eventually Chen, losing heart from Pipsqueak's death and Pan's vanquished financial support as a result of the latter's bankruptcy, takes her own life with sleeping pills, but not before reciting her poet's lines: 'The sun rises, leaving the darkness behind. But the sun is not ours, for we now sleep.' Compared to *Thunderstorm's* airtight structure, *Sunrise's* concentric feature allows character development in their own circles in parallel subplots, including the bank circle that links Pan's ultimate bankruptcy to an offstage underworld boss on the one hand and to Li and Huang on the other, Li's family with his wife and son, Madame Gu and her gigolo, and Pipsqueak and the misery of the low-class brothel.

Comedy also matured in the 1930s and 1940s, as plot-driven well-made plays, as English-style comedy of manners following Ding Xilin, and as satires. As it happens, critics generally agree that it was Li Jianwu's *It's Only Spring* (*Zhe buguo shi chuntian*), published in 1934 – the same year as Cao Yu's *Thunderstorm* – that signified a milestone for huaju comedy because it successfully combined plot construction with characterisation. The play takes place in Beijing during the Northern Expedition (1926–8) when the Kuomintang army in southern China battled with warlords in the north in order to unify the country. It is set in the living room of Beijing Police Chief where his wife is visited by her former lover Feng Yunping, who turns out to be a revolutionary from the south being pursued by the police as soon as he arrived in Beijing. One detective comes to the Chief's home to deliver the letter that ends up in the hands of his wife who, through a series of intrigues, eventually ensures Feng's safe departure from her and Beijing. As a literary scholar who had studied in France and was well versed in Moliere, as well as Victorien Sardou and Eugene Scribe, Li Jianwu was a master of witty dialogue, intriguing plot twists, and intricate character delineation. This last point is especially true in the Chief's wife who shares with many of her stage peers as being trapped in a loveless marriage with an older man. Unlike Fanyi or Bai Wei's Zheng Shaomei, however, she has grown cynical and captive to the vanity until her erstwhile lover rekindles her youthful passion. Instead of letting the fire engulfing all involved, she balances her anxieties with dexterous manoeuver of the specific problem of ensuring her lover's safe escape. In the end, she returns to her web, although her rekindled passion and consequent actions contribute to a sense of rejuvenation, or at least a sense of tranquillity and resolution.

The maturity of dramatic literature also contributed to the re-emergence of professional huaju theatre, most prominently represented by CTTC founded by Tang Huaiqiu (1898–1953), who had studied aviation engineering in France before forming with Tian Han Southern China Society in Shanghai in 1926. In 1933, he founded CTTC with his wife Wu Jing, daughter Tang Ruoqing (1922–83), actor Dai Ya (1909–73) and two other actors. The company debuted in Nanjing in February of the following year with a localised version of Eugene Walter's *The Easiest Way* titled *Mei Luoxiang* (after the play's heroine Laura Murdock) to great success. From the beginning, the company refused support from the government or other institutions and relied on box-office receipt and private support. For the following two years, it moved up to Beijing and toured neighbouring cities to be far from the political centre of Nanjing, which had become the capital after 1927, and the theatrical centre of Shanghai. Indeed, during those two years, it accumulated a solid repertoire that included plays from Southern China Society, *Thunderstorm*, and quite a few translated and adapted plays, particularly a new version of *La Dame aux Camélias* translated and directed by Chen Mian, Tang's friend from their student years in France and a professor of French literature in Beijing. It also trained a solid group of future star actors, including Tang Ruoqing. By the time the company returned to Shanghai in 1936, it shocked the city's entertainment world with *Thunderstorm* and *La Dame aux Camélias*, finally winning long-term contracts for huaju in large-scale theatres such as the Carlton (Ka'erdeng) and Lyceum that were previously open only to movies or occasional Western musicals. During the war, the company went through a number of ups and downs but ultimately survived. It eventually disbanded in 1947. Over its thirteen-year history, it premiered a considerable number of plays with its quality actors and production standard, proving the viability of professional spoken theatre.

Parallel to CTTC were Shanghai spoken theatre artists who were more ideologically attuned to leftist theatre and staged several modern classics. The first group of the leftist movement was Shanghai Art Theatre Society (Shanghai Yishu Jushe), which was established in 1929 by a group of Chinese Communist Party members returning from Japan and was instrumental, together with the radical Modern Society (Modeng She) that had separated from the Southern China Society, in forming the Chinese League of Left-Wing Dramatists in 1931. A seminal event of the movement was Theatre Association's 1933 production of *Roar, China!* by Soviet playwright Sergei Tretyakov (1892–1937), a favourite of international leftist theatre since its 1926 premiere at the Meyerhold Theatre. Based on a true 1924 incident in Sichuan Province, China, where the Captain of the British gunboat HMS Cockchafer demanded the hanging of two Chinese coolies for the accidental death of an American merchant, the play used spectacular stagecraft – including onstage canons from the warship aimed at the audience – to create powerful anti-imperial sentiment featuring a group of defiant coolies and their wives.

Apart from leftist plays, Shanghai also witnessed several productions of European realistic classics that attempted to create 'authentic' *mise-en-scène* with realistic acting, including *Uncle Vanya* (1930) by Xinyou Theatre (Xinyou Jutuan); *A Doll's House* (1935), *The Inspector General* (1935) and *The Storm* (by Russian playwright Alexander Ostrovsky, 1937) by Shanghai Amateur Dramatists Association (Shanghia Yeyu Juren Xiehui); and *Romeo and Juliet* (1937) by Shanghai Amateur Experimental Company (Shanghai Yeyu Shiyan Jutuan). These productions strove for realistic set, costumes and make-up, together with wigs and artificial noses and chins. The actors studied their characters in part by watching Hollywood and Soviet film versions of *A Doll's House*, *The Storm* and *Romeo and Juliet*. For his Uncle Vanya, the actor Yuan Muzhi (1909–78) observed white Russian émigrés in local Russian restaurants, whose demoralised mood as refugees of the Soviet revolution led to his continually downcast and melancholic facial expression. The latter four plays, all directed by Zhang Min (1906–75), were part of a conscientious effort to elevate the actors' performance skills through challenging plays. Zhang had translated several articles on acting and directing, including an introduction of Gordon Craig and Adolphe Appia in 1935, and was one of the first directors to adopt the Stanislavski system. During the war, he co-translated *An Actor Prepares* from Elizabeth Reynolds Hapgood's 1936 English version. Admittedly, neither he nor his actors were well versed in the system during these pre-war productions.

One of the best-known plays depicting life in pre-war Shanghai is *Under Shanghai Eaves* (*Shanghai wuyan xia*) by Xia Yan (1900–95), which he wrote in 1937 right before the war but debuted in 1940. Set in an alley, it uses a cross section of a two-story building to portray the lives of its five tenant families, starting from the sublessor Lin Zhicheng and Yang Caiyu who are confronted with the return of Lin's friend and Yang's husband Kuang Fu, a communist recently released from the Kuomintang prison. Kuang had asked Lin to take care of his wife and daughter Baozhen while serving as a political prisoner. After reminiscing with his friend, wife and daughter, Kuang chooses to quietly leave them alone. Another family that has its life turned upside down by an outsider is that of Huang Jiamei, whose father visiting from the countryside had hoped to see his son succeed in Shanghai, only to find the latter and his wife pawning clothes and quarrelling with each other. The father finally leaves for home but not before leaving his only change for the couple. Another tenant Zhao Zhenyu is a born optimist who is married to a loud cynic. Of the two single tenants, Shi Xiaobao is a deserted woman who is forced into prostitution by a gangster and Li Lingbei has lost his son in the civil war but refuses to accept the reality and keeps singing a famous jingju aria line in which a defeated general sings of his son who has gone to seek support forces but will never return. With a set design that reveals a cross section of the building capable of showing each room, the play maintains a remarkable mixture of tragic and comic elements and ends with the alley's children singing 'We're all brave little children,/All uniting to save our country! Save our country!'[11] While an ostensibly forced ending, it nevertheless reflected an anti-Japanese sentiment that guaranteed thunderous reactions from the audience at the time.

One notable theatrical experiment that stood out during this period was the success of Xiong Foxi (1900–65), a Columbia graduate and head of the Theatre Department of National Academy of Arts in Beijing, in leading the theatre division of a high-profile rural reconstruction campaign in the villages of Ding Xian County in northern China between 1932 and 1937. There, he and his colleagues staged outdoor productions that utilised traditional, folk and Western theatrical techniques and incorporated mass participation of the peasant audience. Radically different from the realistic and modernist proscenium plays that were dominating huaju at the time, their productions were seen as providing a new model for bringing huaju to China's eighty-five per cent rural population. While Ding Xian peasants had only experienced traditional and folk theatre and street entertainment before Xiong and his colleague from the Academy set foot in Ding Xian, they eventually not only enjoyed huaju, but also volunteered to put on their own productions. Xiong, who had studied theatre at Columbia University, was well aware of Max Reinhardt's combination of stage and audience areas with circus space as well as Vsevolod Meyerhold's biomechanics, constructivism and experiments with theatrical space and its relations with the audience. He found these methods the perfect fit for the peasants' sense of participation shaped by such street performance forms as stilts, land boats and dragon lanterns. Xiong created outdoor theatres in the villages and wrote plays to take advantage of the peasants' strong physique, their uninhibited willingness in participatory theatre and their affinity with traditional and folk theatrical forms. One of the plays, *The Trumpet* (*Laba*), ends with a dance procession by the audience in celebration of a couple's imagined (in a dream) reunion. Another play *Cross the River* (*Guodu*), about the struggle between the villagers and a local landowner around the construction of a bridge, involves the audience in a number of ways and its theme song 'Song of Crossing the River' used a popular local tune in order to encourage the peasants to sing with the actors from the beginning. Furthermore, group action became the dominant mode of performance as the ferry crossers, boatmen and bridge builders formed three group characters. His next production *Dragon King Canal* (*Longwang qu*, 1937) made more progress in combining traditional and folk art and huaju with scenic inspiration from folk art, traditional theatre, and ritual singing and dance. Unfortunately, Japanese invasion in northern China cut short his experiment in July 1937, making Ding Xian one of the rare success stories of huaju popularisation in rural China.

## Huaju during and after the War of Resistance against Japan (1937–49)

When the war broke out in July, huaju practitioners quickly mobilised to collectively stage a three-act play *Defend the Marco Polo Bridge* (*Baowei Lugou qiao*) in Shanghai. Soon, they formed thirteen performance troupes that moved to the front and the interior, performing agitprop theatre such as the living-newspaper piece *Put Down Your Whip* (*Fangxia nide bianzi*). Eventually, two huaju centres formed during the eight years of war, one around the temporary capital of Chongqing in the south-west interior and the other remained Shanghai. Most well-known huaju practitioners moved to the interior with the wartime government, including the National Theatre School, which eventually settled in the small town of Jiang, about 150 miles from Chongqing. Huaju in Shanghai underwent the 'isolated island' years between 1937 and 1941 when the Japanese did not occupy the concession area controlled by Britain and France, and the 'fallen' era after December 1941 when Japan occupied the whole city after Pearl Harbor.

Despite the war, this period is often regarded as huaju's golden era, in part as a result of natural progress of spoken theatre's decades of experimentation in dramaturgy and production. Cao Yu, for example, finished his third play *The Savage Land* right before the war and fourth – arguably his last quality original – play *Peking Man* in 1940. At the same time, the war also created opportunities for the development of spoken theatre in certain directions. One of them is the proliferation of historical plays, extolling historical heroes against foreign invasions or those making patriotic choices during similarly taxing times, particularly Southern Ming Dynasty (1644–62) when the issue of resistance or cooperation with the Qing (1644–1911) – after the Manchu capture of Beijing – by the ethnic Chinese in the south mirrored the choices facing every Chinese under Japanese occupation, and the Warring States period (475–221 BC) with its many stories of patriotic heroes among frequent interstate wars. The latter period was the focus of several Guo Moruo's plays, including *Qu Yuan* (1942), which appropriated the legendary poet and patriotic official Qu Yuan (340–275 BC). The highlight of the play is the hero's long soliloquy 'Ode to Thunder and Lightning' (Leidian song) in the last act before his prison burns down, a highlight that is highly reminiscent of King Lear's passage in the thunderstorm. Several plays focused on Southern Ming as a metaphor to extol anti-Japanese heroes and castigate traitors. These plays include two adaptations of the famous *kunqu* play *The Peach Blossom Fan* (*Taohua shan*), which uses the love story between the high-class courtesan Li Xiangjun and the famous scholar Hou Chaozong before and after the fall of Ming to depict the effect of a fallen nation on the lives of its people. One of the more influential adaptations was written by Ouyang Yuqian, which contrasted Li Xiangjun's unbending patriotism to the fallen Ming with Hou Chaozong's eventual submission to the new regime.

These new versions of *The Peach Blossom Fan* also point to a re-evaluation of the role of traditional theatre in spoken drama. This was in part a practical question during the war as theatre sought popular recognition both with the working masses for the purpose of agitation and as a survival strategy in urban theatre, especially in Shanghai. For example, one of the most popular huaju plays of this time, *Qiu Haitang*, enjoyed an unprecedented five-month run after its premiere in Shanghai in December 1942. Based on a novel about the life of a jingju actor Qiu Haitang whose face is deformed as a result of his love relations with a warlord's concubine, the play was adapted and directed by three leading directors of the era, Huang Zuolin (1906–94), Gu Zhongyi (1903–65) and Fei Mu (1906–51). Apart from its meandering and sentimental plot, the extensive infusion of jingju performance also added to the play's appeal, especially as performed by the actor Shi Hui (1915–57) who was tutored by a jingju actor of female roles. During the span of the five-act play, he performed three arias that became the emotional highlights of the play.

Another aspect of huaju popularisation was localisation of Western plays, a reversal of pre-war efforts of staging authentic Western mise-en-scène with literary translations, which had proven less accessible to the average Shanghai audience. Consequently, when professional theatre relied solely on the box office for their livelihood during wartime, they reverted to localisation of Western plays to ensure favourable reception. For example, the playwright, translator and scholar Li Jianwu localised Victorien Sardou's *La Tosca* to the Chinese civil war era of the 1920s with a title *Jin Xiaoyu* and recast *Macbeth* to China's Five Dynasties (907–960) era in an adaptation titled *The Hero of the Turmoil* (*Luanshi yingxiong*).

However, this trend of huaju popularisation did not survive the end of the war in August 1945 because huaju lost ground to the flooding of Hollywood movies banned during Japanese occupation and mainstream huaju practitioners returning from the interior rejected such attempts as artistically inferior. The most notable play written and produced after the war was *Promotion Scheme* (*Shengguan tu*) by Chen Baichen (1908–94). Apparently inspired by Nikolai Gogol's *The Inspector General*, the play was a biting political satire of official corruption that diverged from the previous social commentary comedies exemplified by plays from Ding Xilin and Li Jianwu. The play is set in the dream of two thieves who become a County Head and his secretary after the real County Head is killed by an angry mob. They scheme with corrupt officials and the former Head's wife to deceive the inspecting governor who turns out to be equally corrupt and ends up promoting the wife to his own. The play ends with the County Head being beaten up again by the angry mob. Such biting satire was enthusiastically embraced by the audience immediately after the war when corruption was rampant and civil war between the nationalists and communists was imminent.

In a way, it was a highly appropriate satire of its time and signalled the end of an era in both political and cultural terms for China, especially its modern, spoken theatre that started with a strong social conscience and went through periods of anti-imperial, anti-feudal and anti-Japanese movements as well as dramatic and theatrical evolution that witnessed the maturity of its practitioners, dramatic forms and production systems. Throughout this first half-century, several trends remained constant. One of them is the relationship between huaju and traditional theatre, starting with wenmingxi as a deliberate and eventually failed attempt at hybridising the two forms; through the amateur and professional movements the 1920s and 1930s that sought to establish 'authentic' Western dramaturgy, performance and productions; followed by another era of hybridisation in wartime

Shanghai in professional theatres; and the rejection of this effort by the returning mainstream huaju practitioners after the war. A related issue is the dynamic between huaju's ideological functions – as manifested in its nationalist root, leftist movement, and anti-Japanese agitprop – and its professional and commercial undertakings through wenmingxi, CTTC and wartime Shanghai theatres. Still another important factor in huaju's emergency and growth is the role of Western and Japanese – as a conduit of Western – influence on some of the most important figures of the era. Japan influenced the Spring Willow Society of the wenmingxi era (and Ouyang Yuqian in later decades); Tian Han, Guo Moruo, Bai Wei and others in the neoromantic era of the 1920s; and Xia Yan and Shanghai Art Theatre Society in the leftist theatre movement of the 1930s. The United States educated Hong Shen at Harvard and the Columbia graduates of Hu Shi (*The Main Even in Life*), Zhang Pengchun (Nankai Middle School) and Xiong Foxi (Ding Xian), among others. Europe was especially important in fostering huaju's comic writers, including the British-educated Ding Xilin and Yuan Changying and French-educated Li Jianwu, as well as the director Huang Zuolin.

As we will see in the next chapter, some of these issues continued to impact huaju in one way or another in the second half of the twentieth century. However, the change of government after 1949 ushered in fundamental transformations to huaju practitioners and established systems as well as new directions in its ideological, dramatic and theatrical ecosystems.

# CHAPTER 4
## MODERN CHINESE THEATRE AFTER 1949

On 1 October 1949, the People's Republic of China (PRC) was established under the leadership of the Chinese Communist Party (CCP). Over the following half-century, arts in China, including its modern theatre known as huaju (spoken drama), were heavily influenced by the shifting domestic and international political environment. While there is no doubt that strong ideological demand on theatre restricted dramatic and theatrical creation, the dynamic between theatre and the state during this half century was often complicated – a relationship that periodically produced fascinating pieces. This chapter is divided into three sections that follow PRC's political history. Section 1 discusses the seventeen years between 1949 and 1966 that was marked by the establishment of state-owned spoken theatre system as part of the state ideological apparatus, although it produced occasional frank depictions of social realities. This section is followed by a short discussion of huaju in the Cultural Revolution decade (1966–76), during which huaju remain in the shadow of revolutionary model jingju (Beijing opera) plays with the exception of a few propaganda pieces. The final section discusses huaju in the decades after the Cultural Revolution ended in 1976, through experimental theatres of the 1980s, pro-government 'main melody' theatre and avant-garde performance of the 1990s, and urban theatre of the 2000s.

## The Pre-Cultural Revolution Years (1949–66)

Unlike traditional theatre, which was the target of reform after 1949,[1] huaju flourished in the 1950s as part of the state-sponsored theatre system. Most major cities established its own theatre and important figures of pre-1949 leftist huaju movement such as Tian Han were entrusted with the task of overseeing both modern and traditional theatre. At the same time, unlike traditional theatres where private companies occupied the majority of theatre for at least a decade, private huaju companies essentially disappeared. Tang Huaiqiu, who had headed the China Traveling Theatre Company, was discouraged from forming a private company, although one such company did manage to survive in Beijing until the late 1950s. As the political and cultural centre, Beijing saw the establishment of three huaju theatres: Beijing People's Art Theatre (BPAT, Beijing Renmin Yishu Juyuan), Central Experimental Theatre (Zhongyang Shiyan Huajuyuan) and China Youth Art Theatre (Zhongguo Qingnian Yishu Juyuan).

During these seventeen years, several forces were at work that shaped the political environment for modern theatre: To start with, the dominating theory governing literature and the arts was Mao Zedong's thoughts on the subject developed in the 1940s, which defined the arts as a cog in the revolutionary machine. It should represent workers, peasants and soldiers as the driving force of history and expose their class enemies as reactionaries against social progress. From time to time, this official policy was affected by domestic and international politics that allowed closer scrutiny of social problems and official corruption, although such 'thawing' periods were inevitably short-lived and followed by ideological tightening and persecution of the artists who had spoken their mind.

In terms of practitioners, many established playwrights, directors and actors occupied influential positions, although most of them, especially playwrights, struggled to create new works that fit official ideology. Cao Yu, for example, served as the Artistic Director of BPAT but ultimately failed to write enduring works comparable to his early masterpieces. Tian Han, who was in charge of national theatre affairs, turned his efforts into writing for traditional theatre and only created one memorable huaju play with a historical theme. Guo Moruo also wrote several historical huaju plays with varying artistic quality. The only established author who thrived in this period was Lao She (1899–1966), who turned his talent as a novelist into writing several notable plays, especially *The Dragon Beard Ditch* (*Longxu gou*, 1951) that celebrated an urban reconstruction project in Beijing and *Teahouse* (*Chaguan*, 1958), which used a fictional Beijing teahouse to depict the lives of ordinary Chinese from late Qing (1898), Republican warlord era (1920s) and the late 1940s.

*The Dragon Beard Ditch* was representative of early 1950s' optimism of the new republic as well as huaju's embrace of its role in expressing such feelings, both genuine and with official prodding. As a Beijing native who had recently returned from four years in the U.S. where he wrote a novel on the lives of ordinary Beijing residents during Japanese occupation, Lao She was asked by Premiere Zhou Enlai to write about a reconstruction project that covered up an open ditch but was facing public complaint. While Lao She only went to see the project once and finished the script before the end of the project, the play, once staged by the newly inaugurated BPAT under the direction of the French-educated Jiao Juyin (1905–75), became a smashing success that solidified the reputation of the artists and the theatre.[2] The play involves the fate of several low-class families who live in a compound near the Dragon Beard Ditch. It contrasts their lives before 1949, when a folk artist Madman Cheng is driven to near insanity by local gangsters and a girl drowns in the open ditch, with life under the communist government that disciplines gangsters, provides Cheng with a new livelihood and covers up the open ditch with a wide road. The play earned Lao She the honour of 'People's Artist' from Beijing municipal government, established BPAT as the leading national theatre and nurtured a group of famous actors led by Cheng's performer Yu Shizhi (1927–2013). In 1958, many of the same group of artists, again led by Lao She, Jiao and Yu, created *Teahouse* in which Yu played the manager of a Beijing teahouse that was the canvass to the fate of various characters in the first half-century in Beijing: an upright Manchu banner man, an industrialist who tries but fails to save the country through his factories, a girl sold to a eunuch as his wife, a priest, a politician, a prostitute and, most memorably, a group of father/son pairs of scums performed by the same actors: pimps, fortune-tellers and hooligans. It is a brilliant panorama of Beijing society filled with witty dialogue, trenchant commentary and unforgettable characters that could (and have) only be staged with the local colour and ensemble talent of BPAT.

In a way, though, Lao She's characters in these two contemporary classics were atypical of the representatives of 'new China' – workers, peasants and soldiers – who populated a proliferation of one-act plays under the active support of cultural authorities in Beijing. The official magazine *Play Script* (*Juben*) organised one-act play competitions for several consecutive years and its editor Zhang Guangnian advised playwrights to make their plays 'sharper, simpler, and livelier'.[3] While typically focused on bolstering heroes of the new society and criticising backward thinking and habits, some of the best plays did stand out with realistic characters, well-constructed plots and lively dialogue filled with local colours. The best known of the group include Jin Jian's *Zhao Xiaolan* (1952) and Sun Yu's *The Women's Representative* (*Funü daibiao*, 1953) that focus on new rural women, and Cui Dezhi's *Liu Lianying* (1955) that portrays textile workers. Both *Zhao Xiaolan* and *The Women's Representative* are about cultural and economic independence of women provided by the Marriage Law of 1950 that mandated freedom of choice, which allows Zhao Xiaolan to marry a fellow villager despite her father's insistence on arranged marriage. The law also provides equal property rights, which gives Zhang Guirong, the protagonist of *The Women's Representative*, the ultimate power to persuade her husband and mother-in-law of her right to work outside home. In a way, these plays formed a sharp contrast with gender-focused plays of the 1910s and 1920s that treated the feudal family as a prison from which to escape. In comparison, the new women of the 1950s exhumed a calm confidence in the new system that would thwart whatever feudal elements in their family – husband, father, mother-in-law or matchmaker. This confidence also makes them optimistic, reasonable, caring and smart in their tactics, all winning characteristics for these working-class representatives of new China in its initial years.

By contrast, *Liu Lianying*, written several years later on the subject matter of factory workers, is less sunny and more didactic despite its more mature dramaturgy. Having lost the easy target of feudalism, the play instead turned to the greyer issue of mutual growth versus selfish competition against other production teams. It tells the story of Liu Lianying, the party secretary of a production team in a textile factory, helping Zhang Deyu, the head of the team, to realise his selfishness in refusing to support their competing team with a competent worker. The story is complicated by the fact that Liu and Zhang are about to go on a movie date for the first time. In the end, the two reconciles when Zhang regrets his selfishness. The link between love and work is tightly woven in the play and further enhanced by careful depiction of Liu's inner conflict between tender feelings for Zhang and disappointment of his backward behaviour.

At the same time, the play is reminiscent of the era's stale dramatic formula: 'Workers plays: struggle between advanced and backward ideologies; peasants plays: struggle between joining or not joining the commune; and army plays: military struggle between our and enemy forces.'[4] This criticism is from a newspaper article in June 1957 titled 'The Fourth Type of Script' (Disizhong juben) in which the author praised what he saw as the fourth type of play that strove to break out of this formula. Specifically, he discussed the Shanghai production of *The Cuckoo Sings Again* (*Buguniao you jiaole*) by Yang Lüfang and an earlier play *Through Thick and Thin* (*Tonggan gongku*). Indeed, while still focused on the life of peasants in a commune, *The Cuckoo Sings Again* was a fresh breath of air by pitting a pair of vibrant youths – the female Tong Yanan (the 'cuckoo') and male Shen Xiaoya – as both model workers and lead singers among the young villagers against two leaders of their work unit: Wang Bihao, a member of the Communist Youth League local committee and Tong's boyfriend at the beginning of the play, and Kong Yucheng, a party member and head of the Youth League committee and youth production brigade. In the play, Wang wants to keep Tong to himself by asking her to sign a restrictive pledge and, when rejected, schemes with Kong to stop her from going to study driving the tractor and strip her of her Youth League membership. Their selfish actions are possible because the unit's party secretary only focuses on production routines and refuses to care for the welfare of the villagers. The situation is addressed only after the interference of another party member. At the end of the play, Wang and Kong are removed from their leadership positions and Tong shows Shen the introduction letter for her to go study tractor driving while other youngsters start singing around them.

The criticism of local leaders of the CCP and the Youth League is obviously an important reason for the play's designation as the fourth type of play. So is the theme of the cuckoo (Tong)'s experience of singing, being silenced and singing again, which, while still broadcasting an uplifting message of vibrancy in the new society, is nonetheless under the shadow of selfish and bureaucratic local leaders for the major part of the play. Combined with a brilliant production under the direction of Huang Zuolin, the famous Shanghai director of the 1940s and now Associate Artistic Director of Shanghai People's Art Theatre, the play was a smashing success, reproduced all over the country and made into a movie, also directed by Huang.

While still a minority, social critical plays, especially those directed towards bureaucratic officials, were on the rise in the mid-1950s right until the summer of 1957, when it was abruptly halted by the Anti-Rightist Movement that first invited open criticism of the Party and then persecuted half a million people nationwide for speaking their minds in the process. Until then, both one-act and multi-act plays were written and staged to expose emerging conflicts of the new society. The reason behind their emergence was CCP's growing confidence following political and economic stabilisation and the post-Stalin liberal art policies in the Soviet Union. Apart from *The Cuckoo Sings Again*, two other multi-act plays are also considered the 'fourth type of plays'. One of them, *The Vertical Flute is Played Horizontally* (*Dongxiao hengchui*, by Hai Mo, 1956), is similar to *The Cuckoo Sings Again* by pitting a retired soldier Liu Jie against bureaucratic and corrupt rural officials during the process of forming communes, only with much darker and realistic depictions of life in rural China. In the play, the county party secretary An Zhenbang is only interested in his own career by promoting successful communes to the media while suppressing other villagers' enthusiasm and ignoring their poor living conditions, thus exposing the phenomenon known at the time as 'darkness in the shadow of light' (*dengxia hei*). The other multi-act play, *Through Thick and Thin* (by Yue Ye, 1956), discusses the phenomenon of communist officials leaving their wives in the countryside to marry young and educated women after entering the cities as high-ranking officials after 1949. Here again, the issue is reminiscent of similar plays of the 1920s, such as Ouyang Yuqian's *After Returning Home* (*Huijia zhihou*, 1922), that discussed men abandoning their arranged-marriage wives for women they met in cities or overseas. *Through Thick and Thin* complicates the issue by creating three sympathetic characters: the official Meng Shijing who is the Deputy Head of the Provincial Agricultural Commission; his present wife Hua Yun who met Meng while nursing him in the military hospital during wartime; and his country wife Liu Fangwen who turns out, to Meng's surprise, to be a highly articulate and capable new woman. The plays starts with Liu accompanying Meng's mother, who has been living with Liu in the countryside and is unaware of their divorce, to Meng's city apartment and discussing with Meng problems of forming the commune. Intrigued by the issues Liu raises, which happen to be a central part of his job, Meng goes to his home village with Liu to investigate, which further disturbs Hua's suspicion of the former couple's rekindled flame. Eventually, Meng does express affection for Liu's new character, only to be rebuked by an old army general who knows them both since wartimes and rejected by Liu who is ready to marry a fellow villager, thus eliminating Hua's suspicion when she visits Liu and Meng in the village and eventually reconciles with Meng.

Apart from multi-act plays, several one-acts also focused on exposing contemporary concerns. For example, Lu Yanzhou's *The Return* (*Guilai*, 1956), although artistically much cruder than *Through Thick and Thin*, also deals with the issue of officials abandoning their wives left in the countryside. A slight variation of the theme of forgetting rural folks who helped party officials during wartimes is the focus of *Something Forgotten* (*Bei yiwangle de shiqing*, by Duan Chengbin, 1957). The play also exposes the sufferings of the weak rarely seen on the PRC stage, as an old man with his leg broken after helping two communist officers during the war lives in a shabby shelter and relies on the meagre salary of his wife working as a maid in the home of one of these officials, who has no interest in locating his saviour. Such rare exposure is also found in *The Vertical Flute is Played Horizontally* where the protagonist Liu's mother is forced to borrow high-interest loans to get by before Liu's return from the army.

Another prominent achievement in social criticism came from several satires on bureaucratic attraction to meetings, central planning, selfish flattery of higher ups while ignoring urgent needs of ordinary people. The earliest piece of this genre was Xing Ye's *The Meeting* (*Kaihui*, 1953) in which a district official insists on holding a meeting of villagers for him to lecture about drought alleviation methods. A prominent playwright of the genre was Wang Shaoyan, who wrote several plays around the corrupt, bureaucratic and incompetent Director Chen of a city's supply and sales system (*gongxiao zongshe*). The best-known of them is *The Grapes Are Rotten* (*Putao lanle*) in which he tries to cover up his disastrous decision to buy half a kilogram of grapes for everyone in the city, which has caused large quantities of grapes to rot with more on the way. The play takes place on a Sunday when Chen has just returned home from another meeting and has no time to go to the movie he has promised his daughter, who lives in a boarding primary school. He then goes through various impractical schemes with his flattering secretary, including selling the grapes to winemakers and ordering his subsidiaries to sell them on the streets. The best-known satire of this period was He Qiu's *Before the New Director Arrives* (*Xin juzhang laidao zhiqian*, 1955), which depicts the head of general services department (*zongwuke*) Liu Shanqi who orders elaborate remodelling of a new office for the arriving bureau director while assigning the existing director's office to himself, ignores leaky dormitories of the workers, and leaves bags of cement in the rain only to be rescued by workers under the direction of the new director who has arrived without ceremony.

These satires carried on the tradition of Chen Baichen's *Promotion Scheme* in criticising growing bureaucracy in PRC, although most of them, as well of the serious plays under the banner of the 'fourth type of plays', almost always end with a bright ending, resolving the conflict with a wise higher-ranking official who corrects the mistakes and gives power to the righteous workers and peasants. In other words, the system ultimately works within the reality of these plays. However, this precautionary mechanism was not enough to protect the plays and their authors, as some of them were condemned during the Anti-Rightist Movement and exiled to the countryside. Although some Party leaders in a 1962 conference on arts and literature in Guangzhou explicitly denounced the restriction on criticising Party officials, the ensuing tightening of political atmosphere meant the further elimination of such social critical plays on PRC stages until the early 1980s.

With social critical plays no longer safe and propaganda plays too formulaic, history plays again became a hot topic in the late 1950s, especially for veteran playwrights. Most of these plays remained true to the tradition of using historical plays to reflect contemporary sentiment. Some of the best-known huaju plays include Tian Han's *Guan Hanqing* (1958) on the Yuan Dynasty (1279–1368) dramatist Guan Hanqing, Cao Yu's *Courage and the Sword* (*Dan jian pian*, 1961) on an ancient king's bitter experience of national revival, and Guo Moruo's *Cai Wenji* (1959) and *Wu Zetian* (1960) on two famous women in Chinese history, a poet and the country's only empress. Arguably the best-known historical play of this period, although more for reasons of its role in political history than artistic merit, was the jingju (Beijing opera) play *Hai Rui Dismissed from Office* (*Hai Rui baguan*, 1961) by the historian and Deputy Mayor of Beijing Wu Han on the upright and incorruptible Ming Dynasty (1368–1644) official Hai Rui. In 1965, Mao Zedong's wife Jiang Qing asked the Shanghai propagandist Yao Wenyuan to write a harsh and distorted critique of the play. Mao seized upon the article and accused the play of denouncing his authority in dismissing Defense Minister Peng Dehuai in 1959 because of the latter's criticism of Mao's disastrous policy of the Great Leap Forward, a utopian economic campaign in 1958 that demanded unrealistically rapid industrial and agricultural growth as well as collectivisation. The campaign left disastrous economic consequences for the nation, resulting in widespread famine. After Mao dismissed Peng, he partially took blame for his policies and resigned from the position of National President, although he retained the title of Party Chairman. By 1965, he was ready for a comeback and utilised the criticism of *Hai Rui Dismissed from Office* as an opening shot of his campaign that soon became the Cultural Revolution.

The early 1960s was a period of tug of war in policies towards the arts, with visible consequences for huaju plays. However, the policies of the late 1950s, including the Anti-Rightest Movement of 1957 and the Great Leap Forward of 1958, had severely harmed national economy and constrained artistic creation. By 1960, widespread famine had forced CCP leadership to adopt more pragmatic economic measures. In the field of literature and arts, CCP's Propaganda Department started drafting a document in 1961 aimed at protecting the arts from extreme leftist policies, which was formally circulated in April 1962 under the title 'Eight Articles on Literature and Art' (Wenyi batiao). In March 1962, the National Symposium on the Creation of Spoken Drama, Opera, and Children's Plays (Quanguo Huaju, Geju, Ertongju Chuangzuo Zuotanhui) was held in Guangzhou, in which Premiere Zhou Enlai and Foreign Minister Chen Yi advocated for the 'emancipation of the mind' and more freedom for artistic creation. Chen specifically allowed criticising party leaders and encouraged 'the fourth type of plays'. However, CCP chair Mao Zedong, while temporarily sidelined, was never happy with such liberal policies and admonished the party to 'never forget class struggle' in the Tenth Plenum of the Eight Party Congress in September 1962. In December 1963 and June 1964, Mao issued two directives on literature and the arts, condemning cultural authorities of ignoring contemporary life and class struggle. As a result of such conflicting messages, huaju experienced another mini-boom that nevertheless focused mostly on the theme of class struggle.

Some of the most representative plays of this period again centred on personal relations in the contemporary world, although the focus had shifted to sacrificing individual or small group gains for collective advancement, either in factories or villages. Some of the most representative plays include *The Young Generation* (*Nianqing de yidai*) by Chen Yun, *Never Forget* (*Qianwan buyao wangji*) by Cong Shen and *After the Harvest* (*Fengshou zhihou*) by Lan Cheng, all premiered in 1963. *The Young Generation* focuses on two young geologists in Shanghai. One of them, Xiao Jiye, returns from the wilderness to treat his leg problem but is determined to return to his team while the other, Lin Yusheng, has faked a sickness report in order to stay in Shanghai and wants his graduating girlfriend to stay with him against her desire to join him in the search for minerals for the nation. Lin eventually realises his selfishness when he learns the possibility of Xiao losing his leg and, more importantly, reads a letter from his biological parents written before their execution as revolutionary martyrs, a personal history his adopted parents have hidden from him. Inspired by their words and ashamed of his deeds, Lin joins his girlfriend and returns to his team in the frontier. *Never Forget* was originally published as *To Your Health* (*Zhuni jiankang*) and staged by Heilongjiang People's Art Theatre in the northeast. It was changed to the present title during the preparation for a tour in Beijing following the announcement of Mao's admonition against forgetting class struggle. Once in Beijing, the play created a sensation and played over 100 times and was restaged throughout the nation. The story is about Ding Shaochun, a motor factory worker married to the daughter of a former grocery shop owner, an urban little bourgeois class deemed suspicious at the time because of their difference from the pure proletariat. Under the influence of his wife and mother-in-law, Ding hunts wild ducks on weekends to pay for his fashionable clothes. Before embarking on another hunting trip, he loses a house key in the coil of an important motor his team is building, which almost causes costly damages. The third play, *After the Harvest*, takes place in a village where a good harvest results in the ideological clash between the party secretary Aunt Zhao, who wants to sell extra grain to the country, and her husband Zhao Dachuan, who insists on selling them on the market to buy horses, thus providing an opportunity for a former peddler and donkey seller to embezzle from the village treasury. The lesson of these plays from geologists, workers and peasants – all pillars of socialist construction – served as warnings to the audience who should remain vigilant against impure ideological deviations and guard against individualism that would cause serious harm to socialist construction.

One remarkable exception from such ideological propaganda is a play based on a wildly popular movie with the same title, *Li Shuangshuang* (1963) by Li Zhun. Based on a short story by the author, the film stars the award-winning actress Zhang Ruifang, who masterfully portrayed a new peasant woman who is capable of laughter and crying, a loving mother and wife who, despite her timid husband's misgivings and threats, remains outspoken for the welfare of the village and its female members. Some of the most memorable sequences of the film and play are around the relations between the couple, during cooking a meal, when the husband threatens to leave the village to find work, or when he returns. In her down-to-earth optimism and frustration, Li Shuangshuang resembles the heroine in *Cuckoo Sings Again*.

## Cultural Revolution (1966–76)

The most notable achievement in Chinese theatre during the Cultural Revolution is the two rounds of revolutionary model plays. The first group includes five jingju plays, two ballets and the symphony version of one of the jingju plays. Several more plays were added to the list after 1969 that are also considered as model plays, including five jingju plays and two ballets. Most of these plays were first created before the Cultural Revolution, especially for the 1963 Festival of Modern Jingju Plays. Differing from the classical themes of traditional jingju plays, all model plays are about modern and contemporary themes, either on CCP heroes during the war against Japan, civil war of the late 1940s and Korean War against the U.S., or about contemporary lives very much in the vein of huaju plays of the 1960s. In terms of dramaturgy, the model plays also pushed the class struggle convention to the point of ignoring normal family life and personal relations that are separate from class.

Huaju productions were greatly limited and reduced to little more than propaganda during the decade. At the beginning of Cultural Revolution, regular theatrical performance ground to a halt, as was the case of all other normal social activities. However, Red Guards of various theatres and universities and schools, including the two theatre academies in Beijing and Shanghai, did put on plays appropriate for the occasion. In the summer of 1967, different factions of the Red Guards from Central Theatre Academy staged several plays and even toured some of them throughout the country, including *Storm of the Harbor* (*Haigang fenglei*), *Storm of the Five Continents* (*Wuzhou fenglei*) and *Dare to Drag the Emperor off the Horse* (*Ganba huangdi laxia ma*). By the fall of 1968, as workers and soldier moved into universities and schools to curtail absolute anarchy, these activities effectively came to an end, as did huaju performance in China for several years.

The return of huaju, as well as most other performance forms other than the revolutionary model plays, occurred after 1972 as a result of CCP's midcourse adjustment after an unsuccessful coup by Mao's heir apparent Lin Biao in September 1971 that ended with the crash of the plane carrying Lin and his family in Mongolia. Some new plays were written starting in 1973, culminating in several notable pieces that focused on the topical issue of the 'two lines' between radicals that were in power during the Cultural Revolution and pragmatists in the previous seventeen years led by Liu Shaoqi, the National President persecuted to death in 1969. One such play, *In Their Prime* (*Fenghua zhengmao*, 1974) by Tianjin People's Art Theatre, pitted a middle school teacher in the early 1960s, who takes her students to learn from fishermen in the docks, against the school principal who insists on traditional classroom education, which the play denounced as following bourgeois ideology.

## Post-Mao Era (1977–2000s)

The Cultural Revolution ended in October 1976 after the death of Mao Zedong and the arrest of his wife Jiang Qing and her clique known as the Gang of Four. In the years since then, China went through tremendous political, economic and cultural changes, all of which had profound effect on huaju.

The first – and to a certain extent last – wave of huaju's post-1976 glory was manifest in several plays that depicted the last days of the Cultural Revolution by staging a national revulsion of the Gang of Four and amplifying an ecstatic mood of liberation. The most famous plays of this group include *In the Land of Silence* (*Yu wu sheng chu*, 1978, by Zong Fuxian) that focused on the days after 5 April 1976 (the Chinese Memorial Day) when mass protest in Beijing in the name of memorialising former Premiere Zhou Enlan was brutally suppressed, and the satire *When the Maple Leaves Turned Red* (*Fengye hongle de shihou*, 1977, by Jin Zhenjia and Wang Jingyu) that focused on the days around the gang's arrest. Soon, this euphoria turned to the daunting social issues of economic and ideological reconstruction, or what was known as 'setting wrong things right' (*boluan fanzheng*), a policy adopted at the 1978 Third Plenum of the Eleventh CCP Congress that turned the party's focus from class struggle to economic development.

One of the plays that focused on the theme of 'setting wrong things right' was *Winter Jasmine* (*Baochunhua*, 1979) by Cui Dezhi, the author of the 1955 one-act *Liu Lianying*. Like his earlier play, *Winter Jasmine* is also about life in a textile factory. In the play, the factory's manager and party secretary Li Jian returns from years of persecution during the Cultural Revolution and focuses on quality control by promoting Bai Jie, who has consistently produced flawless fabric but has been ignored because of her rightist mother, as a municipal-level model worker. However, Li's deputy and friend Wu Yiping and his daughter Li Honglan vehemently oppose his decision and insist on ideological orthodoxy. Li eventually triumphs because his effort turns out to be consistent with the new market economy. Apart from Li, the play also glorifies a group of middle characters rarely depicted in positive light until then, including the class-tainted Bai Jie, the salesman You Gui as Bai's most ardent supporter because of his market experience, and the engineer Han Weidong, who has written propaganda pieces during the Cultural Revolution but is now entrusted by Li for his technical skills. The experience of these so-called 'middle characters' long absent from the stage found great resonance with the audience and added to the play's appeal. At the same time, the fact that their happy ending derived from a conscientious official and correct party policy indicates that the play remains in the pre-Cultural Revolution convention of play resolution.

Throughout the first half of the 1980s, dramatic depictions of social problems remained a politically sensitive balancing act for the government. On the one hand, the authorities studiously avoided high-handed political persecutions reminiscent of the 1950s and 1960s. On the other hand, it censored, altered or delayed the production of a number of plays because of what their critics argued as projecting an overly gloomy view of the reality. One of the first plays to receive such censorship was *If I Were Real* (*Jiaru woshi zhende*, 1979) by the Shanghai playwright Sha Yexin. Based on a real criminal trial Sha witnessed, the play focuses on Li Xiaozhang, a young man desperate to return to Shanghai from the countryside (where millions of 'educated youths' were sent during the Cultural Revolution) by pretending to be the son of a high-ranking official in Beijing. Thanks to a slew of fawning and corrupt officials, he almost succeeds before being exposed by Old Mr Zhang, Li's claimed father who arrives from Beijing as an inspector sent by the central government. The play's sympathetic treatment of Li and exposure of official corruption earned it many potential imitators in other theatres as well as the governmental disapproval. After seeing its dress rehearsal, cultural officials in Shanghai stopped its premiere. The controversy around the play eventually triggered a national symposium on playwriting in Beijing in February 1980, which ended with a long speech by Hu Yaobang, head of the CCP Propaganda Department who would soon become the Party Secretary General. Hu, who was instrumental in maintaining generally tolerant policies towards the arts throughout the 1980s, praised Sha's talent and showed deep reverence for artistic creativity. Ultimately, however, he was unwilling to allow the play staged without revision. Sha refused and the play was never staged. In 1981, Taiwan adapted the play into a film that greatly amplified its social criticism, which further sealed its fate in China. Nevertheless, another play by Sha *Mayor Chen Yi* (*Chen Yi shizhang*) about one of PRC founding fathers Chen Yi and his years as Shanghai's mayor in the early 1950s was staged at about the same time to great critical acclaim. In 1985, Sha was promoted to Artistic Director of Shanghai People's Art Theatre.

The censorship of *If I Were Real* set up a precedent for dealing with other contemporary plays, including *Small Well Lane* (*Xiaojing hutong*) by Li Longyun, which was published in 1981 but was not allowed to be staged until 1985 by BPAT. The five-act play follows Lao She's tradition of Beijing-style plays by depicting a group of residents in a lane through three decades. It starts in January 1949, right before the communist takeover. The second act takes place in 1958, at the height of the Great Leap Forward when some of the residents become rightists and others, in their zeal to help steel productivity, almost topple over a room in order to dig out a canon supposedly buried underneath it to make steel. The play then moves to September 1966, at the onset of the Cultural Revolution when the head of the community committee persecutes a pre-1949 policeman and a former store owner who desperately tries to avoid trouble by throwing away a bolt of fabric, submitting the deeds of his houses, and faking a connection to the People's Liberation Army. Act Four is set in October 1976, before news of the Gang of Four's arrest is publicly known when the community head launches her final tyranny over the neighbourhood. The play ends in 1980 when an election for the community head finally takes place to allow the residents to control their own fate. Written in the tradition of Lao She's *Teahouse*, the play offers a wide range of average folks in Beijing and their fate in the previous tumultuous decades, ending with a plea from its oldest resident to be left alone without further turbulence. It is notable for its straightforward depiction of the dark moments in PRC history and of characters that are by turns upright, selfish, victimised, farcical, scheming and villainy.

Li Longyun, who grew in a Beijing courtyard (*siheyuanr*) like the one depicted in the play, wrote the piece in 1980 as his MA thesis under Chen Baichen, the veteran playwright of *Promotion Scheme*, and published it in 1981. It was picked up in 1983 by BPAT, which had hired Li as one of its resident playwrights, but was only given three 'internal performances' (*neibu gongyan*). The performance led to several discussions and subsequent suspension of the play by the authorities whose only reason was that it was 'controversial'. Similar treatment was meted out to several other plays, including *Bus Stop* (1983) by the Nobel Laureate Gao Xingjian and *WM* (*WM [Women]*, 1985) by Wang Peigong. In fact, while the realistic *Small Well Lane* was eventually given over 100 performances in 1985, these two plays, notable for both thematic boldness and formal experimentation, were allowed only a handful of performances.

Huaju's formal experiment started in the late 1970s as part of the excitement in (re)discovering world theatre in the twentieth century after three decades of fossilised knowledge that froze on Ibsen and Stanislavski. All of a sudden, translations of modern theatre from symbolism to expressionism to Bertolt Brecht to theatre of the absurd became talk of the town. The first glimpse of these techniques on stage came in a 1979 production of Brecht's *Life of Galileo* at the Central Youth Theatre under the direction of Chen Yong, who had studied directing in the Soviet Union in the 1950s. Because Brecht worked in East Germany in the 1950s, he was first introduced to China in 1959, when Huang Zuolin directed *Mother Courage and Her Children* to celebrate East Germany's tenth anniversary. In 1962, Huang delivered a speech in the Guangzhou theatre symposium that promoted Brecht's epic theatre as an alternative to Stanislavski. He also supervised Chen's 1979 production, which shocked the Chinese theatre circle with its distancing devices that forced the audience to ponder the relations between power and individual choice. One poignant moment came when Galileo's student, appalled by his surrender to the Inquisition, claimed: 'Unhappy the land that has no heroes!' To this, Galileo retorted: 'Unhappy the land that needs a hero,'[5] which many in the Beijing audience felt as a direct rebuke against hero worship that led to the Cultural Revolution. That moment crystallised for huaju practitioners the connection between formal and thematic innovation as well as the urgency for non-linear narratives to shatter realistic illusions and force the audience to reflect on their own experience.

One of the most innovative and controversial playwrights who combined formal experiments and ideological provocation – and consequently received more scrutiny and censorship – was Gao Xingjian, who wrote *Absolute Signal* (*Juedui xinhao*, 1982, with Liu Huiyuan), *Bus Stop* (*Chezhan*, 1983), *Wild Man* (*Yeren*, 1985) and *The Other Shore* (*Bi'an*, 1986) before emigrating to France. Gao studied French literature in college in the early 1960s and was a translator before becoming a resident playwright for BPAT. His French background, extremely rare for his generation of playwrights, gave him special insight into the works of Jean-Paul Sartre and Samuel Beckett. His *Absolute Signal* is generally regarded as the first little theatre production in China, which was staged in a banquet room in Capital Theatre, BPAT's home theatre. Directed by Lin Zhaohua, who directed all his plays at BPAT, with simple platforms, railings, chairs and a few lights, the play tells the story of a thwarted robbery of a night freight train. It takes place in the conductor's car between an old conductor, his assistant, an under employed young man, his girlfriend and the young man's gangster boss. The immediacy and unpretentiousness of presentation supported a non-linear structure with multiple flashbacks and out of sequence monologues and dialogues that were from time to time lit only with flashlights.

While the play ran 159 performances and was widely copied throughout the nation, Gao's next play *Bus Stop* was summarily banned after a few performances because of its content that is reminiscent of

*Waiting for Godot*. Written before *Absolute Signal* but delayed by the theatre's leadership because of censorship fears, *Bus Stop* is an allegorical story about a group of people waiting at a suburban bus stop where passing-by buses never stop until they eventually discover, after ten years, that the stop has been cancelled. Among them are an old man who wants to go to the city for a game of chess, a young hooligan who vies for a bottle of yogurt in the city, a middle-aged woman going to spend the weekend with her husband and son, a girl for an arranged date, a young man going for college entrance examination, a carpenter of fine furniture ready to pass on his skills to an apprentice, a local state-owned store (*gongxiaoshe*) manager going for a banquet and a man who reads silently and leaves first before everyone else realises their entrapment. The play reflected a general sense of betrayal towards the previous decade and bewilderment of a fast-changing society, a theme its powerful detractors viewed as spreading grave doubt and distortion of the current state of affairs. Gao's third and last play at BPAT, *The Wild Man* (1995), was another experimental piece of multiple spatial and temporal levels that also employed masks, ritual dances and choruses, although it returned to the proscenium stage.

There were quite a few plays that are also notable for their innovative forms. Among them, *Hot Currents Outside the House* (*Wuwai you reliu*, by Ma Zhongjun, et al. 1980) brings a ghost on stage. *Old B on the Wall* (*Guazai qiangshang de Lao B*, by Sun Huizhu, 1984) lets an eternal understudy in a theatre walk off a wall where he has been hanging as a cardboard cut-out. In *The Dead Visiting the Living* (*Yige sizhe dui shengzhe de fangwen*, by Liu Shugang, 1985), a man stabbed to death on a bus when he tried to stop a robbery and was allowed to bleed to death by indifferent onlookers returns to interrogate the witnesses. Finally, *Rubik's Cube* (*Mofang*, by Tao Jun, et al. 1985) used nine episodes of different performance formats to portray a kaleidoscope of contemporary life. In the same year, *WM* (*WM (Women)*),[6] another play that was hailed as breaking new ground in presentation, was censored after several dress rehearsals. The play was written by Wang Peigong and directed by Wang Gui, both from the theatre affiliated with the Air Force. Written in four episodes titled 'Winter', 'Spring', 'Summer' and 'Fall', the play focuses on the fate of a group of educated youths from the end of the Cultural Revolution to the present time. The several dress rehearsals won high praise from theatre insiders for its innovative usage of the chorus and their movement on a bare stage with a live synthesiser and a drum set as well as bold lighting and costume choices. After the dress rehearsals in June, the production was cancelled for its realistic depiction of the struggling characters and Wang Gui was removed from his position as the head of the theatre, although several performances were allowed in late summer in Shanghai and Beijing by different entities before again being cut short.

Despite the *WM* episode, more formally innovative and thematically provocative plays emerged in Beijing and Shanghai. Of these plays, *Uncle Doggie's Nirvana* (*Gou'erye niepan*, 1986), written by BPAT's Jinyun and directed by Diao Guangtan and Lin Zhaohua, focuses on the plight of a peasant from 1949 to the early 1980s and his cycles of possessing and losing land and other properties, enhanced by imaginative manipulation of temporal and spatial planes. Written by Sha Yexin, author of *If I Were Real*, and staged by Shanghai People's Art Theatre, *Confucius, Jesus Christ, and John Lennon* (*Kongzi, Yesu, Pitoushi Lienong*, 1987) is a satire in which Confucius, Jesus Christ and John Lennon are sent by God from a chaotic heaven to the human world on an investigative mission, only to encounter a ruthlessly materialist state and a 1984-style authoritarian regime where pigment discolouration is a sign of ideological degeneration, citizens are neutered except the Queen, and dissidents are injected ideological shots made from the Queen's brain. Written by Chen Zidu, Yang Jian and Zhu Xiaoping, *Sangshuping Chronicles* (*Sangshuping jishi*, 1988) was directed by Xu Xiaozhong, President of Central Academy of Theatre who had studied direction in the Soviet Union in the 1950s. Staged on and in front of a large and raised turntable, the play takes place in 1968–9 in a remote village in the yellow earth plateau of Shaanxi Province where greed and savage customs lead to the oppression and persecution of outsiders and women. Performed by one of the Academy's graduating classes, the play blended dialogue with dance and singing to tell a despairing story that deeply resonated with the mood of cultural introspection of the late 1980s. This was also the theme of *The World's Top Restaurant* (*Tianxia diyi lou*, by He Jiping, 1988) which, while set in a duck restaurant in early twentieth century Beijing, is ultimately a piece of cultural self-interrogation as it focuses on the sabotage of its reformed-minded manager by the restaurant's owners and employees, ending with the former's ouster and a vertical scroll couplet he sends to the restaurant as a parting gift, which reads: 'Such a precarious building—who is the owner, who are the customers? Just a few old rooms—sometimes fit the moonlight, sometimes fit the wind.'[7]

This sense of urgency for a cultural self-examination was abruptly truncated the following year after the Tiananmen Incident and the ensuing government control for ideological and political stability. For huaju, such measures resulted in a split between 'main-theme' plays by state-owned companies aimed at winning government awards vital for the theatres' financial survival and the rise of avant-garde productions by auteur-style directors that represented huaju's true creative energy. Among the outstanding main stage productions, *Shang Yang* (1996, by Shanghai People's Art Theatre, written by Yao Yuan, directed by Chen Xinyi) dramatised the life and death of a reformer during the Warring States era (476–221 BCE). Another play, *The Field of Life and Death* (*Shengsi chang*, 1999), was adapted and directed by Tian Qinxin for the Central Experimental Theatre from a 1934 novella by Xiao Hong about a group of peasants in a remote Manchurian village under Japanese invasion. Both were powerful and melodramatic productions directed by two of the most active contemporary female directors.

The directors who garnered most attention during this decade were Lin Zhaohua, Mou Sen and Meng Jinghui, all of whom directed translated and original plays that pushed formal and content boundaries. All three also worked outside the state-owned theatre system for their provocative productions even though only Mou was an independent director. Lin Zhaohua, for example, created his own studio which allowed him to stage bold experiments impossible for BPAT where he served as Deputy Artistic Director and directed such hit proscenium productions as Guo Shixing's *Bird Men* (*Niaoren*, 1993), a stimulating and farcical study of cultural misunderstandings between China and the West. Written by the former reporter Guo Shixing as part of his 'loafers' trilogy – the other two being *Chess Men* (1995) and *Fish*

*Men* (1997) – the play is about a group of bird lovers who train birds to sing in a Beijing park where a Chinese American psychoanalyst opens a clinic to treat their 'obsession' and the representative of an international animal protection association accuses them of animal cruelty. In his studio independent from BPAT, Lin staged his own interpretations of *Hamlet* (1990), Friedrich Dürrenmat's *Romulus the Great* (1994), *Faust* (1994), *Three Sisters Waiting for Godot* (1998, a postmodern combination of the two plays) and several other Chinese and European plays.

In the early 1990s, subversive staging of European plays became a notable strategy that challenged official ideological hegemony. Lin's 1990 *Hamlet* contested the dichotomy of good and evil by having 'To Be or Not To Be' delivered by the three actors who play Hamlet, Claudius and Polonius and, at the end of the play, letting the actor who plays Hamlet fall as Claudius is stabbed by Hamlet and then the actor who mainly plays Claudius deliver Hamlet's final lines to Horatio. His choice of *Romulus the Great* went even further to challenge the concept of patriotism because Dürrenmat's pseudo-historical play depicts the last Roman emperor as intentionally sabotaging the imperialist empire by focusing exclusively on hen-rearing during German invasion. Lin's subversive choice was enhanced by doubling Romulus, his wife, daughter and courtiers with marionettes that appear on stage with or without the actor playing the role, although Romulus was the only character who was never substituted by a puppet, the only voice of reason on stage.

In 1991, Meng Jinghui, in his last year as a Master of Fine Arts (MFA) directing student at the Central Theatre Academy, directed two theatre of the absurd plays, *The Bald Soprano* and *Waiting for Godot*, the latter after failing to receive permission to be staged on a coal pile on campus. These two plays resonated with the audience with their absurdity and desperation, as the former ended with three minutes of pause that confused the audience and the latter taking place in a white-washed hospital-like room and ending with Vladimir breaking the windows with his umbrella. Both Lin and Meng would continue with their increasingly subjective and postmodern adaptations of European plays. Meng's 1998 adaptation of Dario Fo's *Accidental Death of an*

*Anarchist* (adapted by Huang Jisu) layered the original play's farcical denunciation of police brutality with intertextual allusion to Chinese realities and theatrical classics such as famous scenes from *Teahouse*, which made the play both politically poignant and culturally relatable to the Chinese audience.

Meng's signature blend of provocation and entertainment started soon after he joined the Central Experimental Theatre, although many of his productions were independently produced, including the 1992 *Worldly Pleasures* (*Sifan*), which combines scene from a Ming Dynasty *kunqu* play about a nun escaping from the nunnery and falls in love with a monk with two stories of tasting forbidden love from Boccaccio's *Decameron*. The production stood out for its fluid staging and cheeky irreverence that included no set and plenty of physical and verbal jokes and allusions, all wrapped up in anti-authoritarian defiance in the pursuit of love and sexual libertarianism. This defiance is further demonstrated in his 1994 'anti-play' *I Love XXX* (*Wo ai XXX*), which has no plot or characters and is exclusively composed of declarative lines that each starts with 'I love . . .'. In a bare stage lined with TV sets and folding chairs on the background, he used various combinations of the chorus to comment on world and Chinese events of the twentieth century such as mindless adulation of Mao and abortion policies, interrogate collectivism and ideological brainwashing, and, towards the end, directly challenge the audience and celebrate the crashing of symbols, routines and stars. Meng's ingenious combination of youthful passion, irreverent mockery of social realities and imaginative staging that combined the farcical and the dramatic with creative usage of music – sometimes with a live band onstage – has largely contributed to the revived interest in huaju among urban audience.

At the other end of the spectrum was Mou Sen, whose three productions in the early 1990s went further than his peers in separating performance from the dramatic script. As arguably the only theatre director without proper training from the two theatre academies in Beijing or Shanghai, Mou Sen, who studied literature at Beijing Normal University and a devotee of Jerzy Grotowski's poor theatre, directed Ionesco's *Rhinoceros*, Stravinsky's *A Soldier's Story* and Eugene O'Neill's *Great God Brown* between 1987 and 1989 with his independent Frog

Experimental Theatre (Wa shiyan jutuan). These productions inspired a number of independent performances of post-war European plays, which provided safe release in the stringent atmosphere of the early 1990s. In 1993, Mou trained a group of students who had failed to enter professional performance programs to stage a physical production based on Gao Xingjian's *The Other Shore*. Through such actions as tumbling, climbing ropes, carrying imitation rocks from one end of a room to the other, the performance shocked Beijing arts circle as a deeply spiritual piece on the meaning of self-doubt, physical labour and awakening. In May of the following year, he created *File Zero* (*Ling dang'an*) for Kunsten Festival des Arts in Brussels, which subsequently toured Europe and North America but did not perform in China. Based on a long poem by Yu Jian, the three-performer piece broadcasts Yu's poem about personnel files as a looped audio recording that was stopped and restarted repeatedly by an actor and actress. Layered on top of it is the recollection by one of the actors about growing up in the interior to find out his account father was in reality a former air force officer of the nationalist army who had been exiled to the remote province after 1949. Meanwhile, the other actor welded steel bars onto a metal scaffold and a TV monitor showed a video of a child's open heart surgery. Once the welding was done, the actress stuck apples and tomatoes onto the steel bar, only to be pulled out by the three performers and fed to a blower that spitted out the bloody liquid while the actress – who had remained silent until then – screamed and threw boxes of apples onto the stage, bringing the show to a raging and chaotic end. While Mou started the creative process with three professional actors, they could not understand his improvisational process and he had to replace them after a week with two documentary filmmakers and a choreographer. The father's story by one of the film directors Wu Wenguang became the central story that Wu narrated on stage.

In December of the same year, Mou Sen created *Related to AIDS* (*Yu aizi youguan*), which was closer to a happening than theatrical performance. Sponsored by the Ford Foundation as a piece about AIDS, Mou ended up giving the audience something seemingly unrelated to the subject, except for an informative programme that discussed the dos and don'ts concerning AIDS. For three nights, which constituted the entire run of the production, Mou had thirteen amateurs, including the poet Yu Jian and his actors from *File Zero*, and the dancer Jin Xing who was about to undergo transgender surgery, to perform the task of frying meat balls and making stuffed steamed buns – while chitchatting – for thirteen real labourers who were building a brick wall at the sides of and behind the audience. In the end, the labourers were invited to a long table on stage to have super and, during one of the nights, dance with Jin Xing. This combination of mundane daily routine of cooking and suggestive building of an enclosing wall made the production an important piece of provocation, albeit understandably within a highly selective group of cultural elite.

The mid- and late 1990s also witnessed the re-emergence of Chinese nationalism in contrast to the cultural introspection of the 1980s and oblique provocation of the early 1990s, as evident in such anti-American books as *China Can Say No* (*Zhongguo keyi shuo bu*, 1996, by Song Qiang et al.). The most prominent theatrical manifestation of this phenomenon is the 2000 production of *Che Guevara* (*Qie Gewala*, by Huang Jisu et al.) that glorified the Argentinian revolutionary as an anti-imperial hero in Cuba and Bolivia, anti-corruption crusader in Cuba and devoted lover of family and humanity. Its initial performance in Beijing created a sensation and was widely copied by amateur groups, which testified to the rising tide of nationalism and a desire for social justice.

In a way, *Che Guevara* pointed to the full circle huaju traversed in the second half of the twentieth century that started with state-induced optimism and class struggle and ended with anti-imperialism that at least partially aligned with a remerging nationalism. Such sentiment has lingered into the new millennium and peaked around time of the 2008 Beijing Olympics. At the same time, globalisation and a state policy to turn theatre into part of the cultural industry have added a great deal of ideological, organisational and performance diversity to huaju at the beginning of the twenty-first century.

At the forefront of market-oriented reform are the National Theatre of China (Guojia Huaju Yuan), which was established in 2001 by combining China Youth Art Theatre and Central Experimental

Theatre, and Shanghai Dramatic Arts Centre (Shanghai Huaju Yishu Zhongxin), which was formed in 1995 through the merger of two local theatres – Shanghai People's Art Theatre and Shanghai Youth Huaju Company (Shanghai Qingnian Huaju Tuan). From the beginning, the National Theatre instituted a producer system. Its most successful director Tian Qinxin has collaborated with her producer Li Dong to orchestrate savvy promotional campaigns for all her productions. Her 2010 adaptation of Lao She's novel *Four Generations under One Roof* (*Sishi tongtang*, also translated as *The Yellow Storm*), about life in Beijing during Japanese occupation, included an all-star cast and debuted in Taiwan in order to emphasise the play's affinity with Republican China. The production reportedly grossed over ten million *yuan* within four months, before its debut in Beijing. Similarly, Shanghai Dramatic Art Centre has a strong department of publicity, marketing and programming under the direction of Nick Rongjun Yu (Yu Rongjun), a prolific playwright whose plays combine popular elements of 'white-collar theatre' for Shanghai's middle-class audience and serious observations of contemporary life. Under Yu, the Centre has expanded in pan-Asian and international collaborations.

The other side of the effort to push huaju into the cultural industry was the privatisation of most state-owned companies and the emergence of purely private theatres. An example of the latter category is the Penghao Theatre (Penghao Juchang) in Beijing, which was founded by Wang Xiang, a dentist, with an investment of twelve million *yuan* in 2008. Located right outside Central Academy of Theatre near downtown Beijing, the theatre has leveraged talents from the academy to stage independent plays, including a self-reflective piece on the relation between the theatre and local cultural history, which is entitled *The Story of Gong and Drum Lane* (*Luoguxiang de gushi*, 2009). Another notable phenomenon is the rise of campus theatres as universities have begun to establish theatre programs, often together with media studies. One recent production by the Department of Theatre, Film, and Television Arts of Nanjing University, entitled *Face for Mr. Chiang Kai-shek* (*Jianggong de mianzi*, 2012), has become talk of the nation. Written by an undergraduate student Wen Fangyi and directed by the department head Lü Xiaoping for the university's

110 anniversary, the play depicts three professors debating in 1943 whether to honour a dinner invitation by Chiang Kai-shek, who has recently assumed the university's presidency – whether to 'give him face'. The independence of these intellectuals in the 1940s and their hesitance to cooperate with the government sharply contrast with their persecution during the Cultural Revolution in 1967 at the beginning of the play. The play also reminds the audience of today's intellectuals' dependence on the government.

Such a question, although raised obliquely, represents a far cry from huaju in the early decades of the PRC when theatre suffered from much tighter ideological control. As this chapter has demonstrated, forcing theatre to serve as a weapon of the state ideological apparatus has significantly hampered its development while periods of ideological relaxation allowed – sometimes grudgingly and with consequences – inspired creative energy to stage real concerns of an era and make searching provocations with innovative formal experimentations. It was these moments that created some of the best plays and productions of modern theatre in China.

# CHAPTER 5
## CHINESE DRAMA OUTSIDE THE MAINLAND: TAIWAN AND HONG KONG

Modern spoken theatre in Taiwan and Hong Kong are inexorably linked to huaju (spoken drama) in mainland China because they emerged from the same root and have continued to interact with each other, particularly since the 1980s. At the same time, the specific circumstances of history in these two regions in the twentieth century – particularly the colonial history and its aftermath as well as Taiwan under and after martial law in the latter half of the century – have largely determined the trajectories of their perspective theatres. Indeed, some of the most potent theatrical achievements resulted from defining moments of their histories, such as Taiwan's ideological openings in the 1980s, particularly the revocation of the martial law in 1987, and Hong Kong's apprehensive response to its reunion with China in 1997. At the same time, spoken theatre in Hong Kong and Taiwan went through similar stages as China and other Asian countries, through hybridity (and Japanese influence in East Asia), theatrical realism, little theatre movement influenced by post-war European theatre and globalisation of the twenty-first century. The crosscurrents of their social, political and artistic histories have largely shaped the present form of modern theatre in Taiwan and Hong Kong.

## Taiwan

Spoken theatre in Taiwan has been closely tied to its tumultuous history in the twentieth century. The island was ceded to Japan in 1895 as a result of China's defeat in the Sino-Japanese War (1894–5) and remained under Japanese control until 1945. In 1949, the nationalist government lost the civil war in mainland China, retreated to Taiwan and declared martial law, which remained in effect until 1987. Consequently, early spoken theatre in the island was closely linked to the Japanese community and local practitioners who had studied in Japan. While connections to the mainland grew in later decades and briefly erupted after the restoration of Chinese rule in 1945, martial law again censored all major huaju playwrights who remained in China after 1949 and encouraged propagandist anti-communist plays. Starting from the 1960s, introduction of post-war Western theatre and the return of a group of practitioners/scholars with advanced degrees from Euro-American theatre programmes gradually led to the emergence of the little theatre movement, which gained momentum after 1980. The floodgate of creativity was finally released by the formal revocation of the martial law in 1987.

Like the mainland, the earliest modern theatre productions in Taiwan were by Taiwanese students in Japan, including a production in 1919 of the Japanese shinpa (new school drama) classic *The Gold Demon* (*Jinse yecha*). There were also productions by the Japanese community in Taiwan. One of the early activists, Zhang Weixian,[1] twice studied in Japan between 1927 and 1929 before starting the Minfeng Theatre (Minfeng Jutuan), which was later merged with Japanese new drama groups to form Taipei Association of Theatrical Companies. Their spoken theatre productions were known as *xinju* (new drama) or *wenhuaju* (cultural drama) as they were staged by so-called 'cultural societies'. They were heavily influenced by Japanese shingeki (new drama) and Chinese wenmingxi (civilised drama) and huaju. Because of Japanese imperial policies that only permitted Japanese and Taiwanese, but not Mandarin, productions of Chinese plays were translated into Taiwanese. Some notable huaju productions include those by the touring wenmingxi company The Prosperity Society (Minxing She) in 1921 and local productions of Tian Han's one-act *A Night at the Café* (*Kafeidian zhi yiye*) in 1924 and the anti-imperialist play *Roar, China!* in 1943.

The end of Japanese occupation in 1945 led to a small boom of huaju from the mainland. From late 1946 to early 1947, the huaju veteran Ouyang Yuqian brought Shanghai's New China Theatre Society

(Xin Zhongguo Jushe) to Taiwan where it created a sensation with a two-month run and instilled new life into local theatre. This new life, however, was soon curtailed after the 2/28 Incident of 1947, in which the nationalist government brutally suppressed a local anti-government uprising. Martial law and the retreat of the nationalist government to the island only exacerbated the subsequent censorship, even as a couple more huaju companies from the mainland were allowed to tour the island before 1949.

Throughout the martial law era, professional huaju companies were affiliated with army branches or the ruling Kuomintang (KMT) party. There were also amateur groups in the universities. In the early decades of this era, the major dramatic theme was anti-communism, which was true in both contemporary and historical plays. Most of these plays were written and staged in Mandarin by practitioners from the mainland and supported by government policies. As a result, earlier Taiwanese 'cultural drama' largely disappeared.

These anti-communist plays were mostly melodramas that either used historical events to instil a utopian resolution for territorial restoration or followed formulaic depictions of 'good' nationalists fighting against 'evil' communists. One representative play is *Between Man and Beast* (*Renshou zhijian*, 1950) by Wu Ruo (1915–2001), which depicts a Shanghai courtesan Xun Wenqing who is turned into a spy for the nationalists by her secretary, with whom she fights against 'brutalities' of the new communist government, eventually by sacrificing their lives. They are contrasted with the misery of Xun's innocent maid as well as the submission of a group of spineless dignitaries to – and their eventual purging by – the new government. By contrasting the fate of the 'heroes' with that of the innocent and the 'traitors', the play emphasised sacrificing the 'small self' (*xiaowo*) for the sake of the 'great self' (*dawo*), a message of stoicism and ideological exorcism.

By the 1960s, such ideological formulas had become stale and new themes and techniques in literature and the arts were introduced to the island, which led to a breakthrough in 1980. The preparation for the breakthrough started in such pioneering endeavours as the annual Festival of International Plays (*Shijie juzhan*, 1967–84), where college students staged plays in English from around the world, and Festival of Youth Plays (*Qingnian juzhan*, 1968–84), which allowed university talents to showcase their new works. Both these festivals and several other similar activities were created by Li Mangui (1906–75), a playwright, translator, scholar and professor well versed in world theatre and widely acknowledged as the mother figure of contemporary theatre in Taiwan.

In 1960, a group of English students at the National Taiwan University published the magazine *Modern Literature* (*Xiandai wenxue*). The magazine became an important base in translating modernist works, including plays of Jean-Paul Sartre and Albert Camus, among others, and publishing the writings of Taiwanese writers in similar styles. Several members of the group, including Bai Xianyong (Kenneth Hsien-yung Pai), Li Oufan (Leo Ou Fan Lee) and Chen Ruoxi, honed their skills from the magazine, went on to study in the U.S. and became influential writers, playwrights and scholars. Two other similarly influential magazines were published in 1965: *L'Europe* (*Ouzhou zazhi*) and *Theatre* (*Juchang*). The former, created by a group of Taiwanese students in France, was devoted to avant-garde European literature, plays and films, and introduced French absurdist dramatists Camus, Eugéne Ionesco, Samuel Beckett and Jean Genet. The latter discussed the works of Luigi Pirandello, Beckett, Harold Pinter and Edward Albee. This wave of introduction of post-war Western theatre was instrumental in the eventual rejection of theatrical realism and the rise of the little theatre movement.

The most important playwright of the pre-1980 generation was Yao Yiwei (1922–97), known for such plays as *Red Nose* (*Hong bizi*, 1969) and *A Suitcase* (*Yizhi xiangzi*, 1973). *Red Nose* is an allegorical play set in a resort hotel where the guests are stranded by a road closure, which exacerbates their current problems. Among them are two owners of a factory who will not be able to make promised product delivery, a tycoon who worries that his son is killed in a plane accident, a composer struggling with writer's block and a couple fighting over a child with developmental problems. Enter a travelling circus and its clown Red Nose, who miraculously resolves their problems and brings laughter to everyone. However, Red Nose's seemingly magically power is soon deflated by a woman who removes the red clown nose from his face to reveal a scared, timid and childish face. The woman turns out to be Red Nose's wife from whom he ran away several years ago in an attempt to search for the meaning of life. Now he has found it in bringing happiness to others, however briefly, by hiding behind the clown's red nose. When the road is cleared the following day and the guests are ready to move on with no sense of gratitude towards Red Nose, he chooses to drown himself in a swimming pool instead of returning home with his wife, ostensibly in an attempt to save one of the circus dancers. The play's incisive probe of the meaning of identity and happiness, its biting criticism of selfishness and snobbery, and its reliance on such metatheatrical devices as role-playing brought a breath of fresh air into Taiwan theatre.

Yao's 1973 *A Suitcase*, written after a brief visit to the U.S., is often seen as being inspired by Beckett's *Waiting for Godot* and John Steinbeck's *Of Mice and Men*. In the play, two unemployed workers keep running away from their pursuers who suspect a big old suitcase on the back of one of their bicycles belongs to a doctor who has promised $20,000 for its return. In the end, one of the two unemployed is pushed to death from an observation tower with the suitcase, which turns out to only contain old clothes, books, toys and a certificate.

A few playwrights of this time studied theatre in Europe and North America, although some of their writing careers had started before their overseas education. Among them, Ma Sen (b. 1932), who studied acting and directing in France and received a PhD in sociology at the University of British Columbia, wrote a group of avant-garde plays that became highly influential in the little theatre movement. One such play, *Flower and Sword* (*Hua yu jian*, 1977), is a highly symbolic one-act involving two characters: a son who returns to the tomb of his father after twenty years abroad in answer to his father's beckoning voice, and a ghost who wears four layers of masks that are peeled off one after another during the course of the play as, sequentially, the mother, the father, the father's male friend and a skull. The son, having fallen in love with a man and woman, returns to his father's Tomb of Two Hands, one holding a flower and the other a sword, which are also the gift the father had given the son. Through a Rashomon-style reconstruction of the past, we learn from the mother, the father and the friend varying versions of a story about triangular love that ended in the deaths of two of these three. Eventually, we see the flower as representing love for a woman and the sword as love for a man. The son, asking for advice, is told to kill both of his lovers instead of choosing one because love and hatred are residing simultaneously in his heart. In the end, confronting the skull and rejecting his father's empty voice of beckoning, he takes off the robe his father gave him, swears to cherish both his lovers by giving the flower to one and the sword to the other. He refuses to follow his father, even as he is lost in the search for his ways. A powerful play of soul-searching that is open to multiple interpretations, the play is remarkable in its combination of symbolist fixation on the flower and sword, nightmarish reconstruction of the older generation's triangular love and death, and creative adoption of masks as an economic device for high-strung drama that is reminiscent of mask-changing techniques in *chuanju* (Sichuan opera). Apart from its non-realistic presentation, the play can also be read as an indictment of arranged marriage that fell on the old generation, moral rigidity against bi-sexual love and the Chinese tendency for emotional concealment between generations and genders.

The breakthrough point for Taiwan's little theatre movement came in the 1980 Festival of Experimental Plays (*Shiyan juzhan*) that saw the emergence of a group of artists who have since dominated Taiwan theatre. Their works broke away from realistic huaju conventions by combining Chinese and Western theatrical conventions, the serious and the comic, and, eventually, artistic pursuit and commercial success. The most remarkable play that emerged from the 1980 festival was *Hezhu's Marriage–New Version* (*Hezhu xinpei*). Written and directed by Jin Shijie (b. 1951) for his Lanling Theatre (Lanling Jufang), the play is based on a short jingju farce in which He Zhu, a maid who is married to an official by disguising herself as her mistress, is exposed as an imposter with the return of her mistress but is eventually pardoned for having originally helped the couple. The jingju play is well known for its comical dialogue and performance routines between the maid and a clown servant, farcical slapsticks of the official's parents and satirical depiction of Hezhu's pedantic master who almost drove his daughter to death upon discovering that she (in reality Hezhu in her name) had given money to her crestfallen fiancé, whom he had disavowed and who is now the official after successfully passing the civil service examination. Jin Shijie updated the play into a spoken theatre play set in the contemporary era in which Hezhu is a prostitute who, after hearing about the lost daughter of a rich man, goes to his family as the daughter, thus setting forth a farcical exposé of the modern materialist world. The play adopted jingju movement, blocking and musical/percussion accompaniment conventions, such as when Hezhu talks to her father on the same stage when the latter is supposed to be away back home. The actors also adopted Grotowskian movement routines taught by Wu Jingji, a psychologist who had trained in the Growtoskian method at New York's La MaMa Theatre.

The Experimental Theatre Festival continued for four more years and became an incubator for Taiwan's little theatre movement that created a whole generation of playwrights, directors and companies. One of the best-known playwrights and directors is Lai Shengchuan (Stan Lai, b. 1954), who was born in the U.S. but grew up in Taiwan. After receiving a PhD in theatre from Stanford University, he returned to Taiwan in 1983 and created the Performance Group (Biaoyan Gongzuofang) which created a number of hit productions out of group improvisation, including *That Evening, We Performed Crosstalk* (*Na yiye, women shuo xiangsheng,* 1985) and *Secret Love in Peach Blossom Land (Anlian taohuayuan,* 1986). Packaged with a prologue and five pieces of the Chinese two-person stand-up comedy *xiangsheng* (crosstalk), *That Evening, We Performed Crosstalk,* the group's first production, traces backwards Chinese and Taiwanese history through Taipei in 1985 ('The Love of Taipei') and 1962 ('TV and Me'), Chongqing in 1943 ('Air Raid') and Beijing in 1925 ('Remembrance and Forgetting') and 1900 ('Terminus'). This format was so popular that the company followed up with a series of plays based on crosstalk. Like *Hezhu's Marriage-New Version*'s successful appropriation of jingju, the popularity of folk performance became a stepping stone for modern theatre's reorientation from huaju's adherence to realism.

Made into a movie and repeatedly restaged in Taiwan and China, *Secret Love in Peach Blossom Land* has become an iconic representative of Taiwan's little theatre movement. It is structured around two theatre companies that are double-booked for the same rehearsal space. As a result, the companies take turns rehearsing their play, a farce and a melodrama. The farce, entitled *The Peach Blossom Land*, is the deconstruction of an ancient Chinese story about a person lost in a utopian world called the Peach Blossom Land but cannot find it again after leaving it. In the modern farce version, a poor fisherman escapes from his wife and her lover only to find the utopia where he lives harmoniously with a couple who resembles the wife and lover. However, once he returns to reality in the hope of bringing his wife to the utopian land, he also fails to find it. The melodrama, titled *Secret Love*, tells the story of a pair of lovers from the mainland being separated after the end of the civil war in 1949. When they finally see each other years later in a hospital ward in Taiwan, the man still clings to their erstwhile love while the woman has moved on. This section is performed in conventional huaju style, which by 1986 had become stale and melodramatic, even as the director, the basis for the male character, is continually frustrated by the actors' inability to portray his emotional world. The play's metatheatrical frame and juxtaposition of the farcical and melodramatic, as well as its irreverent observation of such themes as separation and unity, utopia and reality, have made it a contemporary classic in Taiwan and China.

Another veteran of Lanling Theatre and Performance Group Li Guoxiu (Lee Kuo-hsiu, Hugh K. S. Lee, b. 1955) went on to create his own company The Pingfeng Acting Troupe (Pingfeng Biaoyan Ban) that has been as successful as Performance Group. Most of his early plays were farces although the best of them were also profoundly self-reflective, as evidenced by the 1992 production of *Shamlet* (*Shamuleite*). Loosely based on Michael Frayn's *Noises Off* and elements of Mel Brook's film *To Be or Not to Be*, the play is about a mediocre touring troupe that stages *Hamlet* – performed as *Shamlet* because of a printing error – that is filled with technical and performance blunders, backstage intrigues and stabbings behind each other's backs. In a way, the play provides a mirror to the mixed qualities of burgeoning theatrical companies since the 1980s. As Catherine Diamond argues: '*Shamlet* is uniquely Taiwanese, and therefore reflects not only Taiwanese theatrical conditions, but the society as well . . . a response . . . to the selfish materialism of contemporary Taiwan society which threatens to subvert the collaboration necessary for theatrical performance.'[2]

In recent years, Taiwan theatre companies have toured mainland China where they have been enthusiastically received. Large-scale commercial theatres have also been successful in the island, together with independent theatres that also receive government support.

## Hong Kong

Hong Kong was colonised by Britain in 1841 and remained its colony until 1997, when the Chinese government reclaimed the territory as Hong Kong Special Administrative Region (SAR) of the People's Republic of China. The dominant theatrical form in Hong Kong is Cantonese opera. Earliest spoken theatre started by British army officers as early as 1844 with the Hong Kong Amateur Dramatic Club. Chinese language spoken theatre, which is the focus of this section, started roughly at the same time as wenmingxi in Shanghai. As early as 1908, spoken drama productions, known at the time as *baihuaju* (vernacular drama), started advertising in the *Huazi ribao* (*Chinese Daily*) newspaper. The earliest productions advocated for social change and supported the anti-Qing Dynasty movement before the Republican revolution in 1911. Performance in the 1910s was similar to wenmingxi in using scenarios and improvisation, and the actors were all amateurs.

After the name huaju was adopted in Hong Kong in the late 1920s following its usage in the mainland, the first boom for spoken theatre came in 1937 when the territory's status as a British colony made it a safe haven for many theatre artists from the mainland and base for anti-Japanese theatrical mobilisation. The highlight came in 1939 when large-scale performances combined the forces of local practitioners with leading huaju playwrights, directors and actors from the mainland, including the huaju veteran Ouyang Yuqian, the best-known professional company China Touring Theatre Company

(Zhongguo Lüxing Jutuan) headed by Tang Huaiqiu, and stage and film stars such as Jin Shan and Wang Ying. Another highlight came in late 1941 when a group of top artists from Shanghai and the interior staged several famous plays, including Cao Yu's *Peking Man*, under the name of Associated Dramatists in Hong Kong (Liugang Juren Xiehui). While the Pacific War after Pearl Harbor and the subsequent Japanese invasion on 25 December ended Hong Kong's safe haven status, the infusion of creative energy in the previous four years left a profound impact on the local huaju scene.

Between the end of Japanese occupation in 1945 and the establishment of Hong Kong Repertory Theatre (Xianggang Huaju Tuan) in 1977, spoken theatre was mostly the domain of amateur artists, especially performance by college and high school students. After 1949, a group of established playwrights immigrated to Hong Kong where they continued writing plays. The best-known among them include Xiong Shiyi (Hsiung Shih-I, 1902–91), Hu Chunbing (1907–60) and Yao Ke (1905–91). Together with local playwrights such as Lee Woon Wah (Li Yuanhua, 1915–2006), they were the veterans who fostered Hong Kong's theatre during this period. Because of censorship policies by the colonial government, many of the productions were plays on historical themes or translated Western drama. Contemporary-themed plays emerged in the 1960s, as best represented by Yao's *The Dark Alley* (*Louxiang*, 1962) that focuses on the danger of drug addiction. After 1966, when the mainland was embroiled in the fever of the Cultural Revolution, Hong Kong, while inevitably affected by the seismic event and even witnessed a riot initiated by leftist organisers in 1967, nonetheless witnessed the rise of college and high school theatre festivals that provided fertile ground for a new generation of theatrical activists. Like Taiwan theatres at this time, many of the productions were one-act plays that were heavily influenced by post-war Western theatre, especially theatre of the absurd.

Professional theatre eventually emerged in the late 1970s with the support of Hong Kong government, specifically when it directly sponsored the Hong Kong Repertory Theatre in 1977. By following a strategy of staging mostly Western and Chinese classics, the theatre greatly enhanced the stature of spoken theatre in Hong Kong. This strategy was further boosted by the hiring of Daniel S. P. Yang (Yang

Shipeng, b. 1935), an experienced Shakespearean director who had served as professor of theatre at the University of Colorado and Artistic Director of Colorado Shakespeare Festival, as its long-term Artistic Director (1983–5 and 1991–2000). Yang translated and directed plays for the company, and invited actors, directors and designers from China and around the world as guest artists. Yang's successors, Chung King Fai (Zhong Jinghui, b. 1937) and Joanna Chan (Chan Wanying, Chen Yinying, b. 1939) were also educated in the U.S. and were themselves important local directors and playwrights. This government sponsorship led to a proliferation of professional and semi-professional theatres, most of which received some degree of support from the government. Another important step in sustaining professional theatre is the establishment of the School of Drama within Hong Kong Academy of Performing Arts in 1984.

That year also marked a significant turning point for Hong Kong's spoken theatre world, which had until then been struggling to define a unique voice. In 1984, China and Britain agreed to end Hong Kong's colonial status and reunite it with the mainland in 1997, as a SAR that would retain its government and economic systems. The uncertainty over the region's fate after 1997, known as the '97 syndrome', created a large group of plays that reflect the territory's identity crisis. One play that directly tackled the issue is a 15-act piece titled *I Am Hong Konger* (*Ngo hai Heung Gong yan*) by Raymond To (To Kwok Wai, Du Guowei) and Hardy Tsoi (Cai Xichang) in 1985. It was staged as a bilingual production by the Sino-British Repertory Company (Zhongying Jutuan) under the direction of the Australian director Bernard Gross, with an ensemble of seven local characters, six Chinese and one British, although they also play other roles. At the beginning of the play, it asks the question: What is the right tone to say 'I am Hong Konger,' which it later suggests may be flat, passive and worried, lost, or confident and loud, revealing the range of emotions emanating from the residents. The play is divided into two parts. The first eight acts stage the history of Hong Kong from the beginning of colonialism, when a local fisherman's pigtail is cut by a British sailor who in turn gives him a tie, through the 1984 Sino-British talks, which leads to the residents' reactions in the second half. One of the scenes is an International

Students Party in the U.S. where a rich woman has sent her son. At the party, students from different nations are expected to sing a song form their home country. As the Hong Kong students are reluctant to sing either 'God Saves the Queen' or the anthem of mainland China or a pop song, one student starts to sing a famous Chinese folk song 'In That Place Far Away' (*Zaina yaoyuan de difang*), which brings together all the students emotionally and suggests the cultural bond between Hong Kong and the mainland that was at once inseparable and remote. At the end of the play, the actors stepped out of their roles and resumed their status as performers who register to vote, exhibiting a resolution to take the fate of the city into their own hands.

While *I Am Hong Konger* stayed away from a linear realistic structure, another representative play that sought to interrogate Hong Kong's identity followed the realistic tradition. Written by Joanna Chan and titled *Crown Ourselves with Roses* (*Huajin gaolou*, 1988), the play focuses on the life of two immigrant friends from the mainland for over three decades. Often compared to Lao She's *Teahouse* in its structure, the three-act play uses the same spot in the waterfront of Hong Kong Island during the Mid-Autumn Festival in 1955, 1972 and 1987 as a gateway to the immigration experience. The three acts examine the influx of mainland immigrants after 1949; the beginning of Hong Kong's economic take-off in the early 1970s shortly after the 1967 riot that resulted in armed collisions and made local residents weary of political influence from China; and the uncertainties of the mid-1980s about the territory's future. The play is noticeable in its message that while the fate of Hong Kong is out of the hand of its everyday residents, true salvation ultimately lies in self-reliance. One passage by the protagonist Jiang Ziliu in Act Two on the effect of the 1967 riot crystallises the issue:

We used to think that Hong Kong was the heaven providing our little patch of peace. Overnight we learned no matter what we did or how hard we tried, it made no difference. In a crisis, who spoke up for us? Not China, not Great Britain, no one! So with no tomorrow to speak of, we threw ourselves into today. Gradually and without really thinking much about it, we turned away from others to concentrate on ourselves. So we prospered, in just a few years. We've changed . . . but beneath it all maybe we're not all that proud of what we've become.[3]

Jiang's final line also displays a warning against the dogged pursuit of material success, which is the other side of Hong Kong's success story embodied by his friend Ding Feng. Coming to Hong Kong together with Jiang, Ding has succumbed to the philosophy of chasing after wealth by all means, even manipulating Jiang's friendship for a large sum of illegal commission from selling Jiang's old house. The play includes a large group of supporting characters, including a girl named Song Shuwen, who is a friend of both Jiang and Ding but is unfortunately drowned at the end of Act One, making her a lasting reminder of their youthful ideals that is sustained by Jiang and abandoned by Ding.

Another noticeable play of this era is a short allegorical play titled *Metamorphosis under the Star* (*Xingguang xia de tuibian*, 1986) by Anthony Chan (Chan Kam-kuen, Chen Ganquan). The play only has two characters, a cabbage named Vincent and a caterpillar named Charlotte. At first, the two friends live in perfect harmony, which gradually turns to conflicting tension because the caterpillar needs to feed on the cabbage in order to grow. Nevertheless, Vincent keeps feeding Charlotte wholeheartedly to the point of fainting as the latter begins to grow wings and morphs into a beautiful butterfly. When Vincent regains conscience and sees the butterfly that he has helped to bring to the world, he is at first ecstatic, only to turn fearful that his friend will fly away and never return. In reaction, Charlotte tears off her wings so that she will forever be together with her friend. At the end of the play, the two friends are huddled under the stars, which are transformed into butterflies with wings. The combination of selfless devotion and excruciating sacrifice wrapped up in a fairy tale can be read on many levels, including a story of unconditional love or as another depiction of Hong Kong residents' emotional rollercoaster of love, fear, hope, confusion and resolution.

The combination of government support of theatre and the '97 Syndrome' also led to the rise of experimental theatre companies devoted to postmodern, intercultural theatre and performance art. The best-known company of this group is Zuni Icosahedron (Jinnian Ershimianti) founded in 1982 by Danny Yung (Yung Ning Tsun, Rong Nianzeng, b. 1943) who had studied architecture and urban planning and design in the U.S. Yung's background is evident in the company's early productions that relied mostly on visual effect created by physical movement with few spoken lines, often accompanied by savvy deconstruction of Chinese and Western literary, theatrical and musical icons. Their combined effect produced some of the most potent and provocative interpretations of Hong Kong's identity crisis and anxiety towards 1997. Some of their early works include *One Hundred Years of Solitude* (*Bainian zhi guji*, 1982), *Chronicle of Women* (*Lienü zhuan*, 1983), *Sunrise* (*Richu*, 1985), *Genesis–Hong Kong* (*Chuangshi ji–Xianggang ban*, 1986), *The Story of the Stone* (*Shitou ji*, a.k.a. *Dream of the Red Chamber*, 1987), *The Decameron* (*Shiri tan*, 1988), *The Deep Structure of Chinese Culture* (*Zhongguo wenhua de shenceng jiegou*, 1990), *The Revolutionary Opera* (*Xianggang yangbanxi*, 1991), and *2 or 3 Scenes. . . . Hong Kong* (*Xianggang . . . er san shi*, 1993). Many of these productions have different versions or sequels over the years. Their inaugural piece *One Hundred Years of Solitude*, which borrowed from the novel of the same title that earned Gabriel García Márquez Nobel Prize for Literature in 1982, celebrated Version 10.0 in 2011 with the subtitle *Cultural Revolution*. Their works often shone light on the assumptions of race, identity, nationality or language, and their staging of the city's anxiety is often powerfully effective, as evidenced by *The Decameron*.

Performed in 1988 at the height of Hong Kong's insecurity and wave of exodus, *The Decameron* adopted the classic Italian collection of stories told by a group of youngsters at the height of the Black Death as a perfect backdrop to the performance of Hong Kong residents' similar fear and anxiety. Some versions of the piece also include the subtitle of *Love in the Time of Cholera* – another well-known novel by Márquez – to further emphasise the theme of emotional uncertainty, as punctuated by many poignant stage images. Some of these images are clearly reflecting territorial, national, political and ideological confusions. In one scene, a man holds up a portrait of Queen Elizabeth II in a crowd that subsequently disperse in all directions. Another person holds a portrait of Karl Marx that covers his face when he stands and weighs him to the floor when he lies down. Other scenes showcase the panicking wave of exodus, with crowds moving across the stage with furniture pieces; a woman throwing her suitcases to the floor to hug a man as if before eternal separation; and two women sitting in a chair and bed respectively and then standing up and leaving, with another holding onto the switch of a floor lamp, as if to say the last one leaving the city should turn off the light. Still other scenes demonstrate the psychological toll of the event, with a mad woman running around shouting and being chased by a man; a couple madly making love in bed, only to have the woman murdered later by another woman with a knife; a woman lying down and getting off a blood-stained bed; ten hospital beds lining up with an actor flapping manically on them and a woman walking slowly towards him.

While the years after 1997 have allayed much of the fear in Hong Kong, there is no doubt that the city's uncertainty in the previous decade created a rare opening that unleashed tremendous creativity in its modern theatre. In recent years, theatre productions are generally focused on the daily lives of its residents, although political theatre has not disappeared. One outstanding example is Zuni's *East Wing West Wing* series that has so far staged ten plays. The tile of the series apparently alludes to the separate power centres of Hong Kong and Beijing that affect the lives of the city's residents. The series' inaugural play *2046 CE Bye Bye* (*2046 Teshou bujianle* [literally 'The Chief Executive Disappears']) debuted in 2003 to two events that created the largest political crisis for the Hong Kong SAR. The first was the government's inept response the SARS epidemic. The second event was massive protests against Chief Executive Tung Chee Hwa's (eventually aborted) push to enact Article 23 of Hong Kong Basic Law, which sought to criminalise, among other activities, 'any act of treason, secession, sedition, subversion against the Central People's Government'. Structured as a variety show with over a dozen scenes of monologue, dialogue, singing and multimedia presentations, the play alternates between comedy, farce and serious protest. The piece is both an indictment of Tung and a self-reflection of the citizens' responsibility in the new democracy. In an early scene, Tung's election is portrayed as a sham where an actor who subsequently plays Tung erases three candidate names on a white board and only records vote numbers no matter which name – which eventually includes other than the candidates such as Chinese emperors and leaders till Chiang Kai-shek and Mao Zedong – is announced. This is followed by Tung's inauguration ceremony in which the actor mouths over Tung's swearing of the oath in Mandarin – in contrast to the rest of the play that is delivered in Cantonese – to suggest Tung as Beijing's mouthpiece. It also includes an angry speech, which could be from the rallies, accusing Tung of creating a five-year disaster and pleads with him not to extend it to a 'ten-year calamity', an allusion to the Cultural Revolution. Gradually, though, the piece turns a critical eye to Hong Kong media and residents, exposing the media as flaming the unrest for financial gains and the citizens with dubious moral compass, as evidenced in a farcical debate over peeing in public that ends with a vote of four to one in favour of excusing the action. This scene also complicates power relations when an actress assumes a male voice and uses the royal 'we' when chiding the lone dissenter as being stubborn. The play ends with an open letter to Tung asking whether it is unfair to lay all the blame on him because the government is after all a reflection of Hong Kong and its materialist citizens. The letter is read in a calm tone through voice over to an empty stage with Tung's cardboard figure and a projected documentary film about Hong Kong from colonialism, through its growth and visits from Queen Elizabeth II, ending with the signing of the 'Sino-British Joint Declaration' in 1984 by British Prime Minister Margaret Thatcher and Chinese Premiere Zhao Ziyang.

On the other end of the ideological spectrum are plays that portray life after 1997 in a much more positive light. One such play is the musical *Sweet and Sour Hong Kong* (*Suansuan tiantian Xianggang di*) which also debuted in 2003. The play was written by He Jiping, who had immigrated to Hong Kong from Beijing after writing *The World's Top Restaurant* (see previous chapter). With lyrics by James Wong (Huang Zhan) and music by Joseph Koo (Gu Jiahui) – both icons of Hong Kong music scene – the musical was a joint venture by the city's three top companies: Hong Kong Repertory Theatre, Hong Kong Chinese Orchestra and the Hong Kong Dance Company. The play is about the competition of two restaurants. One of them is a hundred-year-old noodle shop going downhill but being helped by the owner's sister from the mainland and her son with a degree in business administration from Peking University. The other is a new pizza shop owned by an attractive young woman with a business degree from abroad. The competition between the old and the new, between Chinese and Western is disrupted by a typhoon that destroys both businesses until a couple from Shanghai saves both of them with new investment. While the play was positively received when touring in the mainland as demonstrating an uplifting spirit of Hong Kong since its unification with China, local reviews criticised the play – including its *deus ex machina* ending using Shanghai investors as saviours of local business – as revealing a bias towards the mainland and ignoring the common tension between Hong Kong natives and immigrants from the mainland.

This play also reveals a number of features of Hong Kong's modern theatre in the new millennium in several aspects. First, its high production value of music and dance points to the blending of spoken theatre and popular entertainment. He Jiping first wrote the play as a pure huaju. When the Hong Kong government in 2003 provided partial support for the production in order to boost its residents' morale in the aftermath of SARS, it was turned into a musical in order to maximise its popular appeal. Indeed, Hong Kong theatre has a tradition of blending popular entertainment and serious drama, as evident in *I Am Hong Konger* and *East Wing West Wing*. Another reason for the musical version is the pressure on Hong Kong Repertory Theatre to produce more popular productions after the government pushed art troupes to the market in 2001. As a result, the company became an independent corporation, although it is still heavily subsidised by the government.

Still another aspect of this production is its tour in China, an expansion of the greater Chinese market that is increasingly utilised by companies in all three regions. For this production, the theme of harmony between Hong Kong natives and new mainland immigrants was obviously an important factor for it to be invited to Guangzhou, Shanghai and Hangzhou, where it represented Hong Kong in China Arts Festival. Other productions have treated the three regions as part of the marketing strategy, as evidenced by Tian Qinxin's opening of

*Four Generations under One Roof* in Taipei in order to generate buzz of its 'Republican style'. In fact, most of Tian's productions have opened in Taiwan or Hong Kong, including her latest production *Green Snake* (*Qingche*), which debuted in Hong Kong in March 2013. In recent years, a number of Taiwan productions have toured China, including *Silent Love in Peach Blossom Land* and *Shamlet*. As evident from the case of *Sweet and Sour Hong Kong*, reception can vary greatly in these three regions. Yet, the fact that a play has been staged in a different region can be manipulated as evidence of its success.

As has been demonstrated throughout this chapter, social and historical events in Taiwan and Hong Kong in the twentieth century often exerted significant impact on their modern theatre. For Taiwan, Japanese occupation meant close ties with Japanese spoken theatre and the use of Japanese and Taiwanese as stage languages. After a brief period of flourish for huaju immediately after Japanese occupation, the nationalist government conscripted theatre as a weapon in its anti-communist propaganda. Since the 1960s, influence of post-war Western theatre greatly influenced the rise of Taiwan's Little Theatre Movement, which exploded after the revocation of martial law in 1987. Hong Kong's status of a British colony and the way such status ended in 1997 were also key factors in the trajectory of its modern theatre. The territory served as a safe haven between 1937 and 1941 for anti-Japanese artists from the mainland who in turn cultivated local talents. After 1949, playwrights from the mainland, together with local talents who had studied and practised huaju in China, fostered amateur and college productions. Direct support by the government in the late 1970s established a professional theatre system in the city, which quickly found its voice in reaction to the 1984 Sino-British decision of Hong Kong's fate in 1997.

The histories of modern theatre in Taiwan and Hong Kong share similarities with each other as well as mainland China and other Asia cultures, in terms of Western influence both in early twentieth century and after World War II as well as the rediscovery of indigenous theatre and performance as a source of inspiration. Ultimately, though, it was their unique social, cultural and political histories that shaped their modern theatre and their unique place in world theatre today.

# CHAPTER 6
## MODERN KOREAN THEATRE

### Introduction

Korea is 'the shrimp between two whales', having been geographically located between China and Japan and the most logical land link between the two. Much of Korean history has involved negotiating a careful existence between those two nations. That history is a major preoccupation with much Korean culture (especially the modern drama). Korea has fought against colonialism and enforced acculturation, as well as attempts to erase Korean history, language and culture. The Korean language 'is the foundation of a national culture' that has been influenced by China and Japan, including Confucian ethics and an imposed social system during Japanese occupation, but has remained unique and distinctive, including its unique written form (*han'gŭl*).[1]

Modern Korean drama has been shaped by Korean identity, Western models and the experience of successive national traumas, including Japanese occupation from 1910 to 1945, the partition of the peninsula into North and South, the Korean War and repressive regimes of different natures in both Koreas. The evolution of the modern theatre was dynamic, multifaceted and at times, contradictory. Modern drama, as part of a colonial modernity imposed by Japan, was both oppressive and a form of resistance, modernising Korean theatre while creating a forum in which Japanese cultural hegemony might be resisted.

In South Korea, for virtually all of its history, Seoul is the site of modern, spoken drama. Most Koreans, however, have regional roots – most Seoul dwellers are only one generation from farmers somewhere else in the nation. Thus much modern Korean drama reflects life in Seoul, but just as much (certainly in the first half of the century) reflects village life as well. The urban/rural dichotomy forms a strong theme in much of Korean drama.

Many Korean cultural critics identify the dominant emotional mode of Korean culture as '*han*', defined as 'a deep-seated feeling of sorrow, bitterness, or despair that originates in oppression or injustice, accumulates over time and remains unexpressed in the heart; it is believed by some to be intrinsic to the Korean cultural experience'.[2] Modern drama is full of examples of plays that manifest han, as will be seen below. Related to this is a 'victim mentality' that several scholars have perceived in modern Korean culture, resulting in a tendency to portray Korean history not only as a series of catastrophes, but the Korean people as constantly suffering at the hands of all others and maintaining a sense of fatality.

Modernity in Korea is also a colonial modernity, imposed from without by Japan during thirty-five years of occupation and colonial rule (1910–45). At the end of the nineteenth century, the nation's leaders were split between radical reformers and modernists, that looked to Japan as a model for Korea to follow and a conservative, Confucian elite equally determined to preserve the status quo and not modernise. Michael Robinson captures the irony of the situation, noting:

In the end the progressives were caught in a dilemma that informed cultural development in Korea for the better part of the 1900s. That is, modernizers in Korea took their inspiration from the very forces (most notably the Japanese) that threatened the political and cultural autonomy of what they hoped might become a modern Korean nation.[3]

In other words, while Japan was taken as a model, the Japanese, by colonising Korea, threatened to eradicate modern Korean culture and replace it with an imposed modern Japanese culture. The political and cultural annexation of Korea by Japan was itself the product of modernity, one that many Koreans resisted and that others were conflicted, embracing modernisation while resisting the imposition of Japanese culture as part of that modernity.

As elsewhere in Asia, universities were of great significance in the development of modern drama. In the first three decades of the twentieth century, Korean students educated at Japanese universities returned to their homeland and began to develop modern hybrid theatres based on the modern Japanese theatres. The translation of Western plays was carried out at universities by professors and students of literature. Those same students would organise theatre companies and continue to manage them and perform plays after the end of their studies. In the 1960s, Korean students educated at Korean universities began to develop postmodern hybrid theatre, and even today, the theatre district in Seoul is located around University Avenue (*Taehangno*), the neighbourhood that includes Seoul National University and branch campuses for several schools.

Lastly, a dominant theme in Korean culture (and hence in modern Korean drama) is the tendency towards authoritarianism, in both North and South Korea. Korean history has been predicated on a strong authority figure at the head of the nation. Confucianism in Chosŏn-era Korea encouraged the Korean people to look upon the king as national father. With the Japanese occupation, again a strong authority sat above the nation. The Kim family in the North and a series of military dictators in the South following the Second World War means that for almost all of its history, every part of Korea has been under a strong authoritarian rule.[4] This aspect of Korean history is frequently explored in modern drama, especially in the South beginning in the 1990s.

This chapter will now explore the history and development of modern Korean drama from 1900 to 2000. 'Korea' in this chapter refers to the Republic of Korea ('South Korea') unless otherwise specified. The chapter will follow chronological order, considering the contexts of traditional Korean theatre and modern Korean history, and then exploring first the period from 1910 to 1945 when modern drama developed under Japanese occupation and influence, first in the form of *shinp'agŭk*, derived from Japanese shinpa, and then in the form of *shingŭk*, derived from Japanese shingeki. The period from 1945 to 1960 followed, a transitional era in the South marked by American influence and political instability. As elsewhere in Asia, 1960 marked a transformation, as modern Korean drama matures, experimental artists emerge and hybrid forms again manifested on Korean stages. Lastly, the period from 1988 to the present marked the internationalisation of

Korean theatre under globalisation while facing increased competition from cinema, television and the internet. The chapter will close with a few words on the modern theatre of the Democratic Peoples' Republic of Korea (DPRK, 'North Korea').

## Traditional Theatres and Performance Forms

As Richard Nichols observes, during the Chosŏn dynasty (1392–1910) 'a variety of factors joined to preclude the development of drama': a dominant conservative noble class, an agrarian economy with no middle class until the twentieth century, a lack of theatre buildings and the popularity of low, ritual and folk forms.[5] Unlike Japan, China and India, Korea does not have a history of performance forms that create a dramatic literature. There is no equivalent to nō, kabuki, zaju or Sanskrit drama. Traditional theatre in Korea falls into one of two categories: court dance and folk performances.

Sandae gŭk literally means 'mountainside ritual', indicative of its origins, although now it is a term used to describe a variety of masked dance dramas originating during the Chosŏn dynasty. Sandae gŭk can be divided into two types, based on origin: village festival plays and court plays. The former include *hahoe pyŏlshin-gut*, from Hahoe village in east-central Korea, derived most likely from an exorcism ritual, from narratives transmitted orally until the twentieth century. The latter includes *pyŏlsandae*, literally 'separate stage performance', indicating that it began as a court form that evolved into a folk form; *t'alch'um*, masked dance drama from the North, preserved after 1948 in the South; and *ogwangdae*, literally 'five performers', from the Southwest.

*Kkoktu koksi* is a puppet theatre aimed at adults, taking as its themes corrupt Buddhist monks, immoral officials, and jealousy and divorce among peasants. It is a satirical theatre, using both human and animal puppets, comical and bawdy, grotesque and exaggerated. Performers were itinerant and the narratives were transmitted orally. Companies consisting of five or six puppeteers, five or six musicians and a narrator would set up a puppet stage in a public place in a village and perform for the residents. The form was considered low and was never sanctioned by the government. In the present, performances are rare, but elements of kkoktu koksi have been used by avant-garde playwrights and theatre artists since the 1960s.

*P'ansori* is a one-person folk narrative sung to the accompaniment of a single drum. The performer sings, performs spoken dialogue and narration, and gestures. The narrative alternates song with speech. The primary prop is a folding fan. As with other forms, the traditional p'ansori narratives were transmitted orally until the modern era, and performers were also encouraged to ad lib and change elements of the narrative in keeping with context and taste. Performances could last for several hours.

All of these forms are indigenous performance forms that do not rely upon or require written scripts. Thus, there was no tradition of playwriting in Korea. The various forms of traditional performance were also regional, and rooted, except for court dance, in the rhythms and culture of agricultural village life. They were thus challenged by modernity and urbanisation. Furthermore, under Japanese rule, all of these indigenous theatres were threatened with extinction and erasure, but were preserved by the artists and were revived after 1945.

The first modern hybrid theatre form to emerge in Korea was *ch'anggŭk* (singing drama). Based on p'ansori narrative singing, ch'anggŭk used an entire cast rather than a solo singer. P'ansori's drum was supplemented with other traditional Korean instruments, and historically accurate scenic elements and costumes were introduced. The dramatic repertory came primarily from p'ansori, so ch'anngŭk represented an attempt to modernise a traditional performance form by blending it with Western elements. The result has been termed 'Korean opera' by some scholars.

Some scholars argue that it was actually the introduction of indoor performance spaces that brought about the development of ch'anngŭk, as all traditional Korean theatre is performed outdoors. In December 1902, the Hyŏmnyul Theatre (*Hyŏmnyul-sa*) opened as the first indoor theatre in Korea, featuring dancing, singing and p'ansori. It closed in April of the following year, but the idea of indoor theatre had been introduced and made popular. On the site of the Hyŏmnyul-sa, the Wŏn'gak Theatre (*Wŏn'gak-sa*) opened on 26 July 1908. The first ch'anngŭk script, *The Ballad of Ch'oe Pyŏng-tu*, was written in 1908 and performed at the Wŏn'gak-sa. It was followed by the first modern play in Korean, *Silver World* (*Un segŏ*, 1908) by Yi In-jig (1861–1916).

Yi had lived in Japan from 1884 to 1894 and had seen shinpa productions by Sudo Sadanori and Kawakami Otojiro. *Silver World* was didactic, less entertaining than instructive. The protagonists, a brother and sister who go to America for their education, spend much of the play making speeches about the need for political reform in Korea and the value of Western civilisation. His second play, *Plum in Snow* (*Sŏlzung-mě*, 1909), adapted from a Japanese novel, was also highly didactic. As in Japan, the modern theatre was seen as a means to an end to push for progressive reforms of society. Yi's plays are considered by some to be proto-shinpa, but others regard them as closer to ch'anngŭk.[6]

Ch'anngŭk was popular in Seoul for the first two decades of the twentieth century, but was replaced by the more modern theatres and then could be found only in conservative rural areas. The limited repertory and hybrid nature (not quite modern, not traditional) found it hard to keep audiences and so by the 1930s, ch'anngŭk was losing popularity in those locales as well. Although there were revivals in the mid-1930s and early 1960s, and, as noted below a continued popularity in North Korea, ch'anngŭk never developed into a truly modern theatre, remaining a hybrid form closer to its traditional roots.

## Modern Korean History and the Evolution of Modern Drama

At the end of the nineteenth century, the longest ruling dynasty in Korean history, the Chosŏn (from the Chinese name Chaoxian – 'Land of Morning Calm') found itself under internal and external pressures.[7] The Sino-Japanese War of 1894–5 was fought mostly in and around Korea. As a result of Japanese victory, China gave up its stake in Korea. Less than ten years later, Japanese victory in the Russo-Japanese War of 1904–5 resulted in Russia giving up its interests in Korea. Korea was also seen by the Japanese as stepping-stone to Manchuria, the first step in establishing a Japanese empire in Asia. In 1905 Korea was declared a 'protectorate' of Japan with no objection from other nations.

Japan initially seemed a model for Korea's modernisation, but as Japan colonised Korea, the model then became a program of forced colonial modernisation and cultural eradication, especially after annexation in 1910. From 1910 to 1945, the Japanese engaged in cultural suppression as well as forcing a complete loss of Korean autonomy and nationhood. Korea was forced to sign a treaty ceding all domestic authority, foreign relations and defence to the Japanese. The Korean language was banned in education and all official documents and discouraged in all other areas. By 1930 all Korean language newspapers were banned and Koreans were encouraged to take Japanese names in forced assimilation. The theatre that emerged during this thirty-five year period was thus both rooted in Japanese models, serving as a form of Japanese acculturation in Korea, but also served as a form of resistance, presenting models for behaviour under Japanese occupation that were subversive and implicated and critiqued the Japanese.

## Shinp'agŭk

After Yi's early experiments at the Wŏn'gak-sa, *Shinp'agŭk* (new school drama) was imported from Japan in 1911. As the name suggests, it was the Korean version of Japanese shinpa. The first shinpagŭk company in Seoul was the Revolutionary Troupe (*Hyŏkshindan*), founded by actor and producer Im Sŏng-gu (1887–1921), formed in 1911 with their first production, *Divine Punishment for Lack of Filial Piety* (*Purhyo Chŏnbŏl*). Shinp'a dramas were melodramatic, sentimental, tear-jerkers with improvised dialogue. Initially, the quality of plays and performances was poor, as Hyŏkshindan, which lasted as a company until 1920, and those that followed were relying on third-rate Japanese companies that toured Korea as their model. Experimentation and experience, however, raised the quality of performances.

Shinp'agŭk took a step forward with the founding in 1922 of the Earth Moon Group (*Towolhoe*) by Pak Sŭng-hŭi (1901–64), a director, producer and shinp'a playwright. Pak was a university student in Tokyo who returned to Seoul and led the Towolhoe for over twenty years. Pak was a theatre reformer, the first to use fully written scripts instead of improvisation and insisting upon extensive rehearsals. He wrote over two hundred plays, most of which have not survived, lost during the Korean War (1950–3).

Shinp'a plays fell into three categories: military history plays in which Korean soldiers fought to defend the nation (serving as a counterpoint to Japanese propaganda), criminal plays in which a heroic policeman finds and captures a notorious criminal (demonstrating virtue and the dangers of vice), and domestic family plays dealing with conflicts between generations (fathers and sons) and genders (husbands and wives or lovers). Sentimentality ruled, as did a simple morality: virtue, love and self-sacrifice were rewarded, while vice was inevitably punished. Suffering was a big theme in shinp'a, partly for its melodramatic qualities, and also because the depiction of melodramatic suffering became a means around Japanese censorship by showing misery and anguish in seeming domestic or criminal situations, with the implication that the Japanese occupation was the reason why the characters were suffering. Shinp'a thus also became a drama of resistance.

By the mid-1920s, however, shinp'a was in decline, replaced by the development of another modern theatre, also derived from and imposed by the Japanese: shingŭk, the Korean version of Japanese shingeki. This is not to suggest shinp'a disappeared, replaced by shingŭk. The Towolhoe lasted until 1946 with a faithful, albeit small, audience. Likewise, some of Pak's plays are still performed today. In the larger theatrical world, however, shinp'a ceased to develop as a form and was eclipsed by shingŭk.

## Shingŭk

Shingŭk (new drama) was the Korean version of shingeki, the modern spoken drama of Japan that became the dominant modern theatre of Korea as well, long after Japanese occupation ended. Shingŭk is naturalistic/realistic spoken drama modelled after Western theatre as filtered through Japanese practices. In Korea, however, it also took on strong nationalistic and ideological tones. To the present-day shingŭk implies modernity, nationalism and a commitment to Western values such as individualism and democracy. Early shingŭk consisted mostly of translations and adaptations of modern plays from Europe. Indigenous plays did develop, but were outnumbered by the productions of Western plays. Two groups were particularly influential in the development of shingŭk: *Tongwuhoe* and *Kŭgyesul Yŏnguhoe*.

The Society of Comradeship (*Tongwuhoe*) was founded in 1921 by a group of Korean students studying at Waseda University in Tokyo, one of the places where shingeki began. Kim U-jin (1897–1927) was a student at Waseda and an aficionado of shingeki. Upon his return to Seoul he organised the Tongwuhoe. He was the first Korean playwright to be influenced by Ibsen, Strindberg and Shaw, writing five plays and translating three more for production. Tongwuhoe were the first performers of what would come to be called shingŭk. They embraced the principles of freedom, self-determination, and welcoming and adopting the modern, mounting plays by Ibsen, O'Neill, Capek, Maeterlinck, Strindberg, Goethe, Hauptmann, Schiller and Pirandello. The company also produced the first shingŭk play by a Korean playwright: *Kim The Death of Kim Yŏng-il* (*Yŏng-il ŭi chugŭm*, 1923) by Cho Myŏng-hŭi. Kim U-Jin's plays were also performed: *A Woman, Yi Yŏngnyŏ* (*Yi Yŏngnyŏ*, 1925) and *Shipwreck* (*Nanp'a*, 1926), among others. The latter is interesting as it was an experiment in expressionism, not naturalism, which indicates that shingŭk, like shingeki, was dominated by realism, but was not solely realism. Instead, it saw all Western theatre as models for modern drama.

As in Japan, Ibsen and Chekhov were primary models, although Korean dramatists were also drawn to Irish playwrights, especially John Millington Synge and Sean O'Casey, not least of which because the Irish playwrights also sought to develop a modern drama in the face of colonial modernity imposed by an imperialistic island neighbour.[8] After forty productions, the Japanese ordered Tongwuhoe disbanded. Its existence was short, but its influence was enduring as a pioneer of shingŭk.

Another playwright who studied in Japan and strongly identified with Irish dramatists founded the second significant shingŭk company. Yu Ch'ijin (1905–74), 'the father of Korean theatre', studied at Ritkyo University in Tokyo, writing his thesis on Sean O'Casey, and with fellow Korean actor Hong Hae-sŏng (1893–1957), performed at the Tsukiji Little Theatre (see Chapter 1) in Tokyo. Returning to Korea, he was one of the founders of the Dramatic Arts Research Society (*Kŭgyesul Yŏnguhoe*), a university association organised in 1931. Kŭgyesul Yŏnguhoe popularised shingŭk, presenting plays by Chekhov, Ibsen, Gogol, Lady Gregory and Galsworthy. They embraced the Western drama model while resisting sole reliance on Western plays or slavish imitation to develop Korean plays. Yu wrote thirty plays, both comedy and tragedy, but always engaging the social implications of Japanese colonialism. In *The Shack* (*T'omak*, 1932), the bleak and cruel life of Korean farmers under Japanese military rule was exposed allegorically. Similarly, in *The Ox* (*So*, 1934) an old farmer has his land confiscated and learns his son has been killed by Japanese police. The occupation authorities disapproved of these plays, which sought to raise Korean national consciousness against Japanese oppression.

Other universities were also sites for the development of shingŭk. Universities and high schools offered drama clubs that staged Western plays. Between 1929 and 1931, schools in and around Seoul staged *The Merchant of Venice*, *The Taming of the Shrew*, Ibsen's *The Lady of the Sea*, Galsworthy's *Justice* and Tolstoy's *The Power of Darkness*.

Commercial theatres also operated at this time, as did numerous smaller groups. The Oriental Theatre (*Tong'yang-sa*), the sole space devoted to dramatic theatre, opened in Seoul in 1935 with three resident companies: Ch'ŏngch'un-jwa, Tongkŭk-jwa and Hŭkŭk-jwa, offering commercial entertainment with no political content. As in Japan and China, numerous writers otherwise unaffiliated with the theatre began writing plays. These writers were part of a larger programme of social change, using drama to encourage progressive social transformations. For example, Pak Hwa-sŏng (1904–88) was a female playwright who had also studied English drama in Japan and returned to Korea to write plays. *The White Flower* (*Paekwha*, 1932), a feminist socialist play based on her short story, is representative of her work. Although as a leftist she was concerned with ideology, her plays explored the impact of poverty and Japanese repression on the lives of ordinary Korean women.

During this period, shingŭk artists came under particular scrutiny by the Japanese. Censorship followed, along with arrest, detention and torture for artists suspected of being anti-Japanese. Finally, in 1939 Kŭgyesul Yŏnguhoe was ordered disbanded and forbidden to perform by the Japanese. Six years would pass before Yu's plays could be performed publicly again. After the defeat of Japan, a newly freed Korea experienced artistic freedom it had never known under the Japanese. *Fatherland* (*Choguk*, 1946) was the first play by Yu Ch'ijin in a free Korea. Anti-Japanese sentiment is still found in this one-act that celebrates the 1919 independence movement.

## Post-War Theatre in a Divided Korea: 1945–60

At the end of the Second World War, as Japan was facing imminent defeat, the Soviets invaded the Korean peninsula in August 1945 as the Americans occupied the South. The United States, already seeking to contain communism in a post-war world, offered a split at the 38th parallel. The Korean peninsula was thus arbitrarily divided by the West and the Soviet Union into two mutually opposed states in 1948: the communist North and the rightist South. At the time of the division of the Koreas, the North was urbanised and industrial and the South was rural and dominated by agriculture. The North had most of the factories, mines, dams and power plants. Until the 1970s, the North had a greater per capita income than the South, which had a predominantly subsistence agriculture economy. The South was a rural nation that would spend the next four decades developing into a modern economic powerhouse.

Korean modern drama starts to emerge again after the war in the absence of Japanese censorship. Almost immediately, however, the drama also became factionalised, with plays, artists and companies proclaiming themselves either communist or nationalist in opposition to the other. The Theatre Rehabilitation Headquarters (*Yŏngŭk Kŏnsŏl*

*Ponbu*) was a leftist organisation that ran afoul of the American forces in Korea because of its support for communism, while the Theatre Arts Association (*Kŭgyesul Hyŏphoe*) was a nationalist, anti-leftist organisation founded in 1947. Yu Ch'ijin wrote plays for the latter.

This ideological conflict within the theatre was one of two defining characteristics of post-war drama, the other being an assertion of Korean national identity after decades of Japanese colonialism and hope for a better future. The better future envisioned in these dramas was determined by the ideological stance of the artists positing that future as well as the visions of the individual playwrights. Playwright O Yŏng-jin (1916–74), for example, moved past the subject matter of realism for shingŭk and mined folklore for narratives that he transformed into satiric comedies mocking the Japanese during their rule and then mocking Korean politics in the period afterwards.

In 1950 the National Theatre was founded with Yu Ch'ijin as Director with two purposes: to promote new Korean theatre and to foster exchanges with other nations. Two resident companies were established: New Association (*Shinhyop*) and Theatre Association (*Kughyop*). The inaugural productions were Yu Ch'ijin's *Wonsulrang* and a Korean translation of the Chinese playwright Cao Yu's huaju classic *Thunderstorm* (see Chapter 3). With the outbreak of war that year the National Theatre moved to Taegu, returning to Seoul only when the cease fire was signed in 1953.

On 25 June 1950, the North invaded the South believing the United States would not interfere and that the people in the South would rise up and overthrow the government. Neither of these was true and the conflict raged, with foreign support on both sides, for three years. Although the Korean War (1950–3) made conditions difficult for the production of theatre, plays were still staged in the South. During and after the war, however, only the commercial theatre enjoyed prosperity.

The American occupation of South Korea after the war also resulted in an increased presence of American drama on the stages of Korea. Seventy-eight foreign plays were staged in South Korea during the 1950s, over a quarter of them being American: Tennessee Williams, Arthur Miller, Eugene O'Neill and William Inge, among others, were on the stages of Korea more than some indigenous playwrights. Indeed, Richard Nichols reports that the problem with so much foreign drama, coupled with the fact that companies like Shinhyŏp when not presenting foreign plays would mount older, pre-war plays, was that few opportunities were left for young Korean playwrights to develop their craft.[9] Foreign drama once again, as in the 1920s, dominated Korean theatre. An emerging film industry added to the challenge of continuing to develop quality modern drama in post-war Korea.

In 1962 the Drama Center was built in Seoul with the support of the Rockefeller Foundation. Yu Ch'ijin served as director and the choice of first productions was telling. The inaugural show was a production of *Hamlet*, followed by a production of O'Neill's *Long Day's Journey into Night*. Some critics found it interesting that the first presentations at the foremost theatre in Seoul in 1962 were not Korean plays but Western ones. A movement began in opposition to shingŭk's tendency to look to the West that would blossom into the 1960s' avant-garde theatre.

## Emergence of the Korean Avant-Garde: 1960 Onward

As elsewhere in Asia and around the globe, the 1960s marked a period of radical transition, both in society and in the theatre that reflected society. The new generation of artists rejected the earlier versions of shingŭk, perceived to be too Western, and sought a truly Korean theatre through experimentation, hybrids and mining the past and traditional theatre for elements to transform the modern Korean drama. The year 1960 marked the founding of Experimental Theatre Group (*Shilhŏm kŭktan*), 'a company founded by the first generation of Korean theatre artists to be educated in Korea by Koreans', with an inaugural performance of *The Bald Primadona* by Ionesco.[10] As a result of the rise of this new generation, new trends in Korean theatre would include a new nationalism coupled with a desire to interrogate the past, as well as a rejection of the Western models of realism and American naturalism and magical realism. Yet, as the choice of an Ionesco play suggests, although realism was rejected, Western influence was still dominant in Korean drama. Much of the 1960s would be spent moving away from the shaping influence of the West and in a quest to find a truly Korean drama.

Challenging this artistic vision was the repressive society in which it was growing. South Korea lived under military rule from 1961 to 1993. Park Chung Hee became ruler of Korea in a coup d'etat in 1961, subsequently promoting economic growth and modernisation combined with the development of a police state that repressed its citizens and especially its artists and journalists. Control over Korean cultural life was deemed important and all scripts were required to be approved by government censors before public performance or publication would be allowed.

In this environment absurdism as modelled by Samuel Beckett became a dominant mode, not only because it allowed playwrights, actors and directors to present allegorical critiques of society, but also because absurdism flourished in repressive societies, artists recognising the fundamental absurdities underlying the laws and social structures that created lived reality in such societies. The worldwide absurdist movement was popular all over the globe in the 1960s, and Korea was no exception. Most of the major playwrights of the 1960s emerged out of the absurdist movement, creating an antirealist avant-garde that sent the tone for the second half of the twentieth century.

O Tae-sǒk, post-war Korea's leading (and arguably most innovative) playwright, was born in 1940 in rural central South Korea, studied philosophy at Yonsei University, but became an experimental theatre artist in the 1960s despite having no formal theatrical training, only a brief period in New York City in which he encountered avant-garde and experimental theatre. His work, beginning in the late 1960s, was in reaction to the dominant shingǔk, resisting naturalism. Although initially he was influenced by the absurdists, most notably Samuel Beckett and Harold Pinter, he prepared an adaptation of Moliere's *Les Fourberies de Scapin* in 1972 that blended Western text and Korean traditional elements. While appreciating both aspects, O believed there were fundamental differences between Korean theatre and that of the rest of the world and set about searching for 'Koreanness' in his work, insisting 'that Western pictorial realism is inimical to Korean character'.[11]

O decided to interrogate Korean history and its relationship to the present through avant-garde theatre. He believes Korean history is inherently tragic and that the theatre should reflect that. His first play in this new mode was *Grass Tomb* (*Ch'obun*, 1973), employing the image of burial in a grass tomb, an ancient Korean practice, blended surrealistically with elements of both Korean and Western theatre. The show was a success in Seoul and later became the first modern Korean play to be performed in the United States when remounted at La Mama Experimental Theatre Club in New York in 1974.

O's subsequent output (over sixty plays total, to date) continued the search for a Korean ethos, exploring Korean history and relating it to the present through imagery, repetition, ritual and non-linear narrative. O writes and directs based on his theory of 'skips and omissions', in which only the essential is placed on stage and the audience must fill the gaps with their own thoughts and imagination. Involving the audience is key to O, who frequently breaks the fourth wall, having characters directly address the audience and often not even look at each other but focus the entire narrative outward to the spectators.

Key works that followed include *Lifecord* (*T'ae*, 1974), *Ch'unp'ung's Wife* (*Ch'unp'ung ŭi ch'ŏ*, 1976) and *Bicycle* (*Chajŏngŏ*, 1983). *Lifecord* concerned a true story from Korean history in which a usurping monarch who executes scholars for calling for the return of the legitimate ruler, which O relates to executions carried out by the Japanese during the colonial period. *Ch'unp'ung's Wife*, which employs traditional Korean theatre techniques (drawn from t'alch'um and sandae gŭk), is an adaptation of a classical Korean folk narrative concerning a married man who falls in love with a courtesan and who is rescued by his wife when he runs out of money. While the original teaches Confucian virtue, O uses the story to interrogate gender, a colonial past and a postcolonial present. *Bicycle* was based on an event that took place in O's village in the Korean war in which retreating North Korean soldiers locked 127 suspected anti-communists in the town registry building then set it on fire, burning all inside to death. For O, the titular bicycle is the metaphoric vehicle by which we might move back and forth from past to present, to see how history affects current actions.

O founded *Mokwha* (Raw Cotton Repertory Company) in 1984, which he still serves as artistic director, chief playwright, acting teacher and director. With Mokwha, O has remounted many of his older play, directing them himself. Plays written and directed for Mokwha include *Intimacy Between Father and Son* (*Pujayujin*, 1987), *Why Did Shim Chong Plunge into the Indang Sea Twice?* (*Shim-ch'ŏngginŭn wae indangsue tubŏn ŭl tŏnjŏt nŭnga*, 1990), *Bellflower* (*Toraji*, 1992), *By the Paekma River* (*Paekma-gang talbamae*, 1993) and *DMZ My Love* (*DMZ nae sarang*, 2002), all of which have been staged multiple times since their initial productions. O's scripts are, more so than others', perhaps, are blueprints for performance and do not capture the spectacle and experience that O attempts to achieve and for which he is known. O is also known internationally for his productions of Shakespeare, especially a Korean traditional theatre infused *Romeo and Juliet* and *The Tempest*. O's work as a Korean writer and director has stretched across five decades and made him the best known Korean theatre artist outside of Korea.

In the 1970s, artistic experiment and political engagement dominated the modern drama, but the artists were playing a dangerous game. Any play seemingly critical of the government, the police or the military, or supportive of socialism or North Korea would be suspect and often closed down. Martial law, censorship and an overall culture of repression paradoxically made it difficult to speak out and drove playwrights, directors, actors and designers to use the theatre to make political statements, albeit often, but not always, obliquely. Although Pak Choyŏl (b. 1930) wrote several plays about reunification during this period, most notably *O Chang-gun's Toenail* (*O Chang-gun ŭi palt'op*, 1974), that were innovative and significant works, government censors refused permission to perform, citing the play as anti-military and pro-communist in the case of *O Chang-gun*. The play was not performed publicly until 1988. Pak wrote a total of ten plays between 1963 and 1980, but repeated censorship drove him from the theatre until the late 1980s.

Government censorship and a complete lack of artistic freedom was perhaps the greatest challenge to theatre artists during this period, but it also resulted in creativity being used to overcome the limitations it posed. Lee Kang-baek (b. 1947) started his several-decade-long playwriting career with 1971's *Five* (*Tasŏt*), an allegorical one-act that won a newspaper literary contest. Lee's mode was allegorical and metaphoric, mostly as a means of avoiding government censorship in the 1970s and 1980s. *Watchman* (*P'asuggun*, 1973), for example, seems a simple fable of a watchman who cries wolf for his own purposes, but audiences understood it as a metaphor for the South Korean government, using the boogeyman of North Korea to justify its own repressive policies. Lee continued to write after the lifting of censorship in the late 1980s and his more recent work has been less political and more existential, engaging themes of sacrifice, compassion and redemption. If there is one major theme throughout his work it has been to focus on the disempowered within society.

Other playwrights active in the 1970s include the previously mentioned O Yŏng-jin, a comedy writer who employed folklore as a basis for satires of contemporary culture. One of his most popular plays, *Wedding Day* (*Maengjinsadaek kyŏngsa*, 1972), was first performed during this period, satirising social climbers and the importance placed on the superficial aspects of a wedding. Although he began his writing career as a novelist, Ch'oe In-hun (b. 1936) also rose to prominence as a playwright during this period, writing tragedies that mixed poetry in prose based on myth, history and Ch'oe's own ideas about fate in Korean history. Ch'oe had been born in the North during the Japanese occupation and migrated to the South during the Korean War. Much of his drama is occupied by the sense of loss of and nostalgia for his birthplace, his identity as a Korean tied to the broken and dislocated sense of a divided Korea. His plays, such as *Where We Will Meet as What We Are* (1970), *Away, Away, Long Time Ago* (*Yennal yejŏgge huŏihuŏi*, 1976) and *At Mountain and Field When Spring Comes* (1977), expressed both a sense of that broken dislocation and a hope for a unified future.

As the 1970s drew to a close, on 26 October 1979, President Park was assassinated by Kim Jae-gyu, his own intelligence chief. Choi Kyu Hah was appointed acting President but did not last long as a military coup on 12 December by Major General Chun Doo Hwan left the military in charge again. The new government was extremely authoritarian and fiercely anti-communism. New laws regarding censorship and what was and was not permissible content for stage plays (among other cultural forms) were promulgated and repression grew, not just in the theatre but in the nation as a whole. What followed in May of 1980 has become known as the Kwangju Uprising. Citizens protesting martial law and the government rose up. General Chun sent in troops to forcibly end the protests. Soldiers confronted mobs from 18 to 27 May resulting in perhaps as many as 2600 citizens killed.

The theatre was unable to respond directly to the repression of the Kwangju Uprising due to the increased suppression of the arts and the press in its wake, with the exception of madangguk, discussed below. It would not be until the late 1980s that Korean artists were able to directly engage this period on stage. Towards the end of the 1980s, however, sociopolitical theatre became increasingly popular. One of the more dominant voices from this period was playwright Lee Yun-taek, born in Busan in 1952. He matriculated at the Seoul Theatre Institute in 1972, but dropped out later that year, eventually completing a degree in elementary education from the Korean National Open University in 1979. He worked as a reporter until 1986 when he began writing plays and founded the Street Theatre Troupe (*Yeonhuidan Keoripae*) in Busan, directing minimalist productions in the Gamagol Theatre. He rose to national prominence with *Citizen K* (*Shinmin K*, 1989), an episodic drama of six scenes that grew out of Lee's experiences as a journalist. In the play, Citizen K, a reporter, is arrested, interrogated about his politics and literature, and witnesses others tortured by military interrogators. He is ambivalent to the abusive and inhumane system, doing nothing to change it. The play itself is thus an indictment of Koreans under the dictatorship of the 1980s. It is also one of Lee's 'ceremony plays', ritualised dramas that combine realism with enacted rituals.

Lee followed *Shinmin K* with a trilogy of ceremony plays: *O-Gu: Ceremony of Death* (*O-Gu: chukŭm ŭi hyŏng-sik*, 1990), *Mask of Fire: Ceremony of Power* (*Pul ŭi kamyŏn: kwŏllyŏk ŭi hyŏnng-sik*, 1993) and *Dummy Bride, Ceremony of Love* (*Pabo kakshi: sarang ŭi hyŏng-sik*), all of which combine narration, music, dance and elements of traditional theatre (most notably puppets in *Pabo kakshi*) alongside Brechtian techniques. Lee also disavows Western and especially American influences on Korean drama, but has directed numerous Western classics in a Korean style, also employing elements of traditional performance: *Hamlet*,

*Oedipus Rex, The Merchant of Venice, The Tempest, Macbeth* and *King Lear.*

Lee has sought to both popularise the theatre and make theatre that is important to the Korean people. Like O Tae-sŏk, he has relied on developing his own unique hybrid form to speak to contemporary audiences. In 1994 he founded the Uri Kŭkyŏn Kuso (Uri Theatre Institute) to further these aims. In 1999 he founded the artistic experimental theatre community Miryang Theatre Village (*Miryang Yŏnguk Ch'on*) in Busan. Most recently, in 2004, Lee developed the Guerilla Theatre (*Gŏrilla Kŭkchang*), a theatre space in Seoul for *Yeonhuidan Keoripae.* While his plays are performed in the nation's capital, Busan remains Lee's artistic home.

Another development from the late 1970s and early 1980s were two related genres: madanggŭk, an outdoor performance in a yard ('madan'), and its comic version, madangnori. Both forms were performed outdoors or in a tent, but Madanggŭk presented social issues satirically and madangnori treated them playfully through reinterpreted folk tales. Madanggŭk was agit-prop in the service of social change; madangnori was wholesome family entertainment. Beginning on university campuses in the late 1970s and spreading throughout the nation after the Kwangju Uprising, madanggŭk was an anti-establishment, satirical form that focused on individual rights, the problems of rural communities, resistance to the American presence in Korea, environmental problems, class conflicts (especially between labour and management) and the divided Korean peninsula. The contradictions and conflicts exposed by the Kwangju uprising were viciously and satirically lampooned by the performers. Madanggŭk was the most popular dramatic form in the 1980s.

## Postmodern Global Korean Theatre: 1988–Present

The year 1988 marked a transformation of Korea yet again. The Seoul Olympics brought attention and money to South Korea, and democracy and free elections were promised. Immediately the relaxation of censorship and greater artistic freedom followed. The social changes in Korea were compounded by the 1989 collapse of Communism in Eastern Europe. The Soviet Union broke apart and no longer served as a supporter of the DPRK, which suddenly found China its sole ally. As a result, the North Korean economy shrank by half in the 1990s while South Korea experienced what was called 'the economic miracle', developing from a Third World nation to a major economic power with many multinational corporations in a few decades. The decreased threat from communism allowed the conservative, anti-communist government to relax and Korea transformed into a true democracy with an elected civilian government.

Although censorship and repression were gone by 1990, they were not forgotten, yet the newfound artistic freedom allowed for not only criticism of the current government but also the interrogation of the past. Simultaneously there was also an identity crisis within the Korean theatre community, as so many artists had existed in opposition to the government that the new freedoms left them seeking to develop a new identity and performance milieu. Similarly, a decline in audience attendance during the 1980s and the ever-increasing competition from film and television, not only for audience but also for artists, contributed to a state of crisis in Korean theatre in the 1980s.

The identity crisis continued into the early 1990s, with the theatre still trying to identify itself as something other than a theatre of resistance. The government designated 1991 as 'The Year of Theatre' and began providing support for the development of theatrical space. Playwrights used the new freedom to write about relevant topics and continue to explore Korean history, even as they faced competition from the more commercial musicals. Kim Kwang-lim (b. 1952), for example, began his theatrical career in the 1970s, but rose to prominence in the 1980s and became quite prolific in the 1990s, with a focus on interrogating Korea's tragic past and its shaping influence on the present. *In Search of Love* (1993) reflects upon the division of the Koreas in the form of an ill-fated love affair. *Come and See Me* (1996), based on an actual series of serial murders, is an exploration of how we search for truth and know it (or do not know it) when we see it.

At the turn of the millennium, Korean theatre faced many challenges. The last decade of the twentieth century found the Republic of Korea in a state of flux and a time of crisis for theatre companies. Shrinking audiences and greater competition for money and attention from film and television made the market more competitive and required either innovation or pandering to audience tastes. Thus the 1990s saw the rise of comedy and musicals.

The theatre was not particularly political in the 1990s, although some sociopolitical issues were raised. Noticeable was a rising feminism, both in Korean drama and in imports. Stronger roles for women, challenges to patriarchal society and assertions of equality grew in prominence on the stages of Seoul. Whereas women's roles in modern drama for much of the twentieth century had been limited to acting, with men dominating playwriting and directing, the 1970s saw an emergence of a number of female designers, directors and writers. Kim A-ra (b. 1956) is one of the foremost female directors of the 1980s and 1990s, eschewing realism for highly stylised productions. She employed minimalism and effective lighting for a production of Janusch Gwavsky's *Cinders* (1987), set in a rehabilitation centre for teenage girls. Kim subsequently directed *The Elephant Man* (1989), *Equus* (1990) and *Antigone* (1997) to great acclaim, but in the 1990s also began working with a number of Korean playwrights to develop a genuine Korean dramaturgy. She founded the company Muchŏn in 1992, named after an ancient Korean ritual, directing Greek tragedies using traditional Korean elements as well as new Korean plays, frequently working outdoors, as traditional theatre would be performed. Kim Hyun-sook (b. 1954) was a particularly significant costume designer. American-educated, she designed costumes for some of the ceremonies at the 1988 Seoul Olympics, for O Tae-sŏk and for the musical *The Last Empress* (1995), among others. Women have made huge strides in recent decades, although it should be noted that Korean theatre is still male dominated.

The issue of unification also became a theme of the 1990s, especially after the death of Kim Il-sung. For a brief moment there seemed the possibility of the two Koreas becoming one again, and that theme was explored in drama, albeit in an apolitical manner.

Korean theatre has also assumed a greater global presence, although it also still features a large number of foreign plays, most notably musicals.

Yoon Ho-jin (b. 1948), a member of Shilhŏm kŭktan in the 1970s, subsequently studied in the United States and the United Kingdom and returned to Korea to direct a variety of foreign plays, including Athol Fugard's *Master Harold . . . and the boys* and *The Island* in 1982 and John Pielmeier's *Agnes of God* in 1983. In 1992 Yoon founded A-Com to produce musicals in Korea. *Guys and Dolls* (1994) established that Broadway musicals could be performed in Korea in Korean by Korean performers and be a hit. Korea then had its own musical hit with *The Last Empress* (*Myŏngsŏng hwanghu*, 1995), concerning the fall of the Chosŏn dynasty, and dozens of musicals, both domestic and foreign, have followed. Korean production of foreign musicals in the 1990s ran the gamut from *Porgy and Bess* to *Aida*, *Jesus Christ Superstar* to *Les Miserables*. *Phantom of the Opera* was staged in Seoul in 2001 and subsequently toured. It was followed by Sondheim's *Assassins* in 2004 and *The Producers* in 2005, among many, many others. Musicals have proven extraordinarily popular in Korea, and the indigenous musical theatre has now found its own style and milieu, transcending the Western models from which it is derived. Since the mid-1990s the number of Korean musicals produced has exceeded that of productions of Western musicals. In that sense, Korean musicals have followed the path of all other modern Korean theatres: a foreign form is introduced, domesticated and then made distinctly Korean.

## Modern North Korean Theatre and Performance

According to official North Korean state history, modern North Korean drama began before there was even a North Korea. Kim Il-sung, the anti-Japanese resistance fighter who became the ruler of communist North Korea after 1948, allegedly wrote the drama *The Three Pretenders* (*3 in 1 tang*) as a teenager. Set in the fictional country of Songdoguk, the play shows the fall of a nation due to the power struggles of three government ministers after the king dies. The ministers attempt to position themselves to rule the country but a foreign invasion is about to occur, and as a result of their machinations, they do not protect the people. The play is ostensibly an analogy of Korea and a satire of the nationalists and non-Kim-allied communists who fight each other rather than the Japanese. The official story is that Kim wrote and directed the play in middle school. The reality is that he most likely did not, but the play became one of the most popular modern dramas after the Korean War. Modern drama in North Korean shares the same origins as South Korean modern drama: shinpa and shingŭk. Where they differ is the evolutionary path after the Second World War.

After 1948, modern theatre in North Korea developed along a radically different trajectory than that of the Republic of Korea. In the years immediately after the defeat of Japan and before the division of the Koreas, numerous leftist artists used the theatre to promote socialism and communism in both the North and South. When the war began, some leftist writers and actors left for the North, even as others fled South. After the war, the Democratic Peoples' Republic of Korea (DPRK, AKA North Korea) encouraged artists to develop a proletarian culture aimed at educating the masses and glorifying the state. Traditional theatre was and is banned in the DPRK.

After 1948, the political culture of North Korea, according to historian Donald N. Clark, is a fusion of Confucianism, autarky (*Juch'e*, or 'self-reliance'), Stalinism, corporatism and communism, and a hybrid state cult focused around the ruling Kim family: Kim Il-sung (1912–94, ruling 1948–94), Kim Jong-il (1942–2011, ruling 1994–2011) and current supreme leader Kim Jong-un (1983–, ruling 2011 to present).[12] The government and society of North Korea value obedience and loyalty to the state and the Kim family above all. Kim Il-sung is the 'Great Leader' and 'Eternal President', and Kim Jong-il is the 'Dear Leader'. The Kim family has controlled North Korea and its culture from the beginning of the DPRK and much of its theatre either revolves around the adoration of the Kims or the glorification of the State. Government censorship is absolute and no public or private performances may take place without the blessing of the regime. All art, culture, history and public acts became politicised.

What Yoon Min-Kyang says of the visual arts is also true of North Korean drama: 'multiplicity of interpretations is not intended . . . interpretations are singular, creating a sense of unified, collective purpose'.[13] Rather than allowing for varied, individual interpretation,

North Korean art is intended to have a single interpretation, one meaning which is rooted in the metahistory of North Korea. According to official North Korean history, the past is a period of oppression and imperialism against the Korean people, until the Kim family arrives in the twentieth century to lead the DPRK to become the greatest nation in the world, which is the present and future. Anti-Kim, reactionary and imperialist forces (most notably the United States and its supposed puppet government in South Korea) are the forces arrayed against the DPRK, but they will eventually lose and even secretly envy the DPRK. All art, including drama, must reflect this understanding of history. All North Korean culture is thus promulgated from the top down, removing colonialism, imperialism, and bourgeois and Western influence from the arts and ensuring they promote *Juch'e* and North Korean socialism.

Until 1950, the dominant subject of North Korean drama was the struggle against the Japanese, with a particular focus on the leadership of (then) General Kim Il-sung. Once the Korean War began, however, drama began to shift and focus more on propaganda in favour of the new state, the government, the North Korean people, and the person and message of Kim Il-sung. Also, while *ch'anggŭk* remained popular in conservative, rural parts of North Korea for a while after the communist takeover, eventually all forms of theatre and performance were subsumed and surpassed by dramas and performances in support of the Party line.

In the 1950s the 'great revolutionary works' were written: *The Great River is Flowing* (*Taehanun hrunda*), *The Young Vanguards* (*Ch'ungnyon junyu*) and *The Communist Guerilla* (*Kongsan ppalchisan*), among others, celebrating the triumph of the communists in North Korea. Oh-kon Cho reads these works as 'a modern version of *shinp'a*, devoted to political ideology'.[14] By the 1970s, however, celebrations of the revolution transformed into a massive, state-led effort to use the arts (among other cultural elements) to legitimise and celebrate Kim Il-sung's rule.

The two dominant forms include revolutionary plays (*hyŏngmyŏng yŏn-gŭk*) and revolutionary opera (*hyŏngmyŏng kagŭk*), the former a kind of spoken drama, the latter an operatic form modelled after that of China and employing folk songs. The first hyŏngmyŏng kagŭk was *Sea of Blood* (*Pibada*, 1971), rapidly followed by *The Flower Girl* (*Kkotpaneun cheonyeo*, 1971), *A True Daughter of the Party* (*Dang-ui chamdoen ttal*, 1971), *Oh, Tell the Forest* (*Milima iyagihara*, 1972) and *The Song of Mount Geumgang* (*Geumgangsanui norae*, 1973), collectively known as 'the five great revolutionary operas'. In the late 1970s, the five official revolutionary dramas appeared, declared by the state to be written personally by Kim Il-sung in the 1930s and 1940s (although they were not officially performed until the 1970s, when they were most likely actually written). These five are: *The Mountain Shrine* (*Sŏnghwangdang*), *Blood at an International Conference* (*Hyŏlbun man'gukhoe*), *A Letter from a Daughter* (*Ttarekesŏ on p'yŏnji*), *The Three Pretenders* (*3 in 1 Tang 3*) and *A Celebration Meeting* (*Kyŏngch'uk taehoe*), all of which were performed by the State Theatrical Company in P'yŏngyang. Little to no modern drama as it has developed in the rest of Asia exists in North Korea.

Beginning in the late 1980s and 1990s an emphasis on giant performance and spectacle began to dominate theatrical production. Large-scale theatres, more resembling stadiums and large sport complexes, featuring seating in the tens of thousands and stages that can hold a cast of 5000 performers, were constructed. On 26 April 2002, Kim Jong-il launched the Arirang Festival, which features mass performances – highly choreographed shows which involve singing, dancing, the creation of images through the use of thousands of people holding coloured cards which together form giant pictures, gymnastics, acrobatics and theatrics. The festival is held in P'yŏngyang every August and September, attracting audiences in the hundreds of thousands. The name Arirang, which also refers to this kind of performance, comes from a Korean folktale in which young lovers are kept forcibly apart. It is used metaphorically here to refer to the two Koreas.

Suk-Young Kim argues that North Korea is an inherently performative nation: staging massive performances in celebration of its self-image, its history and its ruling family and simultaneously forcing a population to engage in everyday performance in order to comply with the regime's version of reality, resulting in theatre as an institution not of entertainment, but of regulation, education and enforcement.[15] In one sense, North Korea itself is a form of modern drama, if this theory is true. Even if not, the Democratic People's Republic invests very heavily in large public performances, demonstrations and events in order to assert identity, establish history and reinforce a social order, despite an obvious absence of spoken drama in its culture.

# CHAPTER 7
## MODERN INDIAN THEATRE

---

### Nineteenth-Century Theatre in India: Colonisation and Decolonisation

Modern theatre in India began as a colonial enterprise in three ports set up by the British East India Company: Calcutta (now Kolkata), Bombay (now Mumbai) and Madras (now Chennai). In the nineteenth century, the British introduced modern theatre to these cities by touring productions to entertain their expatriate communities, by supporting productions of English plays staged by the expatriates themselves and by teaching English drama in Indian universities. The spread of English drama was part of colonising Indian culture – it was designed not only to shape artistic activity, but also to impose on Indians a way of understanding and operating in the world. Two things happened: the urban middle class learnt to despise their own ritual, classical and popular performances, thereby losing touch with them, and they learnt to appreciate Western plays – 'spoken dramas' – which were performed on proscenium stages for a ticket-buying public at times that were not related to annual festivals, harvests or religious occasions.

### The Development of Modern Theatre in Bombay

In 1820, the audience for Bombay's first theatre, The Bombay Amateur Theatre, was 'society', defined by J. H. Stocqueler, editor of The *Bombay Courier*, as

> a score of civilians, a few merchants, the officers of two, or possibly three, European regiments, the staff, half-a-dozen barristers, [and] three or four clergymen . . .[1]

The theatre imported to Bombay in the early 1800s by travelling theatre companies, as well as the theatre staged by amateur residents, was intended to provide entertainment and escape for the staff, soldiers, officers and attendant civilians stationed there. Physically, these theatres (like the ones built in Calcutta) were exact copies of their English counterparts: they had a pit, gallery, dress boxes, painted perspective scenery, painted backdrops, wings, footlights, a front curtain and chandeliers. In physical structure as well as in choice of presentation, these theatres were designed to remind their audiences of home and homeland. While inside, audiences were in (a) British space.

The earliest evidence of Indians in the audience at the Bombay Amateur Theatre is a record of the purchase of a dress box seat by Balcrustnath Sunkerset on 3 August 1821. Four months later, on 13 December 1822 Hormusjee Bomanjee and Sorabji Framji each bought two tickets to see Richard Sheridan's play *The Rivals*.[2] Indians began to attend the English theatre in increasing numbers, and in 1830, when the Amateur Theatre needed money, eleven of the fifty donors were Indians – among them were Bomanjee and Jugonath Sunkersett.[3] When the Amateur Theatre went bankrupt and was demolished, Sunkersett donated the land on which it was later rebuilt. Significantly, the land he donated was in his own neighbourhood. When the rebuilt Amateur, known thereafter as the Grant Road Theatre, opened on 10 February 1846, there were more Indians in the audience than there had been at the Amateur Theatre. The rising number of Indians attending the theatre empowered the Indian audience to control the theatrical experience. As time went on, the opinion of Indian spectators mattered more and more, and it began to influence the selection of plays.[4]

In the 1860s and 1870s, students at the new British colleges who were studying Shakespeare in their classes began to form dramatic societies – encouraged by their professors, and coached by the professional English actors who toured to, or had settled in, Bombay. When British touring companies brought Shakespeare productions to India they also brought the idea that a playwright best represented British civilisation.[5] At the same time the reverence with which Oriental scholars treated India's classical philosophy, sculpture, literature and drama contributed to a renewed interest in Sanskrit drama as a way of asserting cultural parity with the British. The Indian middle class looked for a Sanskrit dramatist who could function as an equivalent to Shakespeare, and found one in Kalidasa (dates uncertain, 150 BCE to 500 CE) whose plays were translated and performed with 'unprecedented frequency' in the late nineteenth century.[6] The Kalidas Elphinstone Society, an amateur dramatic club formed by students at Elphinstone College in Bombay became famous in the 1870s for their production of Monier Williams' translation of Kalidasa's *Abhijnanashakuntala* (named after Shakuntala, the heroine of the play).

In 1871, students at Deccan College in Pune performed a translation of Narayanbhatta's *Venisamha* [Rebraided Hair] with a prologue in rhymed iambic pentameter. The prologue clearly indicates the attitude these new urban Shakespeare scholars had learnt to take towards indigenous popular performance:

Though some might laugh us out and set at naught,
Because they see no feats no duels fought
No freakish monkey, no delirious yell,
No Lanka's tyrant fierce with fury fell,
No absurd songs, no din, no wild attire,
No meaningless uproar, no senseless ire;
Let them, what can they, indiscretion's tools,
In turn we laugh them down and deem them fools.
Illiterate players have usurped the stage,
With scenes obscene depraved this rising age.[7]

Among this group of Indians, traditional performances based on the story of Rama were obscene and depraved; colonialism had done its work.

Prior to the imposition of text-dominated theatre, the majority of the many and varied performance genres throughout India, while unique and particular in terms of artistic goals and aesthetics, dramaturgical structures, social roles, political agendas, the specific cultures they reflect and the regional languages of performance, were and continue to be similar (only) in that they are not text-driven stagings of dramatic literature. This does not mean they do not work with literary texts, but that they are not 'literature that walks'.[8] *Tamasha, bhavai, jatra* and *kathakali* offer four very different examples of the same point. Tamasha, which developed in the 1600s as a court entertainment for the Peshwa rulers and an entertainment and inspiration for Maratha soldiers, combines elements of *kathak* dance (classical north-Indian dance developed as court entertainment), *dasavatar* (mime, pageantry, music and dance that together tell the story of any one of Vishnu's 10 incarnations, proceeding episodically), *lalit* (devotional entertainment performed as part of several festivals, usually incorporating some kind of social critique) and *bharud* (dramatic songs distinguished by their humorous double entendres), along with other musical and performance genres. It incorporates a section known as *batavani*, jokes that satirised a current event or person in power, and later, in the nineteenth century, a *vag*, or plot-based scenario. A tamasha performance can contain as many as thirty *lavanis*, which are sung poetic narratives with a specific metric form. Bhavai, an open-air Gujarati community theatre honouring the goddess Amba, begins with a Ganesha *puja* (literally, sacred offerings to Ganesha), a dance by the goddess Kali, the appearance of a comic character who functions as society's conscience by pointing out social problems, and then proceeds around midnight with a series of plays depicting social, political or religious themes. While each individual play follows a plot and includes a great deal of text, the evening as a whole is a composite and multi-generic experience. Kathakali follows a poetic text sung by musicians at the back of the stage, but the text is actually an excuse for improvised elaboration on the part of the performers, who are expected to add emotional depth and social commentary through *mudras* (gestures). Narrative sections of a familiar (usually mythological) story are divided into quatrains punctuated by segments of pure dance. While kathakali scripts (*attakkathas*) are valued for their literary qualities, they are valued even more for their ability to inspire the actor's improvisational creativity. An evening of jatra, outdoor theatre popular in both urban and rural areas of Bengal, Bihar and Orissa, is arguably the most text-driven of the examples I have mentioned here. Jatra does follow the plot of a play, but the plot is interrupted by Vivek, who functions as the conscience of a given character by singing about the character's inner moral conflicts, and as well (in the nineteenth century) by fifty to sixty songs throughout each performance, some sung by the actors themselves, some sung for them by musicians. Jatra actors improvise their dialogue, so the length and focus of a scene can vary in performance. Significantly, in common parlance the audience goes to 'listen to' jatra, and 'the actor who delivers monumental prose speeches says that he is going to "sing a jatra"'.[9] These genres, because they were framed in contradistinction to the playwright-initiated, text-based colonial theatre, were devalued as 'theatre', and thought of as rural performance by and for 'the masses'.

Consequently, when members of the college dramatic societies began looking for a new kind of 'Indian' drama, they began by translating Shakespeare from English and Kalidasa from Sanskrit. Eventually they began to write and produce their own plays (in their own languages) modelled on Shakespeare.[10] Vinayak Janardan Kirtane (1840–91), a student at Elphinstone College, wrote the first play to use history rather than mythology as its subject. Written in 1857, the same year as the First War of Independence, *Thorle Madhavrao Peshwe* (The Elder Madhavrao Peshwa) marked the beginning of Marathi dramatists' commitment to serious political issues. This was probably inevitable given the fact that on 2 August 1858, with the passing of the Government of India Act, the British Crown formally took over from the British East India Company and began direct rule over India. In *Thorle Madhavrao Peshwe* Kirtane took the colonial theatrical form and used it as a vehicle for anti-colonial sentiment, simultaneously valorising and disrupting its authority. *Thorle Madhavrao Peshwe* gave rise to an entire body of dramatic writing in prose – in other words, to plays without songs.[11] However, eight years later when the *Belgaum Samachar* reviewed another production of the play, it noted: 'many people did not like it because it was made up entirely of dialogues'.[12] This back-and-forth between those who wanted more songs and those who wanted fewer or no songs eventually led to a split between the straight or 'bookish' play, and the *sangeetnatak* which literally means 'music drama', and best is described either as opera or musical theatre.

The sangeetnatak was extremely popular until it was wiped out by the film industry in the 1930s. It was performed in three languages

(Gujarati, Urdu and Hindi) for a linguistically and culturally diverse audience. But because it played to several communities, Gokhale claims it had no stake in any one community's culture or social life, which meant that its appeal was based on pure entertainment, on 'flamboyant devices and sensationalism'.[13] The first sangeetnatak in Marathi, *Shakuntala* (1875 or 1880), had 209 songs taken from an enormous variety of sources: 'keertan, lavanis, devotionals, lullabyes, bhoopalis, ovis, folk songs from Karnataka and Gujarat, ghazals, dadras, and thumris'.[14] However, playwright Balwant Krishna Kirloskar (1843–85) reduced the role of the narrator (the sutradhar) and had characters sing their own thoughts and feelings. The characters were not archetypes, but individuals. Structurally *Shakuntala* was an innovative mixture of 'Indian' and 'Western' dramaturgy.

Marathi theatre set itself up in opposition to the pure entertainment of the sangeetnatak. Marathi theatre spoke to a relatively homogenous audience, and quickly became a platform for addressing social issues of the one community. From there it became a staging ground for the nationalist movement. Although many people still wanted songs (and dances) these gradually gave way to the straight play as the best medium for a political theatre.

The most famous example of an anti-colonial play in Bengal is *Nil Darpan* (The Mirror of Indigo Planters, 1860), about the ruthless exploitation of indigo cultivators, who were forced to cultivate indigo by British indigo planters. *Nil Darpan* caused riots at one of its performances in Lucknow because the British audience objected to the way the planters were portrayed in a scene in which a white planter rapes an Indian peasant. Indigo planters sued the English translator, James Long, on the grounds that the play gave planters a bad name. Long's trial generated a great deal of publicity for both the play and the issue it portrayed, and established *Nil Darpan* as the first nationalist drama in India. It also marked the moment where both British and Bengali audiences became acutely aware of the power of drama as a tool for resistance in the struggle for independence. In his defence, Long compared *Nil Darpan* to the best social dramas in dramatic history, and noted that 'the Drama is the favorite mode with the Hindus for describing certain states of society, manners, customs'.[15]

British authorities began to fear that other 'subversive' productions were being written and staged. They were right: *Nil Darpan* inspired a wave of anti-colonial plays. Upendra Nath Das' *Surendra-Binodini* (1875) 'showed a European Magistrate McCrindle sexually assaulting a maid, Birajmohini, who jumps out of the window to save her honor.'[16] *Gaekwar-Durpan* (The Trial of Gaekwar, 1875) challenged the purported objectivity and fairness of the British legal system by depicting the 'farcical trial of Malhar Rao Gaekwar of Baroda, who was forced to abdicate his throne on 27 April, 1875 on [trumped-up] charges of attempting to poison Colonel Phayre, a British resident of Baroda'.[17] A third play performed in 1875, Dakshina-Charan Chattopadhyay's *Chakar-Darpan* (The Tea Planter's Mirror), attacked 'the cruel and licentious behavior of British planters towards the natives on the tea plantations in Assam'.[18] This play also threw a very public light on British economic and political policy.

Theatre was deemed dangerous enough to prompt the Dramatic Performances and Control Act of 1876, which empowered the government of Bengal to prohibit dramatic performances that were 'scandalous, defamatory, seditious, obscene or otherwise prejudicial to the public interest'.[19] The Dramatic Performances and Control Act of 1876 made it difficult for playwrights to attack British rulers openly, so they turned to historical dramas and attacked Muslim rulers who, reportedly, were generally understood to represent the British.[20] Playwrights also turned women into symbols of the nation. For example, Girish Chandra Ghosh's 1889 play *Profulla* portrayed a wealthy merchant's wife as 'mother India'. The rape of a Hindu woman became a metaphor for the violation of the motherland – a strategy later exploited by the British, who began to ban plays ostensibly because of their treatment of women rather than their overt criticism of the British Raj. Finally, playwrights also cloaked their attacks in adaptations of Shakespeare and in mythological stories.[21]

While the authorities were keeping such a close eye on the Marathi and Bengali stage, Bhargavram Vitthal Warerkar (1883–1964) approached the owner of a tamasha company and asked for permission to write several political plays that never would have passed the censors. Warerkar wrote four tamasha plays about patriots such as the Rani of Jhansi (c. 1830–1858, who led an uprising to protest the British annexation of her land after the death of her husband, and was killed fighting in the first war of independence) and Vasudeo Balwant Phadke (d. 1883, who led a violent campaign against British rule in 1879, aimed at establishing an Indian republic). Warerkar was proud of his tamasha plays because he was able to spread news of the nationalist movement to a non-literate audience.

Meanwhile, 'bookish' plays were increasingly popular, which meant that actors had to learn their lines, and no longer improvised in and around a story as they had earlier. An 1874 ad for a performance in the Belgaum Samachar promised that 'the actors will generally speak according to the book'.[22] At the same time, stagecraft was changing:

> The drop curtain in the old mythological plays used to bear crudely drawn, gaudily colored representations of deities – Ganapati, Maruti or Shankar-Parvati. But when "bookish" plays were performed, an attempt was made to convey to the audience the exact locations of the scenes, such as roads, temples, gardens, palaces, hills, jungles or rivers, by means of curtains depicting them as faithfully as possible. . . . Earlier a garden used to be represented by means of a few branches stuck on the stage; but now, in addition to the gardens painted on curtains, real trees, potted shrubs and plants would be placed on stage to complete the illusion of the real.[23]

Sets got further and further away from the bare stage of Sanskrit drama, or the open-air three-quarter thrust with a hand-held half curtain that was customary in so many genres of traditional performance.

Dedicated to using drama as a social tool, Warerkar turned to Henrik Ibsen in 1931 for formal inspiration. In 1931 he wrote *Sonyacha Kalas* (The Golden Spire), a play about mill-owners' exploitation of labour. Gokhale says:

> The form of the play was "new," that is, Ibsenian. This meant there was unity of time and space and a single narrative line. No characters were introduced by way of comic relief. The play

began with the exposition which caught the main protagonists just before the dramatic crisis, the middle of the play developed the crisis and brought it to a head, and the end resolved it.[24]

Although Warerkar added a few songs, and painted his characters in black and white, he demonstrated that the Shakespearean structure 'could be effectively replaced by a tighter structure of three acts'.[25]

*Andhalyanchi Shala* (School for the Blind, 1933) is thought to be the first modern Marathi play. It was produced by Natyamanwantar, a company:

> formed with the specific purpose of bringing modern drama to the Marathi stage. What constituted its modernity in the eyes of the playmakers and their critics was not simply the number of songs, but the structure of the play, the stage design and the acting style. A "modern" play was expected to have a cohesive structure of three single-scene acts, a theme that reflected an engagement with the human condition, a credible plot and rounded characters, dialogue that would serve a dramatic purpose while sounding conversational, a real-seeming stage set, a natural acting style and, above all, women playing the roles of women.[26]

By 1933 'modern plays' had been conflated with 'naturalism', and the two had become synonymous.

## The Development of Modern Theatre in Calcutta

The history of modern theatre in Calcutta is remarkably similar to the history of modern theatre in Bombay. However, a discussion of nineteenth-century Bengali theatre adds greater detail and clarity to a discussion of the split between modern theatre and traditional performance, while offering a more complicated picture of what is seen as 'Western', and what is seen as 'Indian', and providing evidence to support the claim that modern Indian drama is characterised by hybridity (and in some cases transculturation).

In 1753 the first English theatre opened in Calcutta. It was called The Playhouse, and was followed in 1775 by The New Playhouse, which catered to Governor-General Warren Hastings and other Englishmen of rank, and produced plays by Thomas Otway (1652–85, author of *Venice Preserved*), William Congreve (1670–1729, author of *The Way of the World*), Richard Brinsley Sheridan (1751–1816, author of *The School for Scandal*) and Farquhar (1677–1707, author of *The Beaux Stratagem*). On 1 May 1789 Mrs Emma Bristow opened a theatre in her Chowringhee residence that catered to the city's elite. She produced *The Poor Solider*, *Julius Caesar*, *The Sultan* and *The Padlock*. In 1813, with the support of Sanskrit scholar H. H. Wilson (1786–1864) and Dwarkanath Tagore (1794–1846, grandfather of Rabindranath Tagore) the Chowringhee Theatre opened. Several of its actresses came from the London theatre, and it presented not only the classics (Shakespeare, Sheridan and Goldsmith), but contemporary English plays. In 1839 the Sans Souci theatre opened. The Sans Souci is famous for its 1848 production of *Othello*, starring Baishnav Charan Auddy in the title role. As theatre historian Sushil Mukherjee says: 'A Bengali youth in an English play in an English theatre catering to an English audience in the middle of the nineteenth century is certainly a memorable event'.[27] Nonetheless, these playhouses, like their counterparts in Bombay, were set up for the entertainment of Calcutta's British residents.

Meanwhile, as in Bombay, Bengalis were beginning to attend, perform in, and write their own plays – although the first play in Bengali was done by the Russian Herasim Lebedeff (1749–1818) who in 1795 translated an English play (*The Disguise*) into Bengali and produced it with a cast of Bengali actors. Playwright/historian Adya Rangacharya writes that this was a significant event because for the first time 'a play without songs and dance, a play having nothing to do with Indian tradition . . . was brought to the notice of the audience'.[28]

Although an editorial appeared in Samachar Chandrika calling for 'a [Bengali] theatre in the English model' as early as 1826,[29] the plea wasn't answered until 1851 when Jogendrachandra Gupta wrote *Kirtivilas*, which has been described as the 'first tragedy in Bengali modeled on the English tragedies'.[30] In 1859 Michael Madhusan Dutta (1824–73) arrived on the scene with his first play *Sharmistha* (centred on the character Sharmistha). Dutta is credited with modernising Bengali drama by breaking away from the structure of Sanskrit drama, and introducing the form and formalities of English theatre – he was the first person to use blank verse in Bengali literature.[31] Clearly, in Calcutta, as in Bombay, nineteenth-century Indian theatre modelled itself on colonial forms.

In *The Parlour and The Streets* (1989) Sumanta Banerjee outlines the colonisation of upper-class theatre culture in Calcutta. Banerjee shows how the divide between high/English/urban culture and low/Indian/rural culture was created. Understanding this split is crucial to understanding twentieth-century Indian theatrical movements. In charting the increasing division between elite and popular culture in Calcutta, based upon an increasing cultural divide between the emerging middle class and the lower class during the nineteenth century, Banerjee begins by defining the elite in Calcutta as

> Composed predominantly of *banians* and *dewans* (intermediaries helping the East India Company to conduct business and administration in relation to the indigenous people) at the beginning; absentee landlords (appointed by Lord Cornwallis as government agents to collect rents from landed estates under the Permanent Settlement) at a later stage; and as we reach the end of the nineteenth century, a middle class consisting of professionals who were products of an English colonial education system . . .[32]

The lower classes consisted of 'migrants who came to Calcutta from the neighboring villages in search of jobs'.[33] The lower classes, then, were the most recent arrivals to the city: the people with the closest, or most recent, ties to rural life.

By the end of the eighteenth century members of the new Indian middle class felt that 'education in English language and norms alone could set them apart socially from their humble origins and associations'.[34] The *bhadralok*, (a new class of absentee landlord created by the Permanent Settlement Act of 1795), in order to create their own 'distinct cultural forms that could be representative of [their] newly acquired economic status and educational position',[35] dissociated themselves from the cultural expressions of the lower classes – from 'urban folk culture' with its connections to rural life. Urban culture became increasingly associated with the upper class and with an English education, while rural culture was increasingly associated with the lower classes. Similarly, 'rural' was coming to mean 'simple', while 'urban' was becoming synonymous with 'sophisticated'.

Like their counterparts in Bombay, college-educated Bengalis were learning a 'healthy' contempt for their own literature and indigenous culture. John Drinkwater Bethune (Chairman of the Education Council), in a letter to a young Bengali, wrote, 'By all that I can learn of your vernacular literature, its best specimens are defiled by grossness and indecency.'[36] Bethune spoke of cleansing the Bengali language of 'grossness and indecency', but he – and other Englishmen – were attacking Bengali culture as a whole, including performance. Soon educated Bengalis began to attack jatra. In 1855 one bhadralok wrote:

> Who that has any pretension to polite taste will not be disgusted with the vulgar mode of dancing with which our play commences; and who that has any moral tendency will not censure the immorality of the pieces that are performed?[37]

The alternative to the un-anglicised jatra was the anglicised modern urban theatre. Jatra was pushed out to the countryside. As Banerjee suggests:

> [T]he *jatra-walas* lost a chunk of their middle class patrons to the new spectacle of the theatre mounted by the bhadraloks. . . . [T]he jatras somehow managed to linger on among the lower orders till the educated gentry launched a concerted campaign against their public performances on grounds of "obscenity." They then sought refuge in the Bengal countryside, where they hoped to rediscover the ties that led to their birth.[38]

Clearly as they move from gas light to torches, and as crickets become one of the accompanying instruments, the exiled popular performances also take on a more rural quality. This explains the separation between the rural culture of 'the folks', and urban 'Westernised' middle-class culture.

However, an 1886 treatise on jatra written by Bhubancandra Mukhopadhyay shows that jatra had changed in order to compete with the popularity of modern theatre:

> With the secular quality of life in Calcutta and with the traditional caste-line fast disintegrating under the impact of colonial free enterprise, the nature of the traditional, devotional jatra itself had started to make way for thematically more generalized performances that would attract all sorts of audiences. Several professional jatra companies had emerged that found welcome consumers among the Calcutta audiences. This, in turn, defined popular taste and very soon secular jatra-plays became the norm and rage of the town.[39]

Sudipto Chatterjee argues that a new 'hybridised' jatra emerged, one that incorporated elements of the modern theatre.

Similarly, Chatterjee tells us that modern drama was so popular because it incorporated elements of jatra.[40] The public theatre, despite an apparent disdain for jatra, was nonetheless being influenced by it, especially by imbibing the musicality and histrionic acting style of the folk form and moulding it to fit its requirements to attract/address a larger audience.[41] As an article published in the literary journal *Madhyastha* recounts:

> Some members of our modern educated community believe that theatre does not require songs at all. They have subjected themselves to such a belief after having noted the lack of songs in the European theatre. However, they have failed to contemplate that India is not Europe, European society and our own society are very different, European tastes and our tastes are credibly independent of each other.[42]

In 1867 Girish Chandra Ghosh (1844–1911), a producer, director, actor, designer and composer, put up a production of Michael Madhusan Dutta's Western-style play *Sharmistha* with a jatra company, epitomising the middle road.[43]

The hybrid theatre that emerged has parallels in other artistic movements: the history of nineteenth- and twentieth-century painting in Bengal reads very much like the history of Indian theatre in the same period. The first formal schools of 'high' art were set up by the British in the 1850s and transformed patterns of patronage, systems of training and ways of thinking about art, artists and individual creativity.[44] Institutions such as the Government School of Art in Calcutta admitted members of the newly created upper and middle classes, and instilled an appreciation for Western art while devaluing such art forms as the Kalighat *pat* (popular bazaar paintings of Calcutta). Pat artists were designated as artisans, a derogatory term for those who learnt by copying a guru, whose work was therefore 'not original', and who had inherited their 'trade' from someone in the same family, caste or community rather than studying in a school. As the taste propagated by these formal schools took hold, there was an increased demand for 'realism' – shading, volume, perspective, naturalistic figures and backgrounds.[45] Art historian Ananda Coomaraswamy believed that 'a single generation of English education suffice[d] to break the threads of tradition and to create a nondescript and superficial being deprived of all roots – a sort of intellectual pariah who does not belong to the East or the West, the past or the future'.[46] He pioneered an 'Indian' view of and approach to art and art history designed to counter British views and influence over Indian art. He sought to establish an 'Indian' aesthetic and a 'national' art, and promoted the painter Abindranath Tagore (1871–1951), brother of the Nobel laureate poet/playwright Rabindranath Tagore (1861–1941) as the best representative of an 'artistic revival' in modern Indian art.[47]

Rabindranath Tagore made his acting debut in his family's courtyard theatre in a production of Moliere's *Le Bourgeois Gentilhomme*. In 1881 he published his first play based on the *Ramayana*, and then went on to write verse plays modelled after Shakespeare. His play *Raja o rani* (King and Queen, 1889) was revived numerous times on Calcutta's commercial stage. Finding this style of writing exaggerated, he later moved to his father's school Shantiniketan in the Bengal countryside, and reconsidered his approach to theatre. In an essay titled 'The Stage' (1902), he wrote: 'The cost which is incurred for mere accessories on the stage in Europe would swamp the whole of historic art in famine-stricken India . . . the creative richness of poet and player are overshadowed by the wealth of the capitalist.'[48] He turned to the aesthetics of Sanskrit theatre and to popular performance for inspiration, and began writing numerous plays. Perhaps his most famous play of this period is *Dak Ghar* (Post Office, 1912) about a little boy's death. This play introduced modern Indian theatre to the international community when it received its world premiere at the Abbey Theatre in Dublin in 1913. This production coincided with the announcement of his Nobel Prize for *Gitanjali*, a book of poems, and he became an international celebrity.

It is interesting to note that within India Tagore is better known for his poetry than his playwriting, although there are attempts to make his plays more familiar to contemporary audiences through festivals of his work – in one of which Kavalam Narayana Panikkar staged a well-received production of *Rakta-karabi* (Red Oleanders). Towards the end of his life, Tagore began to experiment with dance: 'his implementation of dance resulted from a drive to liberate classical styles from strict conformity and sheer virtuosity to a heterogeneous lyricism that appealed to the emotions'.[49] In *Taser desh* (Land of Cards, 1933) he experimented with South-East Asian dance, and in a trilogy about love (*Chitrangada*, 1936; *Chandalika*, 1938; and *Shyama*, 1939) he perfected his style of choreographing musical texts. Although Tagore is not associated with the post-independence movements to 'decolonise' Indian theatre, his work clearly prefigured them and led the way.

## Struggle for Independence: The Indian People's Theatre Association

The first conscious, programmatic break with realism came in 1942 when the Indian People's Theatre Association (IPTA), the cultural wing of the Communist Party, was formed in Bombay and Calcutta with the self-expressed purpose of mobilising 'a people's theatre movement throughout the whole of India as the means of revitalising the stage and the traditional arts and making them at once the expression and organiser of our people's struggle for freedom, cultural progress and economic justice'.[50]

IPTA had two overlapping goals: they used jatra (in Bengal), tamasha (in Maharashtra) and *burrakatha* (dramatic ballad singing popular in Andhra Pradesh) to spread awareness of India's subjugation under the English among the largely non-literate rural populations. They also employed these popular entertainments as a way of legitimising genres of theatre denigrated by the English and the English-educated Indian elite. The result was a raised consciousness in the countryside as well as a democratisation of the urban theatre. For the first time peasants appeared on the modern stage both as actors and as leading characters. IPTA productions provided both a venue and a forum for urban and rural performers and their respective performance genres to work together. IPTA's goal was nothing less than uniting the upper and lower classes by employing them both in common projects.[51]

Most importantly, however, IPTA overtly linked performance to anti-colonial politics. IPTA's most famous production is *Nabanna* (New Harvest, 1944) written by Bijon Bhattacharya (1917–78) and directed by the famous Bengali director Sombhu Mitra (1915–97) about the Bengal famine of 1943. Nandi Bhatia notes that *Nabanna* was 'more than a play about famine. It is also an attempt on the IPTA's part to expose the sordid reality that the famine was not a natural disaster but a man-made calamity'.[52] *Nabanna* was a stridently anti-imperialist play.

## Decolonising Theatre: The Theatre of Roots Movement

After Independence in 1947 a number of playwrights and directors turned to classical dance, religious ritual, martial arts and popular entertainment – genres that had come to be identified as 'Indian' because they had been framed in contradistinction to colonial theatre–along with Sanskrit aesthetic theory, to see what dramaturgical structures, acting styles, and staging techniques could be used to create an 'indigenous' non-realistic style of production that in turn could define an 'Indian theatre'. This impulse became known as the theatre of roots movement, a post-Independence effort to decolonise the aesthetics of modern Indian theatre by challenging the visual practices, performer/spectator relationships, dramaturgical structures and aesthetic goals of colonial performance. The movement sought new ways of structuring experience, new ways of perceiving the world and new modes of social interaction that were not dictated by the values and aesthetics of the colonisers. While many late-nineteenth- and early-twentieth-century productions resisted colonial laws and practices in their subject matter, the roots movement challenged colonial culture by reclaiming the aesthetics of performance and by addressing the politics of aesthetics.[53]

One of the characteristics of the roots movement – and particularly of the work of two of its exemplary and most renowned practitioners, Kavalam Narayana Panikkar (b. 1928) and Girish Karnad (b. 1938), whose work I detail in the next chapter in order to provide case studies of this important theatrical trend – is that directors and playwrights complicate the linear narrative, allowing for multiple voices and perspectives on a particular theme or story. Panikkar's productions elaborate on the text to allow the audience to explore many interrelated thematic threads; Karnad surrounds the central plot of his most famous play with a chorus, two talking dolls and a number of songs and dances, giving the audience multiple ways of experiencing and processing the 'main story'. For both Panikkar and Karnad the production is an opportunity for multivocality, for privileging voices other than just that of the playwright. In Panikkar's case, vocal expression and physicality are not subordinated to the text but serve as equal channels of communication, carrying their own information and commentary on the text. Because the commentary is conveyed through physical movement, vocal gestures, music and percussion, these productions honour non-verbal modes of expression, communication and experience. Panikkar is well known for placing text in the body, where language becomes visual, embodied and experienced. To make sense

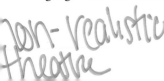
Non-realistic theatre

185

of the physical vocabulary, the spectator has to engage as co-creator of the event rather than passive observer. This is an excellent example of the way the theatre of roots focuses on multisensory, multilayered and performance-driven events for an actively engaged audience. Through their productions, these directors assert the value of other (non–text based, non-linear) ways of perceiving, structuring and processing experience.

In 1985 the Sangeet Natak Akademi (SNA, the National Academy of Music, Dance, and Drama in New Delhi which funds theatre as one of its many activities) developed a 'Scheme of Assistance to Young Theatre Workers' to 'support the endeavors of young theatre workers engaged in exploring and [developing] a theatre idiom indigenous in character, inspired by the folk/traditional theatre of the country'.[54] Five years later the SNA could legitimately claim that the scheme, with its twenty-five festivals (twenty regional, five national) of one hundred thirty-four performances (ninety-eight regional, thirty-six national) of plays in twenty-one languages (including several plays written in dialects that had not, until then, been used for full-length plays) directed by ninety young directors from ninety theatre companies involving 2,500 actors and stage hands, judged by sixty experts and performed for 200,000 audience members had 'made significant contributions to all areas of theatre activities'.[55] However, the scheme provoked numerous criticisms. Marathi playwrights Satish Alekar (b. 1949) and Mahesh Elkunchwar (b. 1939) publicly objected to the scheme on the grounds that a government organisation was inappropriately supporting a specific style of theatre. The Scheme for Young Theatre Directors turned the theatre of roots from a movement into a style, prompting criticism that directors tend to use traditional performance as a 'glove or a coat to be put on and taken off at will'.[56] The goal of creating an 'Indian' theatre using traditional performance was also criticised by Safdar Hashmi, who pointed out that 'Indianness cannot be a matter of form alone. It [must] be a matter of intention, of perception. . . . A play cannot become Indian merely by looking Indian'.[57] Through its series of roundtables, seminars, grant programmes and festivals, the SNA promoted the theatre of roots as a 'national' theatre, effectively sidelining the work of playwrights and directors interested in theatrical realism, as well as various forms of street theatre which were presented as having political rather than aesthetic merit.

## Street Theatre     1940- Now

Most of the street theatre done today grew out of the work IPTA did in the 1940s. As its own movement, street theatre gained momentum in the 1970s with the work of Badal Sircar (1925–2011) and Safdar Hashmi (1958–89). Sircar began performing in the streets to reach audiences that either would not or could not come to a theatre hall to see a performance. He eventually created what he called Third Theatre, which is neither urban proscenium theatre nor traditional performance, but a third kind of theatre (he calls it *anganmancha*, which literally means courtyard stage). Sircar's company Shatabdi performs without sets, lights, costumes, sound or make-up in the street, in bare rooms and in courtyards – anywhere that is free. He charges Re. 1 as a token entrance fee, but waives that for anyone who cannot afford to pay. Thus, he has freed himself from the constant struggle to raise money, and has created a modern people's theatre.

Hashmi dedicated himself to creating a political theatre 'that would effectively express the emotions and concerns of India's working class'.[58] Hashmi defines street theatre as a 'militant political theatre of protest. Its function is to agitate the people and to mobilise them behind fighting organizations'.[59] His company's first piece, the thirteen-minute play *Machine*, has had an enormous impact on the street theatre movement. *Machine* was inspired by a situation at a non-unionised chemical factory: workers wanted a place to park their bicycles and a place to get a cup of tea. Management refused to grant their demands, and the workers went on strike. Guards fired on the strikers, killing six workers. *Machine*, which was first performed on 15 October 1978, is still being performed around the country in a wide variety of languages and adaptations. Both street theatre and Third Theatre have contributed significantly to what Hashmi has called the 'democratisation' of Indian theatre.

Some of the most interesting street theatre work being done in the twenty-first century is being done by women. One example of this work (although it technically dates to the end of the twentieth century) is *Paccha Mannu* (The Newborn, 1996) by A. Mangai, whose work has been influenced by both the street theatre movement and the theatre of roots. *Paccha Mannu* addresses female infanticide and the abortion of female foetuses, and was created to be performed in villages outside of Chennai where female infanticide and the abortion of female foetuses are prevalent. The production begins with members of the company, all dressed in red, parading through the village clapping, drumming and singing 'listen to our story'. When they arrive at an open space in the village centre, Mangai announces the play to the surrounding crowd, inviting audience participation, interruption, dialogue and questions. The company assumes their roles, and begins to enact a series of formative moments between birth and childbirth using a hand-held curtain, a drum, several bamboo sticks and a bundle of cloth as their only set and prop pieces. *Paccha Mannu* was structured around the life-cycle rituals of women in Tamil Nadu; Mangai's premise is that the restrictions of the patriarchy are inscribed onto and embedded in the consciousness of girls and young women through these rituals of socialisation. The rituals were not only the subject of *Paccha Mannu*, but its structure as well. Working in Tamil (her mother tongue), Mangai and her actors 'collected the songs and ritual practices of ceremonies conducted during puberty, marriage, and first pregnancy' (Mangai 1998, p.71). Then they rewrote and recontextualised them to re-present the experiences of women in the area. For example, Mangai placed a popular all-female puberty ritual in the play, but she changed the lyrics to the ritual song and the context in which it was performed:

The puberty ritual . . . is both auspicious and impure—that the girl is now a sexual being is being celebrated. The very same is however seen as threatening and therefore needs control. In most South Indian contexts, this is an elaborate and expensive ceremony. The girl is given special attention but is also taught to restrict movements and social mixing. . . . There is a celebration, feasting, decorations, etc. The songs sung during this ritual speak of purifying a female body and casting off the evil. This mixed feeling of happiness and fear, pride and shame experienced during puberty seems to run all through our lives. We chose a traditional song describing each part of a woman's body from head to toe praying for purification. We retained the tune as it is. The lyric however was changed to express the values of socialization implicated in that ritual. Restriction of free mobility and fear of safeguarding the virginity of the girl became the crux of the song. (Mangai et al. 1998, p.71)

Ultimately, Mangai says the song and the ceremony both serve to imprison the girl, to end her freedom and to place her under the ever more watchful eye of her family. In Mangai's production the girl ends up boxed in by bamboo sticks, each wielded by a person shouting demands and opinions at her. In this way Mangai literalises the way women get stuck in their gender roles through socialisation. Because women participate in immobilising the girl, Mangai's staging highlights the fact that mothers are often the ones who trap their own daughters by passing on traditions, illustrating the ways in which women are complicit in perpetuating the patriarchal system.

Mangai uses traditional performance to critique rather than pass on tradition. Her work is reminiscent of IPTA in its use of popular performance to communicate progressive social messages; but it is new in that Mangai focuses on the private ceremonies of women. By turning the private rituals of women into public forums of debate, Mangai also focuses on genres that she says are 'never recognised as performance' (2002). The rituals are simultaneously the form, subject and means of communication.

## Women's Theatre

Although many women directors do not want to be categorised by their gender, women have been responsible, in the twenty-first century, for releasing Indian theatre from the now-dated concerns of the pre- and post-Independence moment, and from the theatre of roots as the dominant stylistic answer to the question 'what is India/ what is Indian theatre'. Director-scholar Kirti Jain writes:

> Direction in theatre has been the privilege of men down the centuries. . . . Hence the entire notion of directing has been [defined and developed by them]. . . . It is very difficult to say if women's intervention had happened much earlier, would we have an altogether different notion about what a theatrical performance is meant to do?[60]

Director, scholar and former Director of the National School of Drama (NSD) in Delhi Anuradha Kapur asks: 'Does a woman's language produce different narratives, stories, plots and characters? Another perception of time and temporality? An otherwise nuanced experience? Another sort of work process?'.[61] An analysis of the work of women directors over the last twenty years shows they have questioned assumptions about gender, complicated commonplace notions about what it means to be Indian and broadened ideas about what Indian theatre is, can be or should encompass. Their contributions to contemporary Indian theatre exist in the overlapping realms of the political, the social and the aesthetic: they reproduce the world as they see it.

Amal Allana exemplifies the ways in which women are moving Indian theatre forward. A graduate of the NSD, founding Artistic Director of Film and Television Associates in Delhi, and former Chair of the NSD, Allana says she didn't consciously address women's issues until she was in her fifties and began to play with cross-gender casting to explore and explode stereotypes about gendered attributes and behaviour. For example, in Allana's production of *Mother Courage*, she 'seeks to make gender mobile, as it were, by disturbing stereotypes. This she does by shifting and restructuring the elements of gender.' By casting the actor Manohar Singh as Mother Courage 'she reallocated the attributes of femininity and masculinity – passivity, patience, nurturing, sympathy, on the one hand; aggression, courage, bravery, single-mindedness and authority, on the other – from a woman's "role" to a man's "body" and *vice versa*, and thus redefined them'.[62]

In her more recent production of *Erendira* (2005), an adaptation of Gabriel Garcia Marquez's novella *The Incredible and Sad Tale of Innocent Erendira and Her Heartless Grandmother*, Allana split the character of Erendira among eight actors to give body to her own experience of self, which, she says, is not homogenous.[63] Set in Rajasthan, Allana's production focuses on the relentless mistreatment Erendira endures because she is, as a girl and later a woman, devalued – calling into question the ways in which monetary value is placed on lives. One of the most striking scenes is set in a brothel where her grandmother has sold her into sexual slavery, and where men line up to dance her around the stage, grope her body and then walk away without a backward glance. Erendira is yanked around like a rag doll, the dance a cross between a waltz and a polka set to relentlessly happy party music, which seems to mock her all the more. As each man leaves, she collapses, only to be pulled up again by the next man with just enough time to plaster a smile – or grimace – on her face before she is whisked away.

Allana's production *Nati Binodini* (The Actor Binodini, 2006) was adapted from the autobiography of a nineteenth-century prostitute-turned-actor who was one of the first women to perform on the public stage in Calcutta. The production collapses past, present, remembered time and stage time, weaving together numerous realities to demonstrate that moments lived on stage are as rich and formative as 'real' events. We do not experience Binodini's life as a linear progression, but as a series of emotional associations, and as shards of memory. Binodini is played by five actors: sometimes as an old woman watching or talking about her younger self, sometimes as a chorus of dancing selves and once as a self that emerges from the wings to keep herself from revelling too deeply in the applause of her fans. In one extraordinary scene, four Binodinis struggle to play a role, experimenting with different gestures, dance moves and emotions. Again, Allana's work challenges traditional modes of presenting biographical material and apprehending the richness of human experience.

Above-mentioned NSD Director Anuradha Kapur, who has directed numerous productions in India, England and Germany, and founded her own theatre company in 1989 along with a group of painters, musicians, writers and video artists, is also concerned with 'upsetting social and gender hierarchies' and is introducing numerous innovations to contemporary Indian theatre.[64] Her production of *The Job* (1997) a one-woman show with an installation based on Brecht's short story of the same name, centred on a woman who impersonates her husband when he dies, and takes over his job in order to keep her children from starving. Kapur writes: 'This play attempted to look at the repercussions of a woman becoming a man; its dangers and transgressions, and, in the context of the story, its disastrous consequences.'[65]

Another production, *Sundari: An Actor Prepares* (1999), was developed from the autobiography of Jaishankar Sundari, a celebrated female impersonator who performed all over India between 1901 and 1931 and 'became enormously popular especially with women, for whom he became a sort of model, setting the style for everything from dress to deportment'. Kapur writes:

> The performance sought to investigate the enigmatic presence of the man-woman figure in the theatre, and the cross-gender fascination it has characteristically conjured in audiences. Even though the premise of female impersonation almost always rests on the idea of an essential femininity, its performance sought to emphasize that gender is actually constructed in practice, and that it is in fact encoded in demeanor, costume, manner and convention.[66]

Zuleikha Chaudhari graduated from Bennington College in the United States with a degree in Theatre Direction and Lighting Design. Chaudhari describes her work as a 'fragmentation of the linear structure of performance' and asserts that 'an experiential relationship to the text is produced by structuring an environment where the performer creates a physical language which translates text into a series of visual registers'.[67] Chaudhari's 2008 production *On Seeing* was one answer to a series of questions she had about how to articulate memory, experience and what happens in the mind. 'How does one chart or construct an emotional landscape? It's not about emotion, but the landscape. How do you convert words into images?'[68] In *On Seeing* a performer moves in response to a sculptural installation of shifting fluorescent lights placed in an empty room. The spectator travels through the room and her perception of the space – and therefore of its meaning – changes based on the particular way performer, light and spectator interact. Chaudhari writes: 'The performer's presence is negotiated to integrate itself into and extend the visual language of the space . . . the performer's body assumes a life of its own; it becomes a sculptural object interacting with a space rendered dynamic' by both the changing lights and the movement of the spectators.

> For me performance and, more specifically movement, functions less as a mimetic form to illustrate textual content, working instead to expand time so that a moment in a narrative is opened up to the possibility of multiple meanings and resonances. As a result, the visual story performed on stage, while based on and derived from the text, does not attempt to illustrate narrative content. Rather, it offers the viewer a series of visual experiences, which may relate obliquely and elliptically to the textual content, allowing the text and movement to coexist without necessarily always coinciding.[69]

Chaudhari is interested in the interactions between space and actor, and in how narrative unfolds in a visual context.

From the perspective of early 2013, it is clear that women have re-directed modern Indian theatre, and that their ways of working, ways of seeing the world and ways of structuring experience are being recognised, thus opening up Indian society to a much wider range of experiences.

## Contemporary Theatre/Multiple Streams

From this brief survey of modern Indian theatre – its major movements, plays, productions and issues – it is clear that while modern theatre in India began in the nineteenth century as a colonial enterprise, it quickly defined itself in and on its own terms, and has since been a vital part of the social, cultural and political life of the nation. In the next chapter we will focus on two specific post-independence artists whose work demonstrates the heterogeneity of hybridity in modern Indian theatre, and explore them as case studies, investigating how traditional theatre and culture is employed post-Independence to make a truly modern theatre.

# CHAPTER 8
## THEATRE OF ROOTS: POST-INDEPENDENCE THEATRE IN INDIA

*[handwritten margin note: theatre was used to fight colonialism]*

Because theatre was used to disseminate colonial culture and demonstrate cultural superiority in India, it became a powerful tool with which to challenge that very same colonial authority before and after Independence in 1947, when playwrights and directors turned to classical dance, religious ritual, martial arts and popular entertainment, along with Sanskrit aesthetic theory, to see what dramaturgical structures, acting styles and staging techniques could be used to create an 'indigenous' non-realistic style of production that could define an 'Indian theatre'. This impulse became known as the theatre of roots movement, a post-Independence effort to decolonise the aesthetics of modern Indian theatre by challenging the visual practices, performer/spectator relationships, dramaturgical structures and aesthetic goals of colonial performance. The movement sought new ways of structuring experience, new ways of perceiving the world and new modes of social interaction that were not dictated by the values and aesthetics of the colonisers. While many late-nineteenth- and early-twentieth-century productions resisted colonial laws and practices in their subject matter, the roots movement challenged colonial culture by reclaiming the aesthetics of performance and by addressing the politics of aesthetics. While the impetus for the theatre of roots belongs to the post-Independence period, most of the directors and playwrights are still working, and their work continues to have an enormous impact on the contemporary theatre in India. With the financial support of the Sangeet Natak Akademi (SNA, the National Academy of Music, Dance, and Drama in New Delhi which funds the performing arts), the roots movement became one of the most pervasive and influential post-Independence theatrical movements in India. For this reason, I offer case studies here of two of the movement's most prominent practitioners.

One of the characteristics of the roots movement – and particularly the work of two of its exemplary and most renowned practitioners, Kavalam Narayana Panikkar (b. 1928) and Girish Karnad (b. 1938), whose work I detail here in order to provide case studies of this important theatrical trend – is that directors and playwrights complicate the linear narrative, allowing for multiple voices and perspectives on a particular theme or story. These artists offer an opportunity to examine the most important and influential theatrical innovations of the theatre of roots movement. Panikkar's productions elaborate on the text to allow the audience to explore many interrelated thematic threads; Karnad surrounds the central plot of his most famous play with a chorus, two talking dolls and a number of songs and dances, giving the audience multiple ways of experiencing and processing the 'main story'. For both Panikkar and Karnad the production is an opportunity for multivocality, for privileging voices other than just that of the playwright. In Panikkar's case, vocal expression and physicality are not subordinated to the text but serve as equal channels of communication, carrying their own information and commentary on the text. Because the commentary is conveyed through physical movement, vocal gestures, music and percussion, these productions honour non-verbal modes of expression, communication and experience. Panikkar is well known for placing text in the body, where language becomes visual, embodied and experienced. To make sense of the physical vocabulary, the spectator has to engage as co-creator of the event rather than passive observer. This is an excellent example of the way the theatre of roots focuses on multisensory, multilayered and performance-driven events for an actively engaged audience. Through their productions, these directors assert the value of other (non–text based, non-linear) ways of perceiving, structuring and processing experience.

## Panikkar

Kavalam Narayana Panikkar redefined modern Indian theatre by combining the dramaturgical structure of *kutiyattam* (a particular way of performing Sanskrit drama), the actor training methods of *kathakali* (classical dance-drama), the physical training of *kalarippayattu* (a martial art) and aesthetic theory from the *Natyasastra* (the Sanskrit treatise on aesthetics) with staging patterns dictated by the perspectival requirements of the proscenium stage in a relatively fixed, repeatable production. Panikkar redirects the aesthetic goal of performance, the director's relationship to text, the actor's relationship to character, methods of actor training and the spectator's mode of engagement to create a theatre that has the capacity to present many perspectives, defines the self in terms of behaviour rather than essence and as transformative rather than fixed, trains an active and imaginative participant rather than a passive observer, and valorises modes of experience that are beyond language.

In rehearsal and production Panikkar treats text the way a kutiyattam actor does: as a framework for a series of elaborations. Plays in the kutiyattam repertoire, like plays in the kathakali repertoire, are valued for their literary qualities, but even more for their ability to stimulate the actor's imagination to create interesting improvisations on the text. Similarly, what Panikkar values in the plays he directs (both his own and others') is their ability to evoke visual and aural images that can be realised onstage, creating multiple ways of experiencing and processing the themes of the play. The structure of Panikkar's production of *Ottayan* is modelled on the performance structure of kutiyattam, which allows for – in fact, insists on – multiple interpretations of the events in the play on the part of the director, actor and spectator, through elaboration. A dramaturgical structure based on elaboration challenges the notion that ultimate authority lies in the text and with the playwright, and places creative authority with the director, actors and spectators.

While *Ottayan*, like kutiyattam, is not plot driven, it nonetheless has at its centre a simple story about the *Chakyar* Parameshwaran. 'Chakyar' is a caste name for those who traditionally have both the right and responsibility for performing kutiyattam in Kerala temples and stages. Onstage, Chakyars are accompanied by a *Nangiyar*, who keeps the rhythm on a pair of cymbals (*kuzhithalam*). In *Ottayan* the Nangiyar is Parameshwaran's wife. When she makes a rhythmic mistake, causing Parameshwaran to lose his focus and his own rhythm, Parameshwaran runs out of the *kuttampalam*, the building where kutiyattam is traditionally performed, and escapes to the jungle. He runs away because he no longer believes in himself as an actor. In the jungle a wild elephant (the lone tusker) charges at Parameshwaran. Realising he will be killed unless he does something quickly, Parameshwaran decides to save himself with 'a bit of acting': he will transform into an elephant in order to scare off the angry tusker.[1] If he succeeds, he will not only have saved his life, but also restored his faith in himself as an actor. Parameshwaran is successful and the charging elephant takes him for one of his own kind and flees. A passing Woodsman also sees Parameshwaran as an elephant, puts the beleaguered actor in chains and takes him to Moopanar, the Woodsman's leader. Moopanar does not believe Parameshwaran is an actor until Parameshwaran puts on a play. As soon as Moopanar and the Woodsman are deeply engaged in the production, Parameshwaran escapes.

Many of the plays in the contemporary kutiyattam repertoire are based on stories from the epics the *Mahabharata*, the *Ramayana* and other familiar sources. These stories are well known to the kutiyattam spectator. Consequently, the emphasis of a performance is on how a particular performer interprets the text and embodies the narrative rather than on telling the story itself. The elaboration of the drama is so complex that a kutiyattam performance can take anywhere from five to thirty-five nights to complete – the better the actors, the longer it can take; a kutiyattam performance is not the presentation of a text but an elaboration on it. Each scene of the play has its own title and is meant to be performed as its own entity. Within each scene, a performer may spend up to three hours illuminating three lines of text by making political and social analogies, exploring emotional associations and telling related or background stories.

On the first night of a kutiyattam performance a character enters, introduces himself by narrating his personal history and some important details from his own life, presents some of the important events leading up to the play and expands on details found in the first few lines of text. On the second and third nights the same character (possibly played by a different actor) tells stories connected to, but not found in, the main story of the play. On the fourth night a second character introduces himself, presents personal background leading up to the moment the play begins and tells the story from his point of view. On each successive night another character appears until all the characters have been introduced, each offering his own history and version of the story. On other nights the *vidushaka* appears. His job is to translate the Sanskrit text of the play into Malayalam (the language spoken in Kerala) and to make political and social analogies between events in the play and events in the real world. In this way the story is told and retold from many points of view, the background to the story is fully explored, and the story is made relevant to the audience. This process is known as *nirvahanam*.[2] On the final night of kutiyattam, 'the play' is performed. 'The play' – the text sans elaborations – is only a tiny fraction of the total experience.

Consequently, kutiyattam spectators do not have a 'horizontal' experience: they do not follow the plot in a linear fashion across time; instead, they have a series of 'vertical' experiences in which they follow the actor as he delves into each moment, exploring it fully at many levels and in many modes. The responsibility for thorough interpretation and elaboration is handed over to the performers, whose improvisations are based on guidelines set out in the *attaprakaram*,[3] the acting manuals passed from teacher to student. Because the elaborations take precedence over the text, the attaprakarams are even more important to the performers than the text of the play.

While *Ottayan*, unlike kutiyattam performances, tells a new and therefore unfamiliar story, its dramaturgical structure depends upon elaboration of theme rather than revelation of plot, albeit to a lesser degree than in kutiyattam. Panikkar's production of *Ottayan* has a ninety-minute run time, and yet the English-language translation of the Malayalam script is only eight and a half pages long.[4] The fundamental difference between the elaborations in kutiyattam and in *Ottayan* is that in kutiyattam the nirvahanam is prescribed in the attaprakaram, learnt in training and improvised in performance – there is no rehearsal, and no director. In *Ottayan* (as in much modern theatre) the elaboration is worked out in rehearsal between the director and actor and then fixed; the performance is not improvised. Kutiyattam in performance is actor driven; *Ottayan* in performance is director driven. Nonetheless, Panikkar defines his job as director in relation to the text the same way that Chakyars define their jobs in relation to the text.

Panikkar insists that the job of the director is to comment on the play, to focus on what is implied rather than what is stated directly in the text and to bring out the emotional nuances through elaboration. *What* happens is not as important as *how* it happens:

> In [the] interpretation of a play and in realizing the performance text, I also often add new text and create new characters, which is upsetting to those who talk of the sanctity of and faithfulness to text, especially of the classics. I strongly feel that the whole notion of faithfulness to text is meaningless. I, as director, must play a creative role, and I can play that role only by interpreting the play according to my understanding and treat[ing] the text according to my theatrical vision.[5]

Although many have expressed similar sentiments, few directors of modern plays have taken the notion of elaboration to the extreme that Panikkar does: it is rare to see a production of an eight-page play last for ninety minutes.

Panikkar's rehearsal process supports his performance-driven productions. The most significant aspect of his rehearsal process with regard to the treatment of text is that his company, Sopanam, rehearses without a script. Panikkar writes his plays on scraps of paper or in notebooks he has scattered around his house. When he is finished, he puts the scraps in order and gives them to a member of the company to transcribe. This is the script used in rehearsal. It is never duplicated; the actors never have their own copy and they never take it home. Nor do they begin rehearsal by reading it aloud. On the first day of rehearsal, Panikkar discusses with the actors what he has written and reads parts of the play aloud to them. The focus of the conversation is on his vision as director. Thus, the actors begin rehearsal with a more or less full knowledge of what the director wants, but only partial knowledge of the text. This places the emphasis of rehearsal on the interpretation of the text rather than on the text itself.

Because they don't have scripts, the actors learn all their lines in rehearsal, on their feet, while interacting with other actors. They don't encounter the text separately from behaviour. More importantly, they don't ever rehearse with scripts in hand: other actors prompt them from the sidelines, so they work physically from the very beginning, learning the physical life of the character before learning their lines. In fact, the actors don't have a sense of the script as a whole until late in the rehearsal process. They encounter the text in sections, even in fragments, so their focus is on expressing each moment fully as they discover it in rehearsal. Because the actors don't know what comes next, they stay in each moment a bit longer, following and exploring their impulses until they run out of ideas. At this point they are prompted by Panikkar or one of the other actors – which opens up new avenues for exploration. Often, they go in the opposite direction than the script would have taken them: at worst, this is a good acting exercise; at best, the actors find material to incorporate into the production. Most importantly, they are encouraged to find their own way through the material, delving deeply into each moment to mine its full potential.

In most if not all productions, *Ottayan* begins with the actor playing Parameshwaran coming out in costume and introducing himself to the spectators. After he introduces himself, he begins to tell Parameshwaran's story, beginning with the moment Parameshwaran leaves the kuttampalam. The actor does what Panikkar calls a 'rounding', which he has adapted from kutiyattam. Kutiyattam has several movement patterns that signify when the scene is shifting from one place to another: one *is kalappurattu natakkuka*, 'a special movement pattern which is used to indicate going from one place to another'[6]; and another is *vattattil cati natakkuka*, 'a circular movement pattern to indicate moving from one place to another distant place'.[7] In Panikkar's productions, when actors want to show they have travelled a long distance or entered another reality, they walk around the stage in a circle; when they return to centre stage, they are understood to have arrived at their new destination. These moments occur between moments in the text and thus do not illustrate the text, but add to it. Not only do these 'roundings' give the spectator more time to think in greater depth about what's happening, it allows Panikkar to play with time: it takes more time to walk around the stage than it does to say 'I picked up my knapsack and left the place'[8] and yet it takes much less time to walk around the stage than it would to get lost in a jungle. So Panikkar uses roundings to establish the fact that Parameshwaran is operating in theatrical or imaginative time, not literal, real-world time.

Roundings do the same thing with respect to visual reality. A rounding works like a set change: as the actor takes his rounding, his physicality changes to suit the new location; the new location is shown through his character's physical reaction to it, and the spectator experiences a change of locale by observing the body of the actor. What the spectator is really seeing, then, is not a pictorial reality, but an emotional reality: the spectator sees Parameshwaran's surroundings from his perspective. Kutiyattam is performed on a bare stage, and Panikkar works with a bare or almost-bare stage. The focus is on the actor rather than the set, asserting that perceived reality is more important than pictorial reality. It also requires the active engagement of the spectator, who in the case of *Ottayan*, has to imagine the jungle Parameshwaran enters.

The *Natyasastra* divides acting into four main components: *vachika*, vocal expression; *angika*, physical expression through the body; *satvika*, emotional expression through the face; and *aharya*, make-up and costuming. *Natyasastra* scholar Bharat Gupt tells us that angika and satvika are not supposed to support vachika, which is usually but not always vocal expression of or related to the text, but to work as *equal channels of communication* and to have their own integrity,[9] and elaborations that happen between lines of text – such as Panikkar's roundings – have their own integrity.

In many productions, the actors' movements duplicate or illustrate the text. In Panikkar's productions the actors' movements comment on the text, add detail to it or bring out the connotative or poetic meaning in the text. Panikkar believes that theatre should be *drishya kavya*, or visual poetry: 'for me the primary function of the director is to convert the poetic images of the dramatic text into physical images'.[10] In addition to body language, Panikkar uses mudras to create this visual poetry. The word 'mudra' is often translated as 'hand gesture', but in fact these gestures engage the entire body and rely heavily on eye, eyebrow, cheek and lip movements. A mudra is a way of visualising, or embodying, language and thought. There are three kinds of mudras used in kutiyattam: those used to depict nouns and verbs (such as hair, tiger, to see); those that demonstrate emotion (such as love, anger, fear); and those that symbolise concepts (such as time or 'three worlds'). Oral language is linear: only one word can be spoken or received at a time. With mudras, a whole scene can be taken in at once. One can say 'I went to the jungle'. To add information about how one got there, how long it took, how many bends were in the road or how much one enjoyed the walk, one would need to add extra phrases, such as, 'I went to the jungle on a hot sunny day, and it took me two hours to get there.' With mudras, the nature of the journey can be conveyed by the size, speed, duration, quality and directionality of the gestures as well as with body posture and facial expression.

In *Ottayan*, when Parameshwaran enters the jungle and says: 'whither shall I go in this wild jungle?',[11] the story stops so the actor playing Parameshwaran can use gestures to elaborate physically. A good kutiyattam performer would be able to improvise for at least an hour with this one line. Using mudras he would describe the trees he sees, the flowers he smells and the animals he hears; he might, through a technique known in kutiyattam as *anukramam* (flashback), relive a memory of another time he was in the jungle; he might compare the feelings of his character to those of another character in a similar predicament. His nirvahanam would be entirely physical.

Similarly, the elaboration of the actor playing Parameshwaran in *Ottayan* is entirely physical, although he does not go on at such length and uses fewer mudras. He describes the jungle and a few of the things he sees. For example, he sees a tiger: first the actor shows us Parameshwaran's surprise at seeing the tiger; he then jumps away from the spot where he was just standing, turns 180 degrees to face Parameshwaran, (i.e. facing the place he was just standing) and lands in a crouching tiger pose using the kutiyattam gesture for tiger and the *mukhabhinaya*, or facial gesture, of a tiger – becoming the tiger that Parameshwaran sees. The actor then jumps back to his original spot as he transforms back into Parameshwaran and reacts fearfully (through *netrabhinaya*, or eye acting, as well as facial expression and body language) to the tiger he – and all of us – has just seen. In a situation where the space is defined entirely by what the performer describes and evokes, and where spectators see things like tigers from the character's point of view, Panikkar focuses the spectator's attention on the emotional reality of the central character rather than the physical reality of the jungle itself. This makes a larger point about reality in general: people don't act based on reality, they act based on their perception of it. In this sense, perception is more real than reality.

After Parameshwaran describes the jungle, he enacts hearing the elephant. In kutiyattam there is a technique called *kettatuka*:

> When an actor hears something spoken by an unseen character from offstage . . . he feigns to hear it by suitable movements of the head, hands or the mudras. . . . The actor not only enacts hearing the words of the unseen speaker but also brings out fully the meaning of the speech that he has heard by imitating exactly the facial expressions of the unseen speaker and enacts with mudras the meaning of his words.[12]

In *Ottayan* the offstage character is an elephant so there is no dialogue, but the principle is the same. Parameshwaran first enacts hearing the elephant, then shows us the elephant by using the mudra *for* elephant and the facial expression *of* the elephant. Because of the way the hand gesture and the facial gesture work together, he is in fact simultaneously *showing* the elephant and *becoming* the elephant. Thus the spectators see the elephant as Parameshwaran sees him; they experience Parameshwaran's perception of the elephant. Because they are not watching another actor play the elephant, the spectators have a chance to see how Parameshwaran feels about the elephant. Again, the focus shifts from a purportedly objective reality to the emotional reality of the character.

These elaborations require the active participation of the spectators. After hearing the elephant, reacting to what he has heard, and deciding to become an elephant in order to save himself, Parameshwaran transforms himself. His transformation is not accomplished by changing costume, by putting on a mask or by any other literal means. His transformation is accomplished through behaviour: he changes the way he moves and holds his body in order to become *like* an elephant. In theatrical terms, he behaves 'as if' he is an elephant. Again, he uses the mudra for an elephant, adding to it the slow, heavy gait of an elephant's majestic rhythm: takatimi, takatimi, takatimi, takatimi. His steps are underscored by percussion, which is used to help the spectator 'see' the 'elephant' move. In kutiyattam, an actor pouring water from a pot places his hands in such a way that he looks like he is holding a pot. Percussion instruments provide the sound of the water pouring, punctuating the actor's movement and making the objects and actions vivid for the spectator. But it is the spectator's responsibility to provide the 'water' and the 'pot' – to engage with the actor as co-creator of the moment.

Panikkar identifies *thouryathrikam* as the salient characteristic of Indian theatre. *Thouryathrikam* is the combination of *geetha* (vocal music), *nritta* (dance) and *vadya* (instrumental music) to create such multisensory and multidimensional moments in performance. In *Ottayan* themes are played out in the percussion, and spectators listen with their eyes to speeches delivered through the body. In this way Panikkar plays with the senses, and often shifts the sense through which spectators expect to apprehend information. By creating a multisensory theatre of the imagination, Panikkar engages spectators more thoroughly, and offers them the means to more actively absorb information. When seen from this angle, thanathunatakavedi – which literally means "our own theatre" or theatre that reflects our culture and which, in practice is a total theatrical experience – is about rethinking representation to change the way spectators think.

After Parameshwaran has successfully transformed into an elephant he gets so absorbed in his role that he continues to dance as an elephant – until he is spotted by the Woodsmen and taken to the Woodsmen's leader, Moopanar. To escape, Parameshwaran has to prove that he is not an elephant but an actor performing a role. To prove that he is an actor he has to successfully stage a play. The big question of this moment is whether or not the scene Parameshwaran creates will be convincing, whether or not he can make Moopanar believe that he is an actor. In this scene, Panikkar redefines the ideal role of the spectator in modern Indian theatre.

Parameshwaran tells the Woodsman and Moopanar that there is a prerequisite to the performance of a successful drama:

**Parameshwaran**   . . . I shall do drama. But it requires some preparation.

**Moopanar**   What do you require?

**Parameshwaran**   Both of you must at least be ready to see it. Are you ready?

**Moopanar**   I am ready.

**Woodsman**   I am also ready.

**Parameshwaran**   Then half the work is over. . . . Look here, friends, it is not enough on your part to be merely ready to see the play. Watch me closely with your whole mind involved in the performance.[13]

The two woodsmen, and by implication *Ottayan*'s spectators, are being told that the success of the drama depends, in large part, on the spectators, who must be ready to see the play. More than that, the spectators must be ready to engage. As Panikkar says, 'this means that the drama actually takes place in the mind of the spectator, and not on the stage'.[14] For his dramatic presentation to Moopanar, Parameswaran builds a house (elephants in Kerala are often used in construction, so this is an appropriate action to choose). He narrates the various tasks – 'first of all the ground must be cut into and made ready'[15] – as he acts them out to the accompaniment of a drum. He lays the foundation, builds a frame, raises the walls and then secures a beam. But he can't lift the beam alone, so he turns to the two woodsmen and says: 'That is indeed very hard work. How can I do it alone? . . . Please join in this task.'[16] The two woodsmen join the 'elephant' and together they lift the beam. Of course there are no props onstage: the house is built entirely through mime underscored by percussion. Parameshwaran engages the two woodsmen in an act of imagination as they all work together to create an imaginary reality. *Ottayan* offers the powerful lesson that you can create what you can imagine, and supports that lesson by offering an exercise for the imagination – building an imaginary house.

In order for *Ottayan* to be a success, Parameshwaran has to engage the spectator in the same way he engages the Woodsmen. Just as it is the kutiyattam spectator's responsibility to provide the 'water' and the 'pot', *Ottayan* spectators must participate imaginatively or the house will not get built. *Ottayan* works only when the actor and the spectators collaborate – when they engage as co-creators. Here Panikkar does not assume the presence of an educated or involved spectator, nor does he simply instruct spectators in their role: with the building of the house he offers them an opportunity to practice becoming an actively engaged spectator.

## Karnad

If Panikkar's work best exemplifies the rehearsal and production practices of the theatre of roots movement, Girish Karnad's play *Hayavadana* (The One with the Horse's Head, 1971) offers an opportunity to examine the characteristics of the new kind of modern play the movement produced. When *Hayavadana* was published in 1971 it was immediately taken up as a 'poster play' for the emerging roots movement. Suresh Awasthi credited Karnad with having evolved 'a new dramatic form' and singled out Hayavadana as an example of what could be done creatively with 'folk forms' in an urban setting.[17] Later, in his famous article on the roots movement, Awasthi said that the 1972 production by B. V. Karanth (1929–2002) in Delhi 'reversed the colonial course of contemporary theatre'.[18] Five different directors in five different cities staged productions of Hayavadana in 1972. In his review of Karanth's Delhi production, J. N. Kaushal hailed *Hayavadana* as 'not only an event of Delhi's theatre season but an event of the Indian theatre itself'. He said the production 'was a pointer towards the form the emerging [Indian] theatre may take'.[19]

While Panikkar created a hybrid theatre in his attempt to create a 'decolonised' modern Indian theatre, Karnad consciously set out, in almost all of his plays including *Naga-Mandala* (Play with a Cobra, 1988) and *Agni Mattu Male* (The Fire and the Rain, 1994), to create a hybrid theatre that reflects the complex subjectivities of post-Independence reality. For Karnad, erasing all the effects of colonial theatrical culture was neither possible nor desirable. In *Hayavadana* Karnad employs a linear narrative structure, the proscenium stage, the fourth wall and human characters, strategically placing them in a play with a structure of concentric circles, several non-human characters and an acting style that occasionally breaks the fourth wall. By weaving structures, aesthetics and techniques of Western theatre together with structures, aesthetics and techniques from traditional Indian performance, specifically *yakshagana*, a well-known genre of dance-drama performed in Karnataka, Karnad creates a play that is *neither* 'Western' *nor* 'Indian', *both* 'Western' *and* 'Indian'; a new theatre that is more than and different from the sum of its parts. With *Hayavadana* Karnad created a hybrid dramaturgical structure, acting style and visual practice that offers spectators a model for practicing cultural ambidexterity – the ability to successfully and easily operate simultaneously in two or more cultural systems without privileging either one over the other.

The central plot in *Hayavadana* is based on a tale found in the *Kathasaritsagara* (The Ocean of Story), a collection of Sanskrit stories dating from the eleventh century, and on its further development in Thomas Mann's 1940 German novella *The Transposed Heads*. Thus *Hayavadana*'s origins are intergeneric (a folktale transformed into a novella into a play) and intercultural (the story travelled from India to Germany and back again). 'Inter-ness' pervades *Hayavadana* at every level, from its origins to its thematic content to its production history.

*Hayavadana* focuses on Padmini, who is attracted to Kapila, her bookish husband Devadatta's sexy friend. In a jealous fit, Devadatta cuts off his own head. Kapila finds the body and, knowing he will be blamed for Devadatta's suicide, beheads himself. Padmini, terrified of the gossip that will surely ensue, appeals to the goddess Kali for help. Kali agrees to restore the men to life, and tells Padmini to put the heads back on their bodies. But Padmini, desiring the man of her dreams – one with Devadatta's mind and Kapila's body – 'accidentally' switches the heads, leading to the central question of the story: which man is her husband, the one with Devadatta's head or the one with his body? When a *rishi* (great sage) announces that the head is the supreme limb of the body and that the man with Devadatta's head is therefore her husband, Padmini feels that she has the best of both worlds, and happily goes home with the new Devadatta. Kapila exiles himself to the forest. Eventually, unable to tolerate an 'other' body as their own, the two men kill themselves/each other. In the *Kathasaritsagara*, this head/body split occurs between body and soul; in Mann's novella the dichotomy is between intellect and emotion; in Karnad's play the conflict is between self and other. In the *Kathasaritsagara* and in Mann's novella, the split is dealt with philosophically; in *Hayavadana* it is placed in the social and political context of post-Independence India.

Just as Bhagavata (the narrator/singer) is about to introduce Padmini's story, he is interrupted by an actor who runs onstage yelling that he has just seen a talking horse. This turns out to be Hayavadana, the character for whom the play is named – and Hayavadana turns out to have a horse's head and a man's body. His story, which offers another perspective on the divided self, frames the central plot by appearing at both the beginning and end of the play. Hayavadana is trying to unite his body and head, a dilemma he expresses in terms of nationalism and Indianisation: 'I took [an] interest in the social life of the Nation— Civics, Politics, Patriotism, Nationalism, Indianization, [and] the Socialist Pattern of Society,' he says to the Bhagavata. 'But where's my society? Where? You must help me to become a complete man'.[20] As the child of a princess and a celestial being in the form of a horse – as the progeny of miscegenation – Hayavadana comes from two different worlds, but does not feel at home in either. He represents the divided self of the postcolonial subject – a character attempting to decolonise his own mind. He tries to reinvent himself as a fully 'Indian' subject by participating in the most simplistic demonstrations of patriotism: when he appears at the end of act two he has managed to become a full horse, but he still has a human voice which – because he has noticed that people who sing national anthems seem to have lost their voices – he is trying to lose by singing patriotic songs such as 'Vande Mataram' (Mother, I Bow to Thee), 'Sare Jahan se Acchha Hindustan Hamara' (Our India Is Better than the Whole World), 'Jhanda Ooncha Rahe Hamara' (May Our Flag Fly High) and 'Jana Gana Mana' (the national anthem). Because he finds only ridiculously reductive solutions that negate one side of himself, Hayavadana is a comic figure, a foil to the more tragic Devadatta and Kapila whose inability to deal productively with their head/body divide leads to their deaths.

The deity Ganesha, who appears in the Ganesha puja that precedes the play, is an exemplar survivor of the head/body divide. Ganesha's mother Parvati made Ganesha out of mud, placed him at the entrance to her room and told him not to let anyone in while she was having a bath. Shiva returned home after a long period of asceticism and demanded entry, but Ganesha refused. A fight ensued, and Shiva cut off Ganesha's head, which rolled away. Very angry at Shiva for what he had done, Parvati insisted that he repair the damage. Shiva replaced Ganesha's head with the head of the first being to come his way, an elephant. Ganesha's head is extremely important because it comes from Shiva, but he does not become an elephant just because he has an elephant's head. With his elephant head and human body, Ganesha became a third, more powerful, being. Ganesha's story offers another way of looking at the head/body divide that is the subject of *Hayavadana*. His hybridity – and his ability to embrace it – is what makes him powerful. Significantly, Ganesha scholar Paul Courtwright tells us that Ganesha always appears, both iconographically and ritually, in his restored form – *with* the elephant's head.[21] Ganesha worshippers focus not on the act of dismemberment, but on the new Ganesha: a composite – or hybrid – whole being. Ganesha's story is one in which self and other have been combined successfully to make a third entity stronger than either of the original parts, and the opening lines of the Ganesha puja in *Hayavadana* stress this by referring to Ganesha as the 'destroyer of incompleteness'.[22] Ganesha's presence in the play does not simply try to reverse the power dynamic between head and body, it challenges the entire conceptual framework of the head/body divide itself. By implication or analogy (because the head/body divide in this play is a metaphor for cultural difference) Ganesha challenges the production and promotion of cultural difference as both a source/sign of colonial authority and a source/sign of Indian national culture, disrupting the power of both and denying the privilege to either of being representative or authoritative.

Hybridity is not just the subject of *Hayavadana* but its structural strategy. Padmini's story, which is at the centre of the play, is a linear,

210

plot-driven narrative. But the play as a whole is a series of concentric circles. Linear structures lead to single conclusions dictated by the author and more passively absorbed by the spectator. Multilayered structures insist on multiple responses by spectators more actively engaged with interpreting and reconciling the various perspectives arrayed in the performance. In the central circle is the Padmini-Devadatta-Kapila story. This is surrounded by Hayavadana's story, which is in turn framed by the Ganesha puja. Padmini's story is continually interrupted by commentary on her situation, utilising other performance genres, each with its own logic and perspective. For example, Karnad explores Padmini's inner psyche by using two Doll characters that see into and narrate Padmini's dreams about Kapila as she sleeps, revealing the illicit desire she feels but cannot, as a married woman in Indian society, articulate:

**Doll I**   He goes to her . . .

**Doll II**   . . . very near her . . .

**Doll I**   (*In a whisper.*) What's he going to do now?

**Doll II**   (*Even more anxious.*) What?
(*They watch.*)

**Doll I**   (*Baffled.*) But he's climbing a tree!

**Doll II**   (*Almost a wail of disappointment.*) He's dived into a river!

**Doll I**   Is that all he came for?[23]

The Dolls are humorous – particularly onstage. In the 1989 production staged by Karanth they were played by two young masked children who had absolutely no idea what they were saying. But the Dolls have a dark side too: they are gossipy and judgmental, like nosey neighbours – who in this staging were bickering little children.

**Doll I**   As the doll-maker used to say, "What are things coming to!"

**Doll II**   Especially last night—I mean—that dream . . .

**Doll I**  Tut-tut—One shouldn't talk about such things!

**Doll II**  It was so shameless . . .

**Doll I**  I said be quiet . . .

**Doll II**  Honestly! The way they . . .[24]

The Dolls allow Karnad to introduce the voice of 'society' into what is otherwise a three-character story. The Dolls are not at all 'necessary' to the plot, which could move forward without them, but they are important because they remind spectators of the presence of society – and of propriety. Their attitudes contribute to the motivating force for Padmini's behaviour: she does some of what she does *because* of what society will say, and some of what she does *in spite of* what society will say.

The female Chorus provides a contrast to the Dolls' vituperative condemnation of Padmini, and introduces a more mature and sympathetic view of her. They sing:

Why should love stick to the sap of a single body? When the stem is drunk with the thick yearning of the many-petaled, many-flowered lantana, why should it be tied down to the relation of a single flower? . . . A head for each breast. A pupil for each eye. A side for each arm. I have neither regret nor shame.[25]

Although Karanth placed them off to the side of the stage in production, the Chorus literally has the first and last word on Padmini, setting up her story at the beginning and providing the last comment on her at the end. The Chorus offers yet another perspective on the protagonist, reminding us that she is not interested in being like Sita, the long-suffering heroine of the *Ramayana*, often held up as a model of correct female behaviour. The Chorus tells us not to judge Padmini according to orthodox social conventions as expressed by the Dolls, or at the very least to recognise these social strictures as conventions rather than inherent truths. Karnad wants his audience to examine these conventional attitudes and think about whom they serve. Thus, every theatrical device Karnad introduces offers another way of understanding Padmini and another perspective on her situation. Padmini's story is simultaneously centralised by the percentage of stage time it is given, and decentralised by the Dolls, the female chorus, the songs and Hayavadana's story. Because the linear central story is framed by a structure of concentric circles, it is tempting to say that the latter has replaced the former, but it is more accurate to say that Karnad has carefully combined them into a structural hybrid that demands a complex engagement with the multiple modes of production.

When Karnad combines two genres that have never before been put together, his spectators not only experience a new, third genre, but also see the original two in a new way. When Karnad works with elements of traditional performance, he recontextualises them in a way that allows spectators to reconsider their theatrical expectations, social practices and cultural assumptions. For example, Hayavadana's entrance is modelled on the way major characters in yakshagana enter the stage. As in kathakali, the plot stops in order to allow important characters to do an introductory dance called *oddolaga*, in which they appear little by little from behind a hand-held curtain, an elaboration that can last for as long as thirty minutes.[26] The oddolaga focuses on the moral nature of characters from the epics with whom the audience is already familiar. Once the characters have been introduced, they are integrated into the story, which then proceeds. Hayavadana also enters from behind a hand-held curtain, but with crucial differences: his curtain entrance introduces an unfamiliar character and does so in psychological terms. Spectators are not shown who Hayavadana is; they are shown how he feels. Spectators hear sobbing from behind the curtain, which is lowered to reveal a horse's head. As soon as he realises his head is exposed, Hayavadana ducks behind the curtain again. After an extended sequence of hiding and revealing, the curtain drops to the floor to reveal – surprise! – the body of a man. Spectators are not exposed to Hayavadana's moral character, but to his motivation: he doesn't want to appear in public because he is tired of being shunned for having the head of one species and the body of another. In Karanth's production, the curtain entrance was given a further twist: Hayavadana entered with the curtain wrapped around his head – like wearing a paper bag over his head. When he was finally persuaded to take it off, he used the curtain as a shawl. After Hayavadana's entrance, Bhagavata integrates him into the play by posing a series of questions: 'Who are you? . . . What happened? What's your grief?'.[27] These questions are exactly the same as those asked of each major character on their entrance by the bhagavata in yakshagana: 'Who are you? Where have you come from? What is your native place? Why did you come? What is your trouble?'[28] In yakshagana the question and answer section is improvised within a set structure, whereas in Karnad's play the question and answer section is a tightly scripted form of exposition. Bhagavata reassures Hayavadana and then encourages him to tell his story: 'You are not alone here. I am here. The musicians are here.' Gesturing to the spectators, he goes on to joke: 'And there is our large-hearted audience. It may be that they fall asleep during a play sometimes. But they are ever alert when someone is in trouble'.[29] With Hayavadana's entrance, Karnad puts the idea of the yakshagana oddolaga to new use in a modern play.

In addition to stage techniques, Karnad reworks popular performance segments, but his reworking completely changes their politics. In the first scene between Padmini and Kapila, Karnad reworks a farcical scene that exists in the repertoires of many sangeet natak companies, who, according to Karnad, most likely adopted it from tamasha and *Nautanki* (a genre of performance named after the heroine one of its most popular stories). Karnad uses the scene to demonstrate Padmini's spunk and quick wit. Karnad's scene is almost identical to the version of the scene that appears in the tamasha repertoire, except that whereas in tamasha the woman gets outwitted, in *Hayavadana* Kapila is outdone. In the tamasha scene the exchange goes like this:

**Man** Is anybody in?

**Woman** No.

**Man** Then you are alone in the house?

**Woman** No.

**Man** Is your husband in?

**Woman** No.

**Man**   Has he gone out?

**Woman**   No.

**Man**   May I come in?

**Woman**   No.

**Man**   Your husband is not in the house?

**Woman**   No.

**Man**   (*Slyly*) Do you mind if I make love to you?

**Woman**   No.[30]

In *Hayavadana* Kapila offers to find Padmini and ask for her hand in marriage on behalf of the lovestruck Devadatta. When Kapila finds Padmini's door, and she opens it, he instantly falls in love and is tongue-tied:

**Padmini**   You knocked, didn't you?

**Kapila**   Er—yes . . .

**Padmini**   Then why are you gaping at me? What do you want?

**Kapila**   I—I just wanted to know whose house this was.

**Padmini**   Whose house do you want?

**Kapila**   This one.

**Padmini**   I see. Then who do you want here?

**Kapila**   The master . . .

**Padmini**   Do you know his name?

**Kapila**   No.

**Padmini**   Have you met him?

**Kapila**   No.

**Padmini**   Have you seen him?

**Kapila**   No.

**Padmini**   So. You haven't met him, seen him or known him. What do you want with him?

. . .

**Kapila**   I—I can't tell you.

**Padmini**   Really! Who will you tell it to?

**Kapila**   Your father . . .

**Padmini**   Do you want my father or do you want the master of this house?

**Kapila**   Aren't they the same?

**Padmini**   (*As though explaining to a child.*) Listen, my father could be a servant in this house. Or the master of this house could be my father's servant. My father could be the master's father, brother, son-in-law, cousin, grandfather, or uncle. Do you agree?

**Kapila**   Er—Yes.

**Padmini**   Right. Then we'll start again. Whom should I call?

**Kapila**   Your father.

**Padmini**   And if he's not in?

**Kapila**   (*Lost.*) Anyone else.

**Padmini**   Which anyone?

**Kapila**   Perhaps—your brother.

**Padmini**   Do you know him?

**Kapila**   No.

**Padmini**   Have you met him?

**Kapila**   No.

**Padmini**   Do you know his name?

**Kapila**   (*Desperate.*) Please, please—call your father or the master or both, or if they are the same, anyone . . . please call someone![31]

Coming right on the heels of the scene with Kapila and Devadatta in which Devadatta speaks of his love for Padmini in the most clichéd terms ('her face is . . . a white lotus'),[32] this scene actually demonstrates that Padmini is much smarter than her stuffy Brahmin husband who can quote Sanskrit poetry and the Vedas but is neither an original thinker nor a creative artist. The scene also establishes the power dynamic between Padmini and Kapila: Padmini talks rings around Kapila, and although the way she giggles with the two women who hold up her entrance curtain is school-girlish (reminding spectators that she is young), it establishes her dominance over Kapila. Karnad has completely shifted the power dynamic of the exchange.

Although some might call the use of a tamasha scene 'appropriation,' the deliberate 'citation' of the 'original' means that, in fact, the scene is not completely taken out of its original context: the power dynamic in the relationship is clear to anyone watching the scene, but to fully appreciate the political shift Karnad has made the spectator has to be familiar with the 'original' that is referenced – meaning the spectator has to place the Karnad scene in the context of the tamasha scene. Only then is the spectator able to reconsider the political assumptions in the tamasha exchange (when a woman says no she means yes) in light of their comparison to the Karnad scene, while also re-examining his or her understanding of Padmini (she's much smarter and more canny than she appears) in the light of her different responses to the same situation.

Playwright, director and critic Safdar Hashmi (1954–89) objected to the use of traditional performance in modern theatre because, he claimed, it brings along 'the traditional content with its superstition, backwardness, obscurantism, and its promotion of feudal structures'.[33] Others claim that when playwrights or directors incorporate Hindu stories, structural elements from Hindu ritual or characters such as the goddess Kali, they are – consciously or unconsciously, actively or passively – playing into and promoting a definition of India that is synonymous with Hindu culture. However, Kali's appearance in *Hayavadana* does anything but use religion as an opiate of the masses or promote a Hindu monoculture. In fact, Karnad uses Kali to critique mindless religious practice. Although the Ganesha puja at the opening of the play is serious business, Kali appears as a farcical character. Karnad gives the following direction for Kali's entrance:

> A tremendous noise of drums. . . . Behind the curtain one sees the uplifted blood-red palms of the goddess. The curtain is lowered and taken away and one sees a terrifying figure, her arms stretched out, her mouth wide open with the tongue lolling out. The drums stop and as the goddess drops her arms and shuts her mouth, it becomes clear she has been yawning.[34]

With Ganesha the gods are with us. With Kali the gods are asleep. When she is awakened, she is extremely cranky and speaks with a hoarse morning-voice.

Karnad uses Kali to poke fun at the way people turn to the gods only when they want something, and mocks the way people reject the gods if they get what they want too often. At the beginning of the play, in an effort to help Hayavadana become a unified being, Bhagavata sends Hayavadana to the same Kali temple that Padmini, Devadatta and Kapila find. In promoting the temple, he says:

> **Bhagavata**: The goddess there is famous for being ever-awake to the call of devotees. Thousands used to flock to her temple once. No one goes now, though.
>
> **Hayavadana**: Why not?
>
> **Bhagavata**: Because she used to give anything anyone asked for. As the people became aware of this they stopped going.[35]

When Hayavadana arrives at the temple, he falls at Kali's feet and begins to say, 'Mother, make me complete . . . .' But before he can say 'make me a complete man', Kali interrupts him and, following the logic of the rest of the play, turns him into a complete horse.[36] Hayavadana later justifies this by saying that being a horse has its advantages, but the audience knows that Kali interrupted him because she was anxious to get back to sleep. In this way, Karnad treats religion in a serious way with the Ganesha puja only to satirise religious practice and belief through Kali.

Karnad criticises social practices as well: both he and Karanth seem to support Padmini's method of circumventing prohibitions against intercaste marriage. In Karanth's 1989 production of the play there is absolutely no chemistry onstage between Padmini (Tara) and Devadatta (Prakash Shenoi). At first this seems like a mistake – a missed opportunity to show that Padmini is equally in love with both men. But what if she isn't? Padmini is the daughter of a wealthy merchant and Devadatta is the son of a Brahmin, but Kapila is the son of a blacksmith. Padmini can't marry Kapila, but she can marry his best friend. She can get what she wants (Kapila) by switching heads at the Kali temple – a scene that takes place outside the city, where the city's restrictions don't apply. She figures out a way around the rules by keeping Devadatta's head: she can keep Kapila with her even when she goes back to the city as his presence in her house and in her bed is masked by Devadatta's face. In the script the switching of heads is accomplished by switching masks, so Kapila would literally be wearing Devadatta's face. On stage this is too cumbersome and confining for the actors, so most directors have scrapped the masks for Devadatta and Kapila, and Karnad now tells people to dispense with them. But masks do make the point more clearly and visually reinforce Padmini's inventiveness.

Karnad argues that the 'energy of folk theatre comes from the fact that although it seems to uphold traditional values, it also has the means of questioning [those] values'.[37] For example, the end of *Hayavadana* seems to uphold the practice of *sati* while actually undermining it: Padmini's story ends when Kapila and Devadatta, no longer able to stand the presence of the other in themselves, kill themselves/each other, and Padmini performs sati. When a widow joins her husband on his funeral pyre both the act and the victim are referred to as sati. The word 'sati' comes from the Sanskrit *sat*, meaning truth. It originally referred to a woman who was 'true to her ideals' – in other words, a virtuous or pious woman. Because *pativrata*, or loyalty to one's husband in the form of taking on his experiences as one's own, has become an ideal for women, sati came to be seen by some as the ultimate act of loyalty and fidelity, bringing honour to both the sacrificed widow and her husband's family.[38] However, sati is both illegal and widely condemned. At first glance it may seem that Karnad supports sati. He presents it as the only possible end for Padmini: none of the characters or chorus members offer her an alternative. Even though it is highly stylised, the enactment of the sati onstage gives it added weight: Padmini stands behind a hand-held curtain painted with flames, which slowly rises as the curtain is lifted in front of her until she is covered, or 'consumed' by them. However, Karnad added an ironic twist: Padmini's sati marks her devotion not to one man, but to two. Her sati is not an expression of loyal devotion to her husband, but to the fulfilment of her own desire and her disregard for societal convention. She refuses to conform to the 'traditional' image of an 'ideal' woman. These examples prove that creating a new genre involves more than simply cutting and pasting performance practices, production values or characters from one genre to another; it involves a deep interrogation of the contexts, politics and practices of both genres on the part of the playwright, director, performers and spectators in a way that makes all involved rethink their relationship to performance traditions and what they mean.

The character who combines acting styles from yakshagana and Western realism to the best advantage is Bhagavata. The bhagavata is a central figure in yakshagana, which is also called *Bhagavata Ata*, because it often tells stories centring around Vishnu – known as Bhagavan in his several incarnations. The person who leads a dramatic performance telling the story of Bhagavan is called the bhagavata. He is in effect principle performer, director and often producer – the one responsible for the success of the production.[39] The bhagavata as a character type is similar to the sutradhara of Sanskrit drama. Many Sanskrit plays begin with a 'curtain speech' by the sutradhara, announcing the title of the play to be performed, and outlining its plot. The sutradhara brings the audience into the play, linking their world outside the theatre with the world of the play. The bhagavata in yakshagana plays a similar role, as does Karnad's Bhagavata.

In yakshagana the term bhagavata is a title, like 'director' or 'stage manager' – it refers to the actual director, who is onstage as himself. If there had been a 'real' bhagavata in *Hayavadana*, it would have been Karanth. The bhagavata in yakshagana is highly skilled in improvisation; most of his dialogue with the other characters is improvised. In *Hayavadana*, Bhagavata's dialogue is scripted but it is written so that it both seems improvised and has the sensibility of improvisation, referencing and valorising oral storytelling practices that were negated by the colonial culture's privileging of written text. Yet Bhagavata's dialogue is carefully crafted to set up thematic resonances and jokes that pay off in later scenes, extremely difficult to accomplish through improvisation. Karnad's script relies on a highly skilled actor while paying homage to the skill of improvisation – layering the two acting styles in one scene.

More importantly, Karnad's Bhagavata functions in a number of different ways, in a number of different contexts. In yakshagana the bhagavata moves the plot forward by narrating gaps in the story that are not enacted in performance: he serves as commentator on and judge of the action; he articulates the unspoken emotions of the characters; he offers advice to the characters; and he steps into the play to sing as the characters themselves.[40] Karnad's Bhagavata performs exactly the same set of functions – operating in several modes and employing a different performance style for each level of reality. Bhagavata is a skilled practitioner of theatrical and cultural ambidexterity.

Bhagavata becomes the model for someone successfully negotiating many different cultural, linguistic and theatrical realities. He is the character most skilled at jumping in and out of the different frames, or levels of reality, that operate in the play. In act two, after the heads have been exchanged, Padmini has been living with the new Devadatta, whose body, governed by the behaviours of the head, has become flaccid. She returns to the new Kapila, whose body (Devadatta's) has also been governed by the head and gotten into shape. Kapila asks why she has come, but she is unable to speak. Bhagavata steps into the scene and speaks for her, as her, to Kapila: 'How could I make you understand? If Devadatta had changed overnight and had gone back to his original form, I would have forgotten you completely. But that's not how it happened. He changed day by day. Inch by inch. Hair by hair. . . . And as I saw him change–I couldn't get rid of you'. He then steps back out of (her) character, and out of the story, to address the spectators: 'That's what Padmini must tell Kapila. She should say more, without concealing anything.' He steps back into the play to address Kapila, again as Padmini: 'Kapila, if that *rishi* had given me to you, would I have gone back to Devadatta someday exactly like this?' He turns again to the spectators, this time not as an uninvolved narrator, but as someone invested in the outcome of the moment: 'But she doesn't say anything. She remains quiet'.[41] Bhagavata has no trouble jumping in and out of different realities, time frames, personae and characters. He is an expert at handling not just complex seeing, but complex being.

Therefore it is no accident that it is Bhagavata who comes up with a solution to Hayavadana's dilemma. At the beginning of act 1, as Bhagavata (in his role as producer/director) is introducing the play (Padmini's story) to the audience, he is interrupted by an Actor (Prakash Shenoi playing the role of The-Actor-about-to-Play-Devadatta) who says he has seen a talking horse (Hayavadana). This is a reference to the way many Sanskrit plays (particularly Bhasa's) begin: the reality of the auditorium is interrupted and engulfed by the fictional reality of the stage. Hayavadana enters, describes his problem, and Bhagavata sends him off (stage) to the Kali temple, accompanied by the Actor. Thus the producer/director of a company (Bhagavata functioning like the yakshagana bhagavata) presenting a play about (the fictional character) Padmini sends one of the Actors who was supposed to appear in that play (Prakash Shenoi as himself) offstage to a temple that is well-known in real-world India, with a fictitious character (Hayavadana) who isn't part of 'the play' (about Padmini) that has been announced. Of course all of this is very obviously part of *Hayavadana*, which has in fact already begun, because Bhagavata and the Actor are clearly characters themselves. Meanwhile, references are continuously being made by Bhagavata to 'the audience' purportedly present in the theatre to see 'the play' – that is, Padmini's story – that Bhagavata and the Actor are there to perform. However, the spectators have actually come to the theatre to see Karnad's play *Hayavadana*, so the spectators are also performing – in the role of an audience seeing a play about Padmini. Bhagavata ties all of these layers together because he is present in and at all levels of reality. Through Bhagavata the play suggests that complexity rather than uniformity provides a more fulfilling answer to the questions of identity raised by Devadatta,

Kapila, Hayavadana and even Ganesha, and that hybridity at all levels is a more useful tool than nationalistic fervour.

## Towards a National Theatre:
## Sangeet Natak Akademi (SNA)

The origins of the roots movement lie in the varied impulses, agendas and experiments of individual artists, but the creative manifestations of this work were formalised, institutionalised and later prescribed by the Sangeet Natak Akademi (SNA), the National Academy of Music, Dance, and Drama in Delhi. The assumptions about theatre and culture that gave rise to the movement were articulated by India's first Prime Minister Jawaharlal Nehru (1889–1964), formalised in the government policy that established the Akademi, and embedded in the Akademi's mission statement and activities. These were designed to create a 'national' theatre that could reflect and constitute a 'national' identity, and in the wake of Independence, partition and the complicated integration of Princely States into the Union, articulate India as a unified, unique nation.[42]

In the 1970s and 1980s the SNA, under the guidance of Suresh Awasthi, who served as Secretary from 1965 to 1975, consciously began to create a 'national' aesthetic. In 1974 Uma Anand, then Assistant Secretary at the SNA, declared the mission accomplished in an article unambiguously titled 'Emergence of a National Theatre in India': '[A] contemporary theatre has emerged, not in any one or other corner of this diverse and large country but simultaneously in all major centers . . . which bears a definite stamp; a unity, if not a uniformity; a character that can only be called national, since it is composed of so many varying facets.'[43] In fact what the Akademi actually created was not a single 'national theatre', but a group of artists spread across the nation who used traditional performance in the making of their modern theatre. Through a series of festivals they produced between 1984 and 1991, the Akademi supported those artists who they determined were working to develop 'a theatre idiom indigenous in character, inspired by the folk/traditional theatre of the country'.[44]

Thus the theatre of roots was from the outset imagined by members of the SNA as a national theatre.

Critics of the movement object to the very idea of a national theatre in such a diverse country. Each of India's twenty-six states has its own political and social history, a large number of culturally diverse subgroups, and its own performing art traditions. Furthermore, each state has its own language: there are seventeen nationally recognised Indian languages[45] and more than 1,652 recognised dialects; while Hindi is the official national language, it is not spoken by a majority of the population. Given India's enormous diversity at the linguistic level alone, a 'national' theatre seems out of the question. What would it be and whose nation would it represent? In fact neither the artists nor the architects of the movement intended to create a uniform national theatre; as Dharwadker points out, 'the quest [was] not so much for a "national theatre" as for a significant theatre *in* and *of* the nation, linked intra-nationally by complex commonalities and mutual self-differentiations'.[46]

To its credit, the SNA supported and promoted a nationwide theatre community. While translation and publication made plays available to readers around the country and contributed to the formation of a modern dramatic canon in India, the seminars organised by the SNA were even more important in terms of establishing a modern Indian theatre: participants from around the country met in person, established contacts and exchanged ideas. This initiated a conversation about the use of traditional performance genres in which artists from a vast number of regions participated, and promoted the spread of a particular theatrical sensibility throughout the nation.

With the financial support of the SNA, the roots movement became the most pervasive and influential post-Independence theatrical movement in India: everyone involved in Indian theatre between the 1960s and the 1990s was either part of it, promoted it, criticised it, worked against it or felt sidelined because of it; everyone working in the theatre since Independence has had to confront it in some way. For many, at the end of the twentieth century, the theatre of roots came to define 'modern Indian theatre' as a whole – and is thus the movement against which people have reacted in the twenty-first century.

## Legacies of the Roots Movement

Playwright Mahesh Dattani has said that without the theatre of roots, without playwrights and directors such as Karnad and Panikkar, 'we wouldn't have a real modern Indian theatre' (2003). He praises playwrights like Karnad who 'have created valuable links between folklore, traditional theatre and the modern Indian audience. They are extremely valuable in creating a modern Indian theatre which is not defined exclusively by urban tastes' (Dattani 2003).

However, in the 1990s, with the theatre of roots so firmly entrenched in modern Indian theatre culture, many people stopped thinking deeply about it, and the movement as a whole began to stagnate. Younger directors and playwrights began to copy artists like Panikkar and Karnad, creating work that was derivative rather than innovative, while many of the artists who had found a satisfactory way of integrating traditional performance into their modern theatre began to repeat themselves, and their work became formulaic. Although the work of individual artists within the movement continued to be interesting and vibrant, the movement as a whole was moribund:

> Unable to "reject" or "kill" (which, in artistic terms, would involve a subversion of the "traditional form"), our theatre artists remain in limbo. They don't know how to free themselves from tradition or live with it without compromising their own truth. In the meantime, they "invent" tradition not so much from an inner necessity, but in deference to larger cultural and political factors that favor a sanctification or dressing up of the past. (Bharucha 1993, p.209)

More than 70 years after Independence, there is no longer a need for a singular answer to the question 'What is Indian theatre?' Artists, as Bhabha puts it, 'are now free to negotiate and translate their cultural identities in a discontinuous intertextual temporality of cultural difference' (1994, p.38). Many theatre artists and institutions are now asking: Why should we be one India? What is the India we are part of? In what way are we a part of it? In this climate, playwrights and directors are challenging and extending the roots movement by addressing the problematics of its working practices, its thematic blind spots and omissions, and the ways in which it has come to define 'Indian theatre'. At the same time, the National School of Drama (NSD) in Delhi, one of the most influential theatrical organisations in the country, is redefining notions of Indian theatre by showcasing a wider range of work in its annual national theatre festivals.

## Challenging the Theatre of Roots: The Plays of Mahesh Dattani

Although Dattani appreciates the contributions individual artists have made to the development of modern Indian theatre, he rejects the way that Indian theatre has come to be defined in terms of traditional performance: 'Does [Indian theatre] mean traditional forms,' he asks:

> Yes, they're wonderful, they're very sophisticated, they're impressive, but are they really India? That's something I would like to question and challenge. Are they really reflecting life as it is now?. . . . What we need to do now is look at those forms and say we're approaching the twenty-first century, this is who we are and this is our legacy, so where do we take that. That's not happening, and that's a matter of serious concern. (1996; see Mee 1997, pp.24–5)

Dattani also rejects the way the roots movement has participated in constructing a set of themes that are considered 'Indian' while others are not: 'You can talk about feminism because in a way that's accepted. But you can't talk about gay issues because that's not India, it doesn't happen here' (1996; see Mee 1997, p.25). Dattani's work challenges commonly held ideas about Indian theatre, Indian subject matter and, by extension, who is considered Indian.

Dattani started out as an actor working in English-language theatre. He wanted to do Indian plays, but didn't like the available translations, so he began to write his own plays, beginning with *Where There's a Will* (1988). Dattani takes as his subject the complicated dynamics of the modern urban family. His characters struggle for some kind of freedom and happiness under the oppressive weight of tradition, cultural constructions of gender and repressed desire. Their dramas are played out on multilevel sets on proscenium stages where interior and exterior become one, and geographical locations are collapsed – in short, his settings are as fragmented as the families who inhabit them. He is concerned with the 'invisible issues' in Indian society: taboo subjects. Homosexuality is one taboo subject that Dattani takes out of the closet and places onstage for public viewing and dialogue. In response to self-proclaimed liberals who complain about his choice of subject matter, Dattani quips: 'I have yet to meet a homosexual who says "I have nothing against heterosexuals, but do we have to watch them onstage?"' (2000, p.xi).

Dattani deals specifically with the ways in which homophobia destroys lives. *Bravely Fought the Queen* (first performed in 1991) centres around two sisters, one of whom is tricked into marrying the man who is having an affair with her brother in order to provide a cover for the forbidden relationship. She escapes by drinking heavily. *Seven Steps around the Fire* (1999) focuses on the murder of Kamala, a *hijra* (the hijra are a community of male eunuchs who, dressed as women, sing and dance at weddings). It turns out Kamala was secretly married to the son of a wealthy government minister. The minister has Kamala killed, and quickly arranges a 'suitable' marriage for his son, who commits suicide at the wedding. In other plays such as *Where There's A Will*, *Dance Like a Man* (1989) and *Tara* (1990), Dattani deals with gender inequality. *Final Solutions* (1993) is about communal hatred between Hindus and Muslims. In *30 Days in September* (2001) and *On a Muggy Night in Mumbai* (1998), he addresses (respectively) incest and the place of gay culture in Indian society.

Dattani's work claims a place for marginalised people onstage and by extension in society, and his work challenges notions of what is acceptable in society and what constitutes acceptable subject matter for Indian theatre. In response to statements that his work is not Indian because of its content, language or style, he states: 'I am Indian: this is my time and this is my place. . . . I'm reflecting that in my work, and that makes it Indian' (1996; see Mee 1997, p.24). Dattani's plays have become part of mainstream theatre in India: his work is produced in Bangalore, Mumbai, Delhi and Chennai; he is the first playwright writing in English to be awarded the prestigious Sahitya Akademi award (in 1998) for his contribution to world drama; and his work is the subject of several critical studies. Dattani has carved out a place for serious English-language theatre that is not at all like the theatre of roots. He is one of a number of artists who are, in various ways, challenging the definition of Indian theatre promoted by the SNA.

## A Global Focus

The roots movement's need to define and talk about India has given way, in some cases, to a wider focus on global issues. Ratan Thiyam's recent production *Chinglon Mapan Tampak Ama* (Nine Hills One Valley, 2005) exemplifies this new trend. *Chinglon Mapan Tampak Ama* takes part in a global conversation about war, violence and prospects for peace. It is an excellent example of an important shift in the theatre: writers and directors are no longer speaking to the world about their region or country (although *Chinglon Mapan Tampak Ama* does that as well), they are speaking to the world about the world from their particular perspective. *Chinglon Mapan Tampak Ama* is also a turning point for the roots movement: it may signal the beginning of an era of roots productions that speak to the world about global issues. In *Chinglon Mapan Tampak Ama* Thiyam positions terrorism and large-scale acts of violence as an indication that society has lost touch with traditions and the teachings of our elders, a message he addresses through the specificity of the Manipuri context. The production opens with seven elderly women who, bent by age and misery, slowly shuffle their way down centre. Programme notes tell us they are guardians of the cultural traditions of the land. Ringing small bells, they invoke the evil spirits in order to dispel them: 'Come, eat your fill and leave us,' they say, stomping and spitting on the ground to scare them away. As they exit, men begin to run in place, exerting enormous effort and getting no closer to the comforting arms of their desperate mothers, who call out 'keep running, my sons!' They collapse, and the mothers call for the *maichous* (scholars, wise men) to wake up and save their children. The grey-haired maichous, lying in a row on their mats, awaken suddenly to cry out the terrors of their nightmares. Frightened, they attempt some *thang-ta* (martial art) arm movements to focus and clear their minds, but when this doesn't work, they decide they belong to a previous age, and go back to sleep. Women begin to perform the *raslila*, a sacred dance often used to represent 'Manipuri culture' at national and international dance festivals, which is both a meditation on the nature of people's relationships to the divine and a practice for interacting with the divine. This representative of a specific culture and embodiment of a worldview is interrupted by Time, a sword-wielding demon who cuts off the dancers' hands by smacking the floor in front of each dancer with his sword. The dancers recoil and turn upstage in pain while Time, who now controls the stage, finishes his wild dance of acrobatic jumping and stomping. As soon as he is gone, the women try to complete their raslila, doing the best they can with flesh-coloured prosthetic stumps from which red scarves dangle. This violent image enters the dreams of the wise men, who wake up and decide to write a new book of knowledge that will speak to the present generation. They learn about modern society and contemporary events by consulting several modern men and women in black trench coats and sunglasses who look as though they belong in a Paris café or a SoHo bar. These men and women take turns reading from actual newspaper headlines that they literally have been bombarded with from offstage: they recite a long litany of bombings and numbers of dead in Daar Es Salaam, New York, Gujarat, Denpasar, London and Baghdad. The wise men use thang-ta movements to drive away the spirits of evil knowledge, and begin writing. In a deeply moving epilogue, lights dim as *diyas* (hand-held oil lamps) are placed onstage, and the actors say together: 'To bring peace and harmony, to put an end to war, let us place our offerings.' While *Chinglon Mapan Tampak Ama* is about violence in the world and the death of specific traditional cultures, what it evokes is a real sense of what will be lost if the events reported in the headlines ultimately become the norm and a way of life. *Chinglon Mapan Tampak Ama* exemplifies the way directors and playwrights are commenting on global issues from their particular perspectives.

## Artists Extending Roots

While Panikkar's work, and by extension the corpus of work belonging to the roots movement, has been called 'decadent' by younger directors in Kerala who want the roots movement to more directly and didactically address social issues, a number of younger directors – most of them women – are using particular genres of traditional performance specifically to address urgent social issues, which they do quite directly. A. Mangai and Tripurari Sharma exemplify this trend: Mangai (whose work I detailed in the previous chapter) uses traditional women's performances to address gender inequalities. Sharma looks at the way women are typically portrayed in khyal, Nautanki, tamasha, *pandvani* (a genre of musical storytelling that originated in the Chhattisgarh region), and attempts to expand their repertoires to include more feminist takes on women, at the same time addressing inequalities in the working relationship between urban theatre artists and these performers. Tripurari Sharma extends the practices of the roots movement by dealing with the politics of working relationships between performers of traditional genres and artists in the modern theatre. Sharma graduated from the NSD in Delhi in 1979, when the political street theatre movement was gaining momentum. Not all of Sharma's work is street theatre, but her work does reflect the concerns and agendas of the movement. She has dealt with a broad range of topics: communalism, the effect of the dollar on the Indian economy, governmental corruption and rape. Sharma's work takes several forms: she and her company Alarippu (Blossoming) perform plays in the streets and conduct theatre workshops with children; she develops plays and productions collectively in community workshops; and she redirects classical plays in mainstream theatre spaces. Sharma is dedicated to giving voice to those who are not often heard and to political issues that are not being discussed. In conversation, as well as in her methods of work and in her productions, Sharma is not interested in providing answers or solutions to problems. She is more interested in opening dialogue, presenting multiple points of view and providing a forum for exchange. Some of her most famous productions include a re-examination of the female characters in Mohan Rakesh's *Aadhe Adhure* (Halfway House) and a production of her own play *Kaath ki Gadi* (The Wooden Cart), which dealt with the stigmatisation of people with leprosy. Sharma's recent work continues her focus on gender. She spent five years, from 1994 to 1999, on a project with performers of khyal, Nautanki, tamasha, pandvani, and the members of Surabhi, a sangeet natak company, to see how women could be portrayed in a new way through these five genres (see Sharma 1999, pp.99–132). Sharma has seen numerous examples of urban artists spending a few months learning a traditional performance, adapting it for their own use and presenting it as part of a production for a Delhi audience. She exemplifies the group of artists that has determinedly rejected that model, using performers trained in traditional genres to present new work for their usual audiences as well as for audiences in Delhi. Her idea was to generate new scripts, or new treatments of old scripts, that would present women in a new light within the techniques and structures of the traditional performance genres. Although her work culminates in public performances, her focus has been on the process, on seeing if she can devise a model of interaction that is not neocolonial. In *Mahabharat Se* (first performed in 2002 at the NSD) Sharma worked with Shanti Bai Chelak, a well-known pandvani performer, and Sapna Sand, an NSD graduate and former member of the NSD Repertory Company. Pandvani is a solo art, an improvisational telling of stories from the *Mahabharata*. Sharma, Chelak and Sand chose two female characters from the epic to focus on: the well-known Draupadi and the relatively unknown Bhanumati (Duryodhana's wife). Sand played Draupadi and Chelak played Bhanumati, a character not in the pandvani repertoire but whose story and perspective were in this case placed centre stage. Here both Bhanumati and Draupadi spoke for themselves rather than being spoken for by men, and their interior monologues were given theatrical time and space. During the workshop and rehearsal process (which took place in three segments over the course of a year) Chelak and Sand exchanged acting techniques. From Chelak, Sand learnt the methods of improvisation, singing and episodic structuring of narrative that are characteristic of pandvani. From Sand, Chelak learnt how to sustain a character; pandvani usually focuses on a single episode, and the storyteller has to jump in and out of several roles, whereas here Chelak had to sustain a single character through several different episodes. Their process of exchange became part of the performance: in an early scene Chelak literally upstages Sand, who can't keep up with Chelak's singing or movement. Here Chelak's expertise and training in pandvani is foregrounded and performed. The actors end up taking turns telling the story, each using her own skills to bring different sections of the narrative alive, and inhabiting her own space on the bare stage (Chelak stage right and Sand stage left), supported by a row of musicians spread across the upstage area behind them. Their costumes emphasise the difference in their artistic backgrounds: Chelak is dressed in a sari and jewellery characteristic of pandvani, while Sand is dressed in what look like rehearsal clothes: leggings and a loose, comfortable top. Towards the end of the piece they begin to work together, joining together down centre; the rehearsal process is mirrored onstage, and becomes one of the thematic elements of the piece itself.

## Unremarked Roots

Most actors involved in the roots movement – either as company members or freelance actors – were not trained deeply in the genres they used. Panikkar and Thiyam have had the time and money to train their actors in the variety of genres they engage with, but most directors have not had this luxury. There is now a new generation of artists deeply trained in the genres they engage. And unlike earlier actors (particularly those who participated in the SNA's Scheme of Assistance to Young Theatre Workers) their training goes largely unremarked; the focus is not on the 'traditional idiom' employed, but on the work it allows the artist to create. In fact, many of them don't consider themselves to be part of the roots movement at all. For example, Maya Rao is known for her episodic multimedia solo performances, which take on political and social issues through physical and musical metaphor. Although trained in kathakali, she has said that she is 'searching for a way to transpose our traditional theatre into a contemporary mode' (in Kumar 1998, p.3); and is 'looking for a physical language where every action may resonate with a multiplicity of meanings. The eventual form is not kathakali, yet inspired by it' (in NSD 2007, p.19). In fact, her kathakali training is not self-consciously foregrounded in the work itself.

In *A Deep Fried Jam* (2002) which she calls a 'socio-political cabaret', Rao weaves rock music (played live by an onstage one-man rock band) with video projections, spoken poetry and movement sequences to comment on 'everything from war to food' in urban life. In this piece, Rao asserts that 'the various actions connected with cooking, like steaming, baking, flattening, become metaphors for events and situations in other spheres of our lives' (NSD 2002, p.88). In one of the sequences, Rao, wearing a purple-sequined outfit with a studded black leather belt, slides her bottom along the floor then turns suddenly to say over her shoulder: 'I'm sorry we don't deal in it any more. We could have it arranged for your . . .' – and she turns to face front again, lies flat on her back, opens her legs, and says: 'satisfaction'. In another episode she chants: 'We're doing fine, fine, fine. . . . We're doing fine, fine, fine . . .' and ends by stomping on the ground as if she is stomping on someone, or stomping out a fire. Although her footwork is typical of kathakali, it takes on an entirely new meaning in this context. Rao's work indicates that the roots movement has gotten to a point where the roots themselves don't have to be demonstrated in an obvious way.

All of the artists discussed here (in addition to the work of women directors discussed in the previous chapter) exemplify the numerous ways artists are now challenging the definitions of India and Indian theatre that the roots movement embodied, in terms of subject matter, style, training, rehearsal practice and marketing.

## *Redefining Indian Theatre at the NSD:* A New National Theatre Festival

In 1999 the NSD organised the first Bharat Rang Mahotsav (BRM), a national theatre festival, to both honour 50 years of independence and expose their students to the most important and innovative work going on around the country.

The BRM was so successful that it has become an annual event. In 1999 there were 32 plays in 11 languages from 13 states; 15 of the productions could be considered part of the roots movement. Other productions at the festival included: *Baraat Chali London Ko*, a two-and-a-half-hour solo performance in which actor Laxman Deshpande uses a single piece of cloth to transform himself into the 52 characters necessary to tell the story of a young man from a conservative Maharashtrian family who goes to London and falls in love with an English girl; *Khanabadosh*, a naturalistic adaptation of the autobiographical writings of Punjabi short-story writer Ajit Kaur that focuses on the romantic relationship between Kaul and an emotionless Oma; *Sundari – An Actor Prepares*; *Gandhi vs. Gandhi* directed by C. Basavalingaiah, about the fraught relationship between the Mahatma and his son, produced with documentary-like pictorial realism in costume and make-up; and Mohan Maharishi's *Einstein* in which the linear story of Einstein's life and contribution to modern conceptualisations of time and space is broken up by the simultaneous presence of three different Einsteins from three different times (child Einstein, young Einstein and the grown Albert Einstein). Thus the NSD festival was significantly different from earlier national theatre festivals organised by the SNA, which were limited primarily to plays, playwrights and directors the SNA determined to be part of the roots movement. Instead, the NSD, as one of the most powerful theatre institutions in the nation, chose to recognise and promote, at the national level, a wider variety of work. The message sent to students and to the Delhi audiences is that there is more to Indian theatre than the theatre of roots.

Although the wide variety of work represented at the 1999 BRM was representative of what had been happening for a long time throughout the country, it was finally recognised at a festival billing itself as 'national'. The second BRM in 2000 featured 82 productions from 20 states in 18 languages, of which roughly 19 could be said to belong to the roots movement. The NSD's stated intention for the 2000 BRM was to mirror 'Indian Theatre in all its variety reflecting its strength and failings, tenor and texture, trends and thematic patterns, diversities and complexities' (NSD 2003, p.17). In 2001 the BRM presented 72 productions from 20 states in 19 languages, of which about 18 were of the theatre of roots – a number that got smaller from year to year as the NSD continued to recognise the entire contemporary theatrical scene, and not just promote one particular movement. In 2002 the BRM featured 139 productions from 24 states and 1 Union Territory, in 22 Indian languages, including a mini-festival on street theatre. This was the first year that the BRM included 5 international companies (from Bangladesh, South Korea, Germany, Israel and Mauritius). This marks an important moment: instead of fiercely guarding and protecting 'Indian theatre' from outside influence, the NSD began to introduce its students to international work, formally and officially opening up to foreign influence. The festivals in 2003, 2004, 2005 and 2006 continued these trends. Other theatre festivals continue to be held in cities such as Kolkata, Ujjain and Mumbai (where the Prithvi Theatre organises a major festival every year) and at the newly constructed Rangashankara in Bangalore. Currently, however, the NSD is the biggest, most heavily attended, widest ranging and the only festival that claims to represent the entire nation's theatre, as it consciously participates in the construction of modern Indian theatre in the new millennium.

### Remaking Tradition . . . Again: The 2007 BRM

The ninth annual BRM in Delhi ushered in a new era in modern Indian theatre. First, organisers did not issue an automatic invitation to the 25 directors considered to be the most important in India as they had earlier, but asked everyone to submit applications, including a video/DVD of a new production (one that had its premiere within a year of the application deadline). Very few of the older generation of directors applied, and fewer still were accepted. The festival cleared a space for the work of a younger generation of artists, allowing audiences to see the most recent work and the newest developments and experiments in theatre.

The title of the associated seminar, 'Theatre: Making/Remaking Traditions', reflected the overall focus of the festival. The 51 productions at the festival included adaptations and reinterpretations of Kalidasa, Aeschylus, Sophocles, Strindberg, Chekhov, Kafka, Gombrowicz, Ionesco, Tagore and others. Whereas many directors such as Rajinder Nath have made it a point to direct only plays by Indian playwrights, and earlier festivals exclusively showcased productions of Indian plays, the 2007 BRM acknowledged that 'modern Indian theatre has come back again and again to the classics of world drama and the works of the major Indian playwrights; and simultaneously dramatised masterworks of fiction, both Indian and foreign' (NSD 2007, p.10). They had begun the process of reconfiguring the canon of modern plays, playwrights, productions and directors to reflect the presence of those productions that deal with 'non-Indian' material.

The biggest change was the 2007 festival's global reach, with 13 productions from outside India: China, Japan, South Korea, Australia, Iran, Uzbekistan, Poland, Germany, Switzerland, Pakistan, Sri Lanka, Nepal and Bangladesh. NSD Chairperson Amal Allana said in her address at the inaugural ceremony on 6 January, parts of which were reprinted in the festival brochure, that 'the presence of an international component in our festival not only affords us the opportunity to see the best of world theatre, but also allows us to draw and make connections between cultures, as well as to see Indian theatre in a global context' (NSD 2007, p.10). Her remarks demonstrate a theatrical self-confidence that has emerged in the last 15 years. While the definition of Indian theatre set forth by the roots movement was problematic, it should be credited for establishing a theatre that artists could claim as 'Indian', even as they fought its limitations. Having established an 'Indian theatre' (however problematic) it was now safe to look outward again.

Festival organisers noted the 'shift over the last two decades from a predominantly verbal theatre to a theatre of mixed means, aiming to reach beyond the limits of a particular language' (10). This shift is a direct result of such directors as Panikkar, Karanth and Thiyam; playwrights such as Karnad; and institutions like the SNA – all part of the roots movement. Concluding that 'dance has thus come to be a major point of reference for theatre' (10), the festival included 13 dance pieces, from Padmini Chettur's *Paperdoll* in which five dancers dressed in white explore physical possibilities and limitations while lined up in a row against the back wall of the theatre and attached by the hands as if they are a chain of paper dolls; to *Behati Ganga*, a physicalised dialogue between a mother and her unborn child, characterised not by hand gestures but by abstract physicalisations of internal emotions and sensations, including an enactment of giving birth; to *The Field*, in which dancers sway while perched on top of flexible four-meter poles.

Theatre productions at the festival that originated in India included Alyque Padamsee's *Macbeth* in tights, fake beards and British accents in which Lady Macbeth literally got off on the idea of her husband as king; a series of Chekhov farces played exclusively for laughs; a historical play about mill workers and their relationship to the complicated politics of Mumbai, played out in front of a cubist rendition of the Mumbai skyline; a vaudeville clown show of Ionesco's *The Chairs*; and a production of *King Lear* that begins on the sandy heath with a group of homeless vagabonds attending to Lear.

Several pieces in the 2007 BRM took the roots movement to new realms. One of the pieces I found most interesting for the way it combined bharatanatyam with rap, puppetry, expressionist lighting and a recorded soundscape with everything from calming music to radio news to the breath sounds of someone clearly terrified, was *Kaikeyi*, a solo exploration of the title character who is usually seen as the villainess in the *Ramayana*, a woman who manoeuvred Rama out of his rightful place on the throne. In this piece performer Geeta Chandran (b. 1962) re-examines Kaikeyi's place in society, offering a new look at the reasons for her political machinations. Chandran brought together her training in bharatanatyam and carnatic vocal music together with her experience working in television, film, theatre, dance education and journalism to create a piece in which she combined bharatanatyam with *tai chi chuan*, and variously spoke, sang and enacted formative moments in Kaikeyi's dealings with the political machinery of Ayodhya.

The future of the BRM and its impact on Indian theatre remain to be seen. Currently, however, the BRM is important because of the way it showcases and therefore validates a wide range of theatre. By recognising the diversity from around the country, and introducing students to theatre from around the world, the NSD continues to redefine Indian theatre and what it means to be Indian in India – a continuation of the work begun by the theatre of roots movement.

# CHAPTER 9
## MODERN SOUTHEAST ASIAN DRAMA

Virtually every chapter until this one has centred upon the drama and theatre of a single nation or culture. This chapter is unique as its focus is an entire geographic area, not a single nation. 'Southeast Asia' as a designation is a bit problematic, as it presents rather different cultures by reason of a linked geography and history. Included in this region are predominantly Hindu, Buddhist, Muslim and Christian nations, nations that have undergone both similar and radically different colonial experiences, and similar and different relationships with China, Japan and the West. All have known internal and external conflicts in the twentieth century, stability and instability, and a variety of governments. As the designation 'Southeast Asia' is, at heart, a geographic one, for our purposes we will divide Southeast Asia geographically into two areas: mainland Southeast Asia, consisting of the nations of Vietnam, Laos, Cambodia, Thailand and Myanmar, and Maritime Southeast Asia, consisting of the nations of Brunei, Malaysia, Indonesia, The Philippines, Singapore and East Timor.[1]

We would also note, however, that the nation states of Southeast Asia are colonial constructs; products of European divisions involving separations of people who were, before colonisation, part of a single group as well as the joining of different ethnicities into a single nation state where before no such thing existed. As a result, the nations of Southeast Asia have also faced unique challenges in the twentieth century in establishing national identities unlike those faced in East Asia.

Most, although not all, Southeast Asian nations follow the same paradigm: first is drama of colonial modernity, a spoken drama patterned after the model of the coloniser which then becomes a drama of colonial resistance. The one notable exception to this is Thailand, which was never colonised, but whose ruler at the beginning of the twentieth century embraced modern Western drama. The second phase is drama of new identity in postcolonial period. After independence, the nations of Southeast Asia sought to define themselves and develop new identities in the face of new challenges, including wars, interracial conflicts and oppressive regimes. More recently, contemporary pluralism defines modern Southeast Asian theatre, with two key developments being the rise of the musical and the evolution of social action theatre, which is theatre for social and political change. The rise of globalism and the post-Cold War global economy, the advent and threat of AIDS and HIV, the growing impact of women in traditionally patriarchal societies, and the challenges of living in multicultural, multilingual and multiethnic societies represent issues tackled with regularity in the theatre. Note that these different types of drama do not represent a progression but rather the types of theatre that develop in Southeast Asia (among others) concurrently.

In this chapter we will begin with a brief overview of each area and then explore the development of the separate nation states and the late nineteenth- and twentieth-century histories of the people of Southeast Asia. The nations will be engaged in alphabetical order. Note that each of these nations has a rich pre-colonial history that, given space limitations, we must surpass and begin with the colonial period as that is when modern drama begins. To do so, however, is not to suggest that Southeast Asia has no history, identity or drama before the encounters with the West.


## Mainland Southeast Asia

As with Maritime Southeast Asia, modern theatre on the mainland is the product of the colonial experience and a manifestation of colonial modernity. French Indochine (Indochina), as it was called, was the French colony that covered much of the Southeast Asian peninsula – Vietnam, Laos and Cambodia, which were treated as a single political entity until separated by independence in 1954. The very name 'Indochina' was formed by combining 'India' and 'China', promptly ignoring the indigenous reality of the peninsula and instead referring to the two larger cultures to either side of the north of the peninsula. As a result, we might see mainland Southeast Asia as a 'space between' – influenced by and influencing India and China, as well as each other, yet each nation uniquely its own. It is also an area that has known many wars and internal conflicts through much of the twentieth century, from early wars of independence, conflicts between nation states on the peninsula, Second World War, further wars of independence from France and then against the United States and its allies from the early 60s until 1975, followed by oppressive regimes within, such as the Khmer Rouge in Cambodia and the Hmong genocide in Laos in the 1970s. Many of the internal conflicts can be directly traced as a result of colonialism, as noted above.

## Cambodia

Cambodia had a robust traditional theatre, itself full of hybrid forms, that was devastated in the wake of the 1970–5 Cambodian Civil War. Modern spoken drama began in Cambodia in the 1950s as lakhon niyeay. Pioneered by Hang Tun Hak (1926–75), a Cambodian student in France in the 1950s who returned to begin writing what he called 'national drama' (lakhon chiet), the new form began as French plays performed sometimes in their original language and sometimes in Khmer translations, directed by Hang, who also taught actors Western-style realism. He also wrote original plays, many of which are considered modern classics, such as *The Sun is Rising* (Preah arthit reah haey) and *Our Elders* (Ream chbong yeung). His plays attacked corruption in the ruling classes and used political satire.

The civil war ended in 1975, with the victory of the Khmer Rouge and the establishing of the so-called 'killing fields'. Under dictator Pol Pot, the Khmer Rouge destroyed social and cultural institutions, executing intellectuals and artists by the thousands, including Hang Tun Hak. An estimated ninety per cent of artists died during the Pol Pot regime. In 1979, the Khmer Rouge government was again overthrown and Cambodia began the slow process of healing. While the government supports the arts and universities offer classes in both traditional performance and spoken drama, lakhon niyeay remains a marginal form. Modern hybrid productions, however, such as *Samritechak* (2002), Sophiline Cheam Shapiro's Cambodian classical court dance (robam kbach boraan) adaptation of Shakespeare's *Othello*, are popular at international theatre festivals and on tour, as they combine familiar stories from the West with 'exotic' performance forms from Asia.[2]

## Laos

Theatre in the Lao People's Democratic Republic (Laos), nominally a communist nation with a strongly Buddhist population, remains dominated by traditional forms, both sung storytelling and royal court dances with strong Thai and Cambodian influences. Modern spoken drama, called lakhon vao (literally, 'spoken drama'), did not emerge until recently. Even dance or sung drama in which multiple performers playing an extended narrative developed only in the 1920s, when Thai Likay companies, discussed below, performed in Lao-speaking parts of Thailand and northern provinces of Laos. Beginning in the 1970s, lakhon vao began to emerge under the influence of Western popular culture, but modern spoken drama remains profoundly underrepresented in Laotian performing arts.

## Myanmar (Burma)

On the west side of the Southeast Asian peninsula, the country was colonised by Britain following a series of wars in the late nineteenth century. Known as Burma, the territory served as a site for major combat during the Second World War between the British and the Japanese. Independence followed in 1948, but a 1962 military coup left the nation under the leadership of a repressive military junta. In 1989, the ruling generals changed the name of the nation to the Republic of the Union of Myanmar, an act that remains controversial and contested. As this is the name under which the nation is officially recognised, we use it here, but many prefer to continue to employ the name Burma.

Traditional Burmese culture has dance dramas and puppet plays. Within Burmese dramaturgy there are no purely tragic plays in the Western sense – dramas always end happily. A modern theatre began to evolve in the beginning of the twentieth century based on British and American realism. When the Japanese occupied Burma during the war, modern plays grew in popularity, particularly as a form of resistance. As in many Asian nations, the modern theatre found only a small, educated audience for much of the twentieth century.

The plays, called pya zat ('new plays'), are modern, spoken drama which use modern costumes and contemporary music and are often comedies. They tend to deal with issues of urbanisation and modernisation. The first pya zat appeared in the 1940s when Thakin Kodaw Hming (1875–1964), called 'the Burmese George Bernard Shaw', used satire and dramas about contemporary life to promote a nationalist agenda. First prime minister U Nu (1907–95) also wrote dramas on social and religious issues. His best known play was *The People Win Through* (Pyi thu aung than, 1951), a critique of communism. Pya zat thrived from independence through the 1980s, but it has declined since due to changing tastes and competition from film and television. More recently, performance art, experimental theatre and hybrid adaptations of Western plays are on the rise in the first decade of the twenty-first century.

## Thailand

Thai drama has been profoundly shaped by Indian, Lao, Burmese, Cambodian and Chinese influences, and in turn has had a profound influence on Laotian and Cambodian culture, among others. Thailand is also the only Southeast Asian nation that was never colonised, which made it an exception to the model of modern drama and theatre present through Western colonisers. As a result, Thailand was slow to develop spoken drama based on Western models, although it had several modern hybrid theatres developed from the combination of the indigenous drama and theatre traditions of its own people and its neighbours. Thailand has a strong traditional theatre at all levels of society, from rural village performance forms such as manora to a variety of court dances, such as lakon fai nai, from masked dance drama called khon to shadow puppets called nang. The modern theatre has gone through waves and troughs of practice and popularity. Bangkok, the capital, is also the centre of modern theatre; historically that is where the modern theatre developed. The National Theatre, built in the 1930s and remodelled in 1967, is arguably the nation's most important modern theatre space.

The most popular modern theatre is a hybrid, commercial form called Likay, which mixes classical dance, modern music, contemporary Western and classical Thai costume, and melodramatic stories. Likay most likely emerged in the late nineteenth century, but scholars and historians cannot agree on an exact origin point. The form itself is improvisational and involves direct address of the audience. The stories can be traditional folk tales, taken from classical Thai literature, borrowed from Western narratives, based on historic incidents, or even from current events. Actors play stock character roles and the dialogue and song lyrics are all improvised. As this description depicts, Likay is a true hybrid theatre, blending both indigenous and imported performance traditions.

Lakon phut, modern spoken drama, was first produced in 1904 by Prince Vajiravudh (1881–1925) in a one-hundred-seat theatre he constructed after attending theatre while being educated at Sandhurst and Oxford. He is known as the Father of Modern Thai Theatre. Early modern drama was for a very small group of educated aristocrats with a taste for things Western. Vajiravudh, who would become King Rama VI, wrote more than one hundred plays, mostly melodramas and farces. He also translated three of Shakespeare's plays into Thai: *As You Like It*, *Merchant of Venice* and *Romeo and Juliet*. Audiences for these plays were limited to a very small group of educated elite and the form did not find a larger milieu, and lakon phut has remained an elitist form for much of the twentieth century. It did, however, benefit from the government policies of westernisation from 1938 to 1944. This policy, however, mainly resulted in the modernisation of indigenous forms, such as the blending of classical Thai dance with modern Western music.

Western-style playwriting and acting did not truly emerge until the sixties, when Chulalongkorn University and Thammasat University established drama departments to promote lakon phut in Thailand. In both cases, the programmes were offshoots of departments of foreign languages and their influence did not move much past the campus and urban environments. Modern drama was dominated in the 1960s and 1970s by university theatre. Teachers and students translated, read and mounted Western dramas, notably post-war American magical realism in the form of *A Streetcar Named Desire* and *Death of a Salesman*, as well as Shakespeare's *Macbeth* and *A Midsummer Night's Dream*. Towards the end of the 1960s, as in the rest of Asia, the theatre grew more political.

In the wake of the 1973 student uprising, the theatre grew socially and politically active. Crescent Moon Theatre Company (Prachansiew), created by students at Thammasat University and led by Widhayakorn Chingkul and Suthart Swardsri, staged a number of protest plays against the older generation and political oppression. Absurdist, surrealist and experimental plays emerged. The right wing coup of 1976 ended radical theatre, and while subsequent generations have been less politically active, the tradition of socially conscious modern drama has been kept alive by a number of theatre companies focusing on the plight of children living in poverty, the dilemmas faced by prostitutes, and AIDS and HIV education.

Lakon phut has transformed into lakon phut samai mhai ('modern spoken theatre'), a more inclusive conceptual category that includes non-realistic experimental theatre, musicals, hybrid forms and drama for social action. Modern Thai theatre expanded between 1980 and 1995, finally becoming popular in the late 1990s. In the 1990s the government promoted the writing of modern Thai plays and provided greater support for modern theatre.[3] Nevertheless, modern drama still does not attract mass audiences and faces challenges from the film and television industries, competing not only for audiences but also for artists, as the best directors, writers and actors are often hired to work primarily in those industries.

## Vietnam

Following the paradigm we have seen so far, modern Vietnamese drama is rooted in Western models established first in written drama and then in theatrical performance. As with Tokyo, Seoul and Shanghai, Hanoi was the urban centre where modern drama began to develop. Modern Western-style drama in Vietnam first appeared under French colonial rule in 1915 when Nguyễn Văn Vĩnh (1882–1936) translated Moliere into Vietnamese. Five years later, on 25 April 1920 the Khai Trí Tiến Đức (Association for the Intellectual and Moral Training of the Vietnamese), a cultural organisation dedicated to the modernisation of Vietnamese culture, gave a performance of Moliere's *The Imaginary Invalid* in Hanoi. Phạm Quynh then translated Corneille's *Le Cid* and *Horace*, which were then published in the journal *Nam Phong*. This new form of drama was given the name kịch nói, which means 'spoken play' or 'spoken drama' in Vietnamese. The playwrights who followed Phạm Quynh used French neoclassical comedy and tragedy as models, such as Vũ Đình Long (1896–1960), whose *The Cup of Poison* (*Chén thuốc độc*) was first performed on 22 October 1921 in Hanoi and is considered the first kịch nói drama.

Social and political conflict as a result of colonialism and French imperialism dominated Vietnam for much of the twentieth century. Nguyễn Sinh Cung, better known by his *nomme d'guerre* Hồ Chí Minh (1890–1969), originally petitioned for independence for Vietnam from French colonial rule in 1919 at the Versailles Peace conference that ended the First World War. Ignored by the West, he began a nationalist movement in Vietnam, the Viet Minh, that quickly transformed into an anti-Japanese resistance at the beginning of the Second World War and Japan's occupation of much of Southeast Asia.

In 1930, nationalist revolts against the French failed and the Communist Party of Indochina was created. The period from 1930 to the beginning of the Second World War was one of rapid transformation and political unrest. The modern theatre alternated between directly addressing the struggle and providing subtle dramas of resistance and providing escapist fare that focused on psychological realism while ignoring the larger social and political issues of the day.

Vũ Trọng Phụng (1912–39), a realist novelist and professional journalist, wrote *Not an Echo* (*Không một tiếng vang*, 1931), a critical and popular success on stage in Hanoi. Vi Huyền Đắc (1899–1976), already well-known as a novelist, achieved greater fame as a realist playwright. His work from this period includes the realistic dramas *Singer Yen* (Cô đầu Yến, 1930), *Miss Minh, Director* (Cô đốc Minh, 1931) and *Money* (Kim tiền, 1938), and the comedy *Mr. Secretary Cop* (Ông Ký Cóp, 1938).[4] More political fare could be found in Monsieur Franco-Annamite (*Ông Tây An-nam*, 1931), an anti-colonial play by Nam Xương (pen name of Nguyễn Cát Ngạc, 1905–58), that satirised Francophile intellectual elites.

During the Second World War, Vichy France was forced by the German occupiers to surrender Indochina to Germany's ally Japan. Japan occupied Vietnam and exploited its resources to aid in the war effort in the South Pacific, leading to a famine in 1945. The Japanese occupation also brought censorship and a considerable reduction in dramatic activity, although dramatist and screenwriter Nguyễn Huy Tưởng (1912–60) wrote the plays *Vũ Như Tô* (1943), which deals with the ethical obligations of an artist in a corrupt society, *Cột đồng Mã Viện* (1944) and *Bắc Sơn* (1945), a critique of collaboration, during the occupation, although the first was not performed until 1995.

In August 1945, after the end of the War, Hồ Chí Minh declared Vietnam independent and took over the colonial capital of Hanoi in North Vietnam. A month later, in September, Nationalist Chinese forces arrived, looting Hanoi and ignoring most of the rest of the nation, while simultaneously in France General Charles de Gaulle announced that France would not abandon any of its colonies after the war.[5] In late 1946, the French began to reassert control over parts of French Indochina, meeting strong armed resistance from the Viet Minh. The French were able to control the cities, but the rural areas remained firmly in resistance control. The French tried to maintain control by reorganising the colony into autonomous (but not independent) vassal states, but the Communist takeover of mainland China in 1949 gave the Viet Minh an ally and supplier of arms and support. While the French attempted to break the link between the

Viet Minh and the People's Republic of China, the conflict escalated and the colonial power was forced to send more and more troops to Indochina. Defeated at Điện Biên Phủ in Summer, 1954, the French began peace negotiations and divided French Indochine into four nation states: Laos, Cambodia, North Vietnam (with its capital in Hanoi) and the Republic of Vietnam (RVN, AKA 'South Vietnam' with its capital in Saigon).

The two Vietnams were never intended to remain separate nation. The powers of the West did not want a single nation under communist rule to exist in Southeast Asia, particularly after the emergence of the People's Republic of China (PRC) five years before and the situation on the Korean peninsula; thus, the country was artificially divided into two in hopes that RVN, a constitutional monarchy, would subsume North Vietnam as a single nation in support of the West. Instead, a military coup overthrew the monarchy and a dictatorship under Ngô Đình Diệm began. A communist rebellion began in the South, aided by the North. In 1963 a second military coup followed, and President Diệm was shot in an alleged CIA-backed assassination.

From the 1964 Gulf of Tonkin Incident through the escalation of the war, the January 1968 Tet Offensive (instead of the traditional cease fire at Tet, a Buddhist celebration, the Viet Cong launched a series of attacks that militarily were a tactical victory for American forces but a significant loss in the public eye, leading to slow drawdown), and the eventual defeat and withdrawal of American forces in April 1975 as Saigon and Phnom Penh fell, the conflict destroyed large parts of the Vietnamese countryside and devastated cities. Theatrical activity slowed, although it never stopped. It is estimated that from 1954 to 1975, 3.8 million violent deaths occurred in Vietnam from war and war-related activities.[6]

During the American War (as it was known in Vietnam), propaganda plays were staged against the Americans in the North, providing a form of theatrical resistance. Following reunification after the war, southern dramatists and theatre artists were charged with anti-communism and 'Americanism' and imprisoned or 're-educated'. Kịch nói remained firmly rooted on socialist realism following the Russian model. After China invaded Vietnam in 1979, Russian plays became the dominant model and a period of anti-Chinese drama followed in the 1980s. In the following decade, however, the Sixth Party Congress in 1986 declared the new national policy of 'renovation' (Đổi mới), which brought about market reforms, decentralisation and de-collectivisation. The government also began to aggressively promote modern drama, sponsoring no less than twenty-three kịch nói companies in which socialist realism dominated.

The new generation of artists to emerge after 1986 combined disillusioned idealism with critiques of corruption, conspicuous consumption and even socialism in general. Emblematic of this period is Lưu Quang Vũ (1948–88), whose play *Trương Ba's Soul in the Butcher's Skin* (Hồn Trương Ba da hang thịt, 1988) uses the allegory of a chess player's soul trapped in a butcher's body to critique how a corrupt government corrupts its people. Lưu Quang Vũ and his wife and son died in an automobile accident that many be controversial, as he was a dissident voice at a time when the government grew more conservative. Other playwrights have engaged the United States in more complex ways than the evil Other depicted in plays of national identity in the 1960s and 1970s. *She Yearns for her Husband at the Sound of the Midnight Drum* (Dạ Cổ Hoài Lang, 1994) by Thanh Hoàng was one of the most popular and long-running plays of the last decade of the twentieth century, and features a Vietnamese-American character called 'The Girl' who interrogates the differences between her two homelands and raises the issue of the identity of the displaced 'boat people' who fled South Vietnam after the fall of Saigon.[7]

In the last two decades, experimental theatre and new hybrids have all developed on the stages of Vietnam. Experimental Little Theatre (Sân khấu nhỏ) was both local spoken theatre in Ho Chi Minh City in the 1990s and modern drama with its foreign content removed. It was both nostalgic and forward-looking. The 5B Vo Van Tan Experimental Stage Club was the most dynamic space and company, staging the most innovative and cutting edge plays in Vietnam. *Dạ Cổ Hoài Lang* premiered there. The performances at 5B were more experimental than traditional kịch nói, and employed more comedy. It should be noted, however, that due to shifts in audience tastes and the attempts to increase audience size, in the twenty-first century some artists feel that *Sân khấu nhỏ* has grown superficially.[8] The modern Vietnamese theatre scene remains vibrant, however.

## Maritime Southeast Asia

Maritime Southeast Asia consists of an archipelago of tens of thousands of islands that can be subdivided into several smaller archipelagos, bounded by the Southeast Asian peninsula to the north, Australia to the south, the Pacific Ocean to the east and the Indian Ocean to the west. Malaysia, Singapore and Brunei share a common history, language and ethnic mix and as a result develop similar modern theatres, which are also shared with parts of Indonesia. Indonesia, however, was also colonised by the Dutch and developed several modern theatres. East Timor, colonised by the Portuguese, and the Philippines, first colonised by the Spanish and then by the United States, developed different modern spoken dramas.

## Brunei

Brunei is a sultanate on the northwest coast of the island of Borneo, surrounded by Malaysia, and predominantly Muslim. Malay is the official language. Although much of the sixteenth century saw Brunei successfully at war with Spain to prevent a Spanish puppet being placed on the throne, in 1888 it became a British protectorate. Oil was discovered in 1929, making Brunei of sudden greater strategic importance. In the wake of the Second World War, as in much of South East Asia, Brunei sought and gained independence in the 1950s.

Brunei had an early hybrid modern drama called *bangsawan* (also known as Malay Opera) which it shared with Malaysia, a popular form that developed in the late nineteenth century as a Malay-language imitation of Indian Parsi theatre. Bangsawan is a form of improvised melodrama to musical accompaniment. During the Second World War, the occupying Japanese created anti-British bangsawan. While bangsawan remained popular after the war, it declined in the 1960s.

'Spoken drama' in the form of *sandiwara* appeared in the 1940s but rose to prominence in the 1960s. The name is a corruption of the Dutch words for 'secret' and 'to make public', identifying sandiwara as a dramatic form with agit-prop potential. Sandiwara, while often improvised, was also a text-based drama, with many plays written between the 1940s and the 1960s.

When the Brunei Revolt broke out at the end of 1962, the British aided the monarchy to end the rebellion. The State of Emergency laws passed in its wake ensured no public theatrical performances would be held until the 1970s. Several writer/directors who had been educated in Cairo returned and wrote one acts called *drama sebabak* that encouraged commitment to Islam and awareness of social issues. Bangsawam, sandiwara and drama sebabak were all hybrid forms, combining indigenous tradition with elements of Western dramaturgy.

Beginning in the 1980s, the government encouraged playwriting competitions on nationalistic themes. The best plays were given public performances and published, although spoken word drama never achieved the popularity of the other three forms. While theatre is offered as a course of study at the University of Brunei Darussalam, no Western-style theatre building exists, government censorship of scripts remains strong, and local audiences are not drawn to modern theatre, leaving Brunei with one of the least extant spoken dramas in Asia.

## East Timor

The Democratic Republic of Timor-Leste ('East Timor') occupies the eastern half of the island of Timor (the western half is a province in Indonesia). Colonised by Portugal, East Timor declared its independence in 1975, but from 1975 to 1999 fought a war against Indonesia, which sought to occupy the entire island and incorporate East Timor into its own nation. Lusaphone East Timor has Malay, Portuguese and Catholic cultural influences, which also serve to shape what limited theatre there is. Beginning in the early twenty-first century, youth theatre groups, frequently with the guidance of Australian artists, have begun developing theatre for social action and theatre for development.

## Indonesia

Indonesia consists of over 17,000 islands, six thousand of which are inhabited by a total of over two hundred million people from over a hundred ethnic groups speaking three hundred languages and countless dialects. It is the fourth most populous nation on the planet, and boasts the largest Muslim population in the world. And yet, as Evan Darwin Winet observes, 'Indonesia did not exist prior to European colonisation'.[9] By this he means that the nation state of Indonesia both is a colonial creation and has developed a national identity in response to the colonial experience. The islands and peoples of Indonesia were and are a heterogeneous group, forged into a single political construct by the occupation of the Dutch and the subsequent war of independence.

After Japanese occupation during the Second World War, Indonesia fought a war of independence from the Netherlands from 1945 to 1949. Sukarno (1901–70) was a freedom fighter against the Dutch who was then the first president of an independent Indonesia, although he eventually came to be seen as corrupt. In 1963 he named himself 'President-for-Life', cancelled elections and declared that parliament would be appointed by the president, not elected, in a policy called 'Guided Democracy'. This was followed in 1965 by an attempted coup. General Suharto (1921–2008) blamed the *Partai Komunis Indonesia* (PKI), the Indonesian Communist Party, and for the next two years there followed a purge of leftists – 600,000 people were imprisoned and over 400,000 killed, including actors, writers, scholars and other artists. The purges had a chilling effect on the theatre. In March 1966, Sukarno stepped down and Suharto became President, aligning with the US bloc during the Cold War.

Western-style realism began in Indonesia in the late 1920s with Western-educated playwrights rejecting indigenous forms and developing modern drama, albeit the plays lacked literary and theatrical sophistication and merit. By the middle of the next decade, however, a realistic theatre has evolved and, as elsewhere, was part of the nationalistic and anti-colonial struggle. The Japanese occupation in the 1940s had an unintended effect. Because all plays had to be submitted for approval, written drama became the norm and playwriting for the modern theatre was normalised. In the war for independence after the defeat of the Japanese, modern plays served to entertain, to rally the people and to reinforce nationalism.

Modern drama in the 1950s was rooted in both psychological realism and the urge to demystify the war of independence and critique the negative aspects of the emerging society. Corruption, endemic poverty, the growing autarchy of Sukarno and the divergence between nationalism, socialism and Islam were the subject matter of playwrights such as Utuy Tatang Sontani (1920–79) and Akdiat Kartamihardja (1911–2010). The 1950s also saw experiments in Stanislavski-rooted American method acting by Asrul Sani (1927–2004), a teacher, writer and director, who founded the Akademi Teater Nasional Indonesia (Indonesia National Theater Academy) in 1955 with film director and fellow playwright Usmar Ismail (1921–71).[10]

As elsewhere, the 1960s brought about experiments and hybrids, including a significant adaptation of *Hamlet* employing gamelan music and other indigenous performance elements directed by Jim Lim (Jim Adhilimas, b. 1936), who also created hybrid productions of Camus's *Caligula* and plays by Ionesco.[11] The culturally mixed audience of Indonesia was receptive to hybrid theatre that showcased Western dramaturgy and indigenous performance culture.

Willibrordus Surendra Broto Rendra (1935–2009), better known as W. S. Rendra and finally, just Rendra, is Indonesia's most influential theatre artist and a major figure in Indonesian culture. After studying at New York University and receiving his only formal training in theatre at the American Academy of Dramatic Arts, Rendra returned to Indonesia in 1967 and, according to Evan Darwin Winet, 'began to produce a kind of modern theatre Indonesia had not seen before: ensemble-based, improvisational, abstract, and theatrical, a theatre that privileges action over text, visual over linguistic composition and the company over the individual actor'.[12] Rendra pioneered a revolutionary approach to actor training and performance that was complimented by his own playwriting.

Rendra has written a variety of types of plays, from 'mini-word' (minikata), developed from improvisational exercises with actors, to adaptations of Western classical dramas, such as *Oedipus Rex*, *Lysistrata*, *Hamlet*, *Macbeth* and even an Indonesian *Waiting for Godot*, to his powerful, satirical dramas such as *The Mastadon and the Condors* (Mastadon dan Burung Kondor, 1973), *The Struggle of the Naga Tribe* (Kisah perjuangan suku Naga, 1975) and *Province Secretary* (Sekda, 1977), all of which criticised the government, frequently leading to censorship. Winet notes, 'Rendra viewed theatre as a form of cultural resistance through which clowns spoke truth to the authorities.'[13] From 1978 to 1986 he was banned from performing in public, but subsequently remounted his protest plays of the 1970s in the 1990s.

By the mid-1990s, the modern theatre consisted of 'a wave of increasingly direct and angry critical works that openly questioned the New Order's aesthetic norms and voiced bitter criticisms of the prevailing political and social system and its leader'.[14] Rendra and other dissidents became cultural celebrities. In 1998 Suharto resigned and government suppression of theatre lessened. The hybrid works of the second half of the twentieth century still dominate modern Indonesian drama, but Indonesia has also taken its place in the first decade of the twenty-first century's multicultural performances in a globalised context.

## Malaysia

Malaysia is a multiethnic nation, consisting of a dominant Malay population with a substantial Chinese and Indian presence. Modern drama has developed in Malay (the official language), English, Mandarin and Tamil. While both the Portuguese and the Dutch attempted to colonise Malaysia, it was the British that succeeded in forcing the Malay to become a protectorate in the early nineteenth century, finally achieving independence almost a century and a half later in 1957.

Indigenous hybrid modern forms such as sandiwara and bangsawan developed in the early twentieth century. Western-style realistic drama began to develop in the 1920s, but would not flourish until the sixties, earning the name drama moden ('modern drama') at that point. Western models began to appear at this point. The Malay Translation Bureau was founded in 1924 to translate Western works into Malay, and productions of Shakespeare and Christopher Marlowe, among others, in Malay followed. The Japanese occupied Malaysia during the war, continuing performances of sandiwara, this time with anti-British and anti-American content. After the war, nationalist playwrights began writing pro-independence plays for drama moden and sandiwara. The 1950s marked the beginning of the first generation of Malay playwrights, who primarily wrote for sandiwara. Kala Dewata (pen name of Mutapha Kamil Yassin, b. 1925) developed a style of realistic writing that became the standard and promoted a form of realistic acting, as seen in plays like *Tiled Roof, Thatched Roof* (Atap genting atap rembia, 1963).

In the 1960s, drama moden came into its own. Realistic plays, modelled after Western naturalism but maintaining Malay identity, became the dominant style. Drama moden artists sought to portray not the past, but an image of contemporary society, both as it is and as it could be. Second-generation playwrights such as Krishen Jit (1939–2005) wrote both English and Malay plays. Jit had founded an amateur drama society while at the University of Malaysia and began writing realistic dramas. His plays, following the current trend at the time, grew less realistic and more avant-garde.

By the 1970s, a theatre grown tired of realism became experimental. Third-generation drama moden playwrights wrote non-realistic political plays in Malay, English and Mandarin Chinese, although the beginning of the 1970s also found multicultural and minority theatre being challenged by new laws and social and political tensions. There has always been strong government censorship, first by the British, then the Japanese, then the British again and then finally by the new government. Scripts must be approved before they can be publicly performed, no play may be performed without a license. In 1969 relations between ethnic Chinese Malaysians and the Malay were tense and following the May elections there were race riots in Kuala Lumpur on 13 May. The government declared a state of emergency followed by new economic policies and rapid urbanisation designed to lift the Malay. The government also created a 'New Cultural Policy' in 1971, defining and privileging Malay culture and language and requiring the presence of Islam and Islamic values in culture. The tensions generated by these events were made manifest in the dramas of the period.

The 1980s and 1990s have brought a number of next-wave playwrights to the forefront. Chinese-descended Kee Thuan Chye (b. 1954) grew up in a Chinese-dominant community and began writing absurdist plays in his early 1920s: *Oh, But I Don't Want to Go, Oh, But I Have To* (1974), *The Situation of the Man Who Stabbed a Dummy or a Woman and Was Disarmed By Members of His Club for a Reason Yet Obscure, If There Was One* (1974) and *Eyeballs, Leper and a Very Dead Spider* (1977).[15] Kee then realised in the 1980s that non-Malay minorities were being disenfranchised from the political, social and cultural spheres of the nation and became a more political playwright, writing *1984 Here and Now* in 1984 and producing it the following year in Kuala Lumpur. The play uses George Orwell's eponymous novel to critique race relations within Malaysia. Kee combined the absurd with the political and employed innovative dramatic techniques in his subsequent theatre, such as *The Big Purge* (1988) in which ordinary characters were played by actors and authority figures were played by shadow puppets, telling a story of individual complicity in the creation of an unequal society. Subsequent dramas also employed satire, bawdy humour and allegory as social and political critique, particularly at the marginalisation of non-Malay citizens.

Indian-descended Huzir Sulaiman (b. 1973), award-winning actor, director and playwright, is known for his inventive plays that are surreal political satires, youth culture celebrations and explorations of contemporary Southeast Asian identity. His major works include *Atomic Jaya* (1998), *Hip-Hopera* (1998), *Election Day* (1999) and *Occupation* (2002). Although drama moden can be found in large cities, capital Kuala Lumpur is the heart of the modern drama in Malaysia.

## The Philippines

The Philippines are unique in Maritime Southeast Asia in that they were first colonised by the Spanish and then by the United States. As a result a unique modern theatre developed featuring hundreds of years of hybrid dramas, eventually joined in the nineteenth century by modern, naturalistic drama.

The Philippines, as a result of conversion to Catholicism under Spanish occupation, developed a culture of religious spectacle. Lenten plays (*senkulo*) that narrate the passion from Palm Sunday to Easter Sunday, Christmas plays (*Panunuluyan*), and plays about the lives of the saints have medieval and renaissance Spanish religious dramas as their origins. Komedya developed in the seventeenth century, flourishing until the twentieth, based on Spanish religious plays as well. Jesuit Father Vicente Puche wrote a Latin play to be performed by Cebuano schoolboys in 1598. Another Jesuit followed with another play based on the life of Saint Barbara in 1608. In addition to providing a model for modern drama, the Jesuits began Cebuano theatre. Religious plays were written in Cebuano and performed in Cebu for the next two centuries. Vincente Sotto (1877–1950), who would go on to become a politician, wrote a series of realistic plays in Cebuano in the first decade of the twentieth century. Contemporary theatre in Cebu includes experimental modern theatre, street theatre and even Broadway musicals. A more realistic theatre also developed in the late nineteenth century for educated Filipinos, including Zaruela, musical plays on contemporary themes.

The 1898 Treaty of Paris that ended the Spanish American War resulted in Spain ceding the Philippines to the United States, and the American military subsequently constructed bases throughout the islands. Vaudeville, performed on those bases beginning in 1916, then became a popular performance form in the Philippines called '*bodabil*'. Modern written drama also emerged at the time of the Spanish American War. The first modern Pilipino play, *The Ideal Woman* (Ang Babaye nga Huaran), was written by Cornelio Hilado (1837–1919) in Ilolo in 1878, one year before Henrik Ibsen composed *A Doll's House*. During the first decade of the twentieth century, 'seditious plays' were written and performed in Tagalog, presenting revolutionary, anti-American allegorical drama. The anti-American aspect of the theatre was rapidly suppressed by the colonisers, and English became the dominant language of modern theatre in the Philippines. *A Modern Filipina* (1915) by Jesus Araullo and Lino Casillejo was the first English language play. As its title implies, the play was concerned with both developing a modern drama and promoting a modern society, particularly for women.

The 1920s through the 1940s saw little innovative modern drama – it was a theatre of bourgeois romance for an audience of educated elites. Modern theatres were based primarily at schools, which employed the dramas to teach English and moral lessons. American plays and musicals as well as Western classics were the typical fare. Local drama was in English and psychologically realistic. After the Second World War, the Philippines achieved independence in 1946, but the next major event in modern drama did not occur until the 1960s, when Pilipino nationalism and growing political unrest pushed theatre artists to stop working in English and begin writing and performing in Tagalog, as well as to write overtly political plays. Martial law was declared in 1972, which only served to further radicalise the theatre. Modern drama in the 1970s was the second wave of hybrid theatre, combining agit-prop, realism, religious theatre and explorations of pre-colonial and traditional theatres alongside and incorporated into Western drama. In short, there is no monolithic, homogenous Philippine theatre, modern or otherwise, but an entire panoply of hybrids.

## Singapore

Originally a small Malay kingdom, Singapore has become a modern, multicultural island nation as a result of British colonisation followed by large-scale Indian and Chinese immigration (organised and encouraged by the British in order to develop a labour force). Singapore has four official languages: Malay, Mandarin, Tamil and English. The nation is comparatively wealthy, conservative and diverse.

The People's Action Party has won every election since independence from Britain in 1963 and independence from Malaysia in 1965, and through the National Arts Council, has provided theatre companies and artists with significant support. Singapore is the world's fourth largest financial centre, and as a result there is substantial backing for theatre in the form of infrastructure and technology.

For much of its early history, traditional theatre from the various ethnic groups that comprise Singapore dominated the performing arts culture. Chinese, Malay and Indian traditional theatres entertained their respective audiences, encouraged by the post-independence government in a separate-but-equal approach to culture. Modern drama in Singapore has, for the most part, been a cultural movement to break down the ethnic barriers and create a uniquely Singaporean contemporary culture.

Chung Cheng High School, founded in 1939, served as a site for the development of modern Chinese language drama in Singapore. After the war, almost a decade before English language dramas were written, the students began an innovative modern drama group, Chung Cheng High School Drama Research Society, influenced by modern theatre in China. Alumni of the school's drama research group eventually founded the Singapore Amateur Players (SAP) in 1955. The plays they presented were left-leaning social realism. The leaders of SAP were Chinese-born journalists and teachers familiar with Chinese huaju and the teachings of Stanislavski. They sought to use the group to both develop a modern Chinese theatre for Singapore while also pushing a progressive social agenda in the years before independence. As Singaporean critic Krishen Jit observes, 'The Chung Cheng drama teachers and students were the heirs of the revolutionary May Fourth Movement of 1919 that had inspired the westernization of Chinese art, literature and drama.'[16] The SAP presented works by Cao Yu, Gogol, Ibsen, Chekhov and Gorky and firmly embraced Stanislavskian principles in acting. Although a few original works by Singaporean authors were occasionally presented, by and large the SAP stayed with 'spoken drama classics' from the West.

Modern drama in English began to develop in the 1960s in response to the drive towards independence. Lim Chor Pee (1936–2006), a lawyer and playwright, began writing modern dramas based on British models in the early sixties. His first plays, *Mimi Fan* (1962) and *A White Rose at Midnight* (1964), were naturalistic dramas that brought him considerable fame. The former is considered Singapore's first play in English and its first modern drama. He founded the Experimental Theatre Club, serving as artistic director from 1962 to 1967, as a venue for original experimental Singaporean works in opposition to the other English-language theatres, which were British-owned and catered to British tastes. He gave up his theatrical pursuits at the end of the 1960s as his law practice began to demand more of his time.

Likewise, Goh Poh Seng (1936–2010) was a poet and novelist from Kuala Lumpur, Malaysia, whose primary career was as a physician. He was dedicated to the artistic and cultural development of Singapore after independence and also wrote naturalistic plays in English set in Singapore: *The Moon Is Less Bright* (1964), *When Smiles Are Done* (1966) and *The Elder Brother* (1967). Stella Kon (b. 1944) won first prize in the National Playwriting Competition in 1983 with *Emily of Emerald Hill*, a one-woman monodrama about the matriarch of a *peranakan* family (Straits-born Chinese) mourning her disappearing culture. Directed by Max LeBlond in 1985, the play became a staple of the Singaporean stage over the next three decades with hundreds of productions.

Known as 'the Father of Singaporean Theatre', Kuo Pao Kun (1939–2002) was a director, writer, administrator, teacher and activist. Born in Hebei Province, China, he moved to Singapore with his father in 1948 after the Second World War. He was educated in English and Chinese at Catholic schools and as a playwright worked initially in Mandarin Chinese and then, beginning in 1983, in English. Kuo is seen as a 'builder of bridges between disparate theatre people', as he looked to create a true Singaporean theatre community, rather than one based on single language and ethnicity.[17]

He founded three theatre centres in Singapore: The Practice Performing Arts School (PPAS) in 1965, The Substation, dedicated to developing experimental works in 1990, and The Theatre Training and Research Programme at PPAS in 2000. He has mentored numerous Singaporean actors, directors, designers and writers. He founded a semi-professional, bilingual theatre company in 1986 called Practice Theatre Ensemble dedicated to developing local talent and plays in Mandarin and English. In the 1960s, Kuo was perhaps the first Southeast Asian to direct Brecht and was also a committed leftist, finding himself one of the leaders in the Singaporean echoes of the Chinese Cultural Revolution. As a result of his political activities, he was arrested by the government in 1976 and was detained without trial until 1980. After his release he immediately returned to his theatre work where he was one of the most active presences. Ironically, less than a decade later, the government began celebrating his work and he received numerous awards from the state and other organisations until his death, including the Cultural Medallion in 1989 and the Excellence for Singapore Award in 2002.

In addition to his work as a teacher, director and activist, Kuo wrote many important dramas in Chinese and English. Regardless of language, Kuo was always looking to develop a specifically Asian idiom that could speak to all audiences in Singapore. His major works include *The Struggle* (1969), a play written in the wake of the Cultural Revolution cautioning about urban development and censored by the government; *The Little White Sailing Boat* (1982), his first play after release from detention; *The Coffin is Too Big for the Hole* (1985), a monologue written in both English and Mandarin in which a man attempting to bury his grandfather must navigate both tradition and bureaucracy; *Kopi Tiam* (Coffee Shop, 1986), which used 23 Mandarin Chinese theatre companies to perform; *No Parking on Odd Days* (1986), a one-man show about dealing with red tape; and *Mama Looking for Her Cat* (1988), a multi-lingual, non-realistic ensemble piece, developed with a group of eleven actors, dealing with the negotiation of tradition and contemporary society.

A shift in practice occurred in the 1990s, moving away from playwright-centred, text-driven theatre. Ensemble-created intercultural work began to dominate the theatre scene, particularly influenced by Ong Keng Sen (b. 1963), a director and the founder of Theatre Works in 1985, a company dedicated to the development of contemporary Singaporean theatre as an international, intercultural theatre and to the evolution of Asian identity. Ong's work mixes Eastern and Western theatre. He is known for his productions of Shakespeare.

Since the late 1980s there has also been a movement to develop musicals in Singapore, with the aim of developing pieces that will also have success in other nations. Numerous Asian-themed musicals have developed as a result with great success in Singapore and several have had overseas tours in Asia, although the Western market has proven more challenging to crack.

The nations and people of Southeast Asia have developed and continue to develop remarkable modern performances and dramas in response to cultural conditions and social changes. In the face of globalisation and the wake of colonialism, these national dramas and theatres both maintain their hybrid identity and reflect the global reality, influenced by popular culture from around the world. As Catherine Diamond observes, these nation states 'are the site of both superficial adaptations of cultural difference, and a profound layering of historical fusions'.[18] Like the other nations explored here, contemporary Southeast Asian theatres remain dynamic, heterogeneous cultural forces that are created by local artists for local audiences, but that are also increasingly available to audiences outside of their respective nation states, thanks to international festivals and the internet. Similarly, their increased presence in scholarly literature has meant greater accessibility for those outside of Asia to encounter and understand modern Southeast Asian theatre and drama in its original contexts.

A few larger patterns may be discerned in this brief analysis of Southeast Asian modern theatre. First, it is clear in simply surveying these brief summaries that modern theatres, like all cultural material, are no great respecters of national borders. Thai theatre influences Laotian and Cambodian; Indonesian theatre has clear overlapping elements and forms with Brunei and Malaysia. Second, the profound and shaping influence of colonialism not only introduces and shapes the modern theatre, but also gives a tool with which to combat colonialism. The pattern plays out in the form of an educated comprador class writing dramas in the form of the coloniser's tradition and often in the coloniser's language. In the Philippines, Spanish plays are written and performed, as French ones are in Vietnam. After the Second World War, however, the modern drama becomes a tool by which colonialism might be critiqued and resisted and by which new identities might be forged.

Third, the nations of Southeast Asia are bound together by a common and shared history beyond and before colonialism. Many are also bound by a shared history of conflict beyond (although just as often caused by) colonialism. The Vietnam War, the Indonesian civil war and purges, the Khmer Rouge era in Cambodia and the ongoing military dictatorship in Myanmar, to name but a handful, would seem to indicate a violent and oppressive century for Southeast Asia. The legacy of that violence and oppression is manifested and explored in the respective modern dramas of those nations, and a comparative study of the remnants of violence and oppression in modern Southeast Asian drama would be a comparatively easy task. Set the Vietnamese dramas of the American war next to Rendra's dramas of Indonesian violence and corruption and similarities emerge, not least of which is a resilient spirit that uses the theatre both to remember the oppression and to offer alternative histories in which to combat it.

Fourth, as noted in the introduction to this study, modern Southeast Asian theatre is mostly a theatre of urban elites. Although, as noted above, the occasional rural form emerges, the predominant location is the city and the artists and the audiences are both highly educated.

Fifth, unlike in East Asia (although shared with parts of South Asia), Islam is both a major cultural influence and a controlling presence in the theatre. With its prescriptions against cross-dressing and its cultural concern over images and representations, Islam can present a challenge to the artists working in modern theatre. Indonesia is the largest Muslim nation on Earth, and Brunei and Malaysia have major Muslim populations.

Sixth, new challenges result in new theatrical themes, forms and concerns. With the global rise of AIDS/HIV and sex tourism, nations such as Thailand, Malaysia and Singapore have seen the theatres respond first and faster than governments or other cultural bodies. The theatre becomes a source of information, a tool of education and a means by which to influence public policy, not least of which because of the afore-mentioned educated elite who make the theatre and who make up the audience.

Seventh, modern theatre is challenged in almost every nation state discussed here by the advent of new media and its appropriation of the best artists. Film, television and now the internet require content and the media industries of Thailand, Cambodia, Indonesia, Vietnam and the others offer inexpensive entertainment compared with theatre, and attract writers, directors and performers who are paid more and reach a much bigger audience. Modern theatre must also compete with popular culture from the West. Changing technology and globalisation represent one of the biggest challenges to the continuing development of Southeast Asian theatre.

Lastly, as with the rest of Asia, globalisation means that Southeast Asian drama is not limited in its influence and performance possibilities to immediate neighbours. Singapore and Malaysia host huge international theatre festivals. A greater modern Asian theatre community is emerging in the twenty-first century, of which Southeast Asia is a significant part. Historic ties to Chinese and Indian cultures allow for ease of transculturation of material into those nations, while festivals in Australia, Europe and the Americas have also expanded the international audience for Southeast Asian drama and performance. The larger global pressures combined with local politics will continue to shape and develop modern Southeast Asian theatre.

# CONCLUSION

The end of a century is an arbitrary marker, and trends continue, as artists continue to work, develop and evolve regardless of the date on the calendar. The end of the twentieth and the beginning of the twenty-first century has seen continuity and radical transformation in the modern theatres of Asia. As noted in the Introduction, the purpose of this book is threefold: to introduce to the English reader the modern theatres of Asia; to present a synoptic history of those theatres, in which parallel developments may be seen and traced; and to contextualise those theatres in the larger intercultural world in which pluralistic theatres develop as a result of cultural exchange in all directions. Now, at the end of the volume, we hope the reader has found these three purposes achieved.

In conclusion, we note several recurring aspects, both between nations and diachronically. Some aspects of modern theatre that were present at the beginning continue to determine its evolution, shape its experience or frame its meaning. During the twentieth century, modernism has shifted into postmodernism, as detailed in these chapters, but colonialism remains an issue, interculturalism remains a defining characteristic, and competition and collaboration with other media continue to transform and challenge the theatre.

First, much modern Asian drama was born out of colonial modernity and yet developed into an anti-colonial dramaturgy. More often than not, modernity was imposed upon the nations of Asia by imperialistic, colonising Western nations. Although modernity can be imposed versus self-determined (i.e. Korea and India vs. Japan and Thailand), the end result is the same: external pressures changing the culture, politics and even social structures of the emerging Asian nation. The modern theatre, as noted in the conclusion of Chapter 9, follows a pattern in which an educated comprador class writes dramas in the form of the coloniser's tradition and often in the coloniser's language for the purpose of modernising the nation on with a progressive agenda. Rapidly, however, modern drama becomes a tool by which colonialism might be critiqued and resisted and by which new identities might be forged. This pattern occurs in Korea under Japanese occupation, India under British occupation, Indonesia under Dutch occupation, Vietnam under the French and the Philippines under Spanish and then American occupation, among others. The anti-colonial drama is initially a drama of resistance. After independence, it becomes a drama of identity, of documenting history and of assertion of unity. Sometimes (more often than not) it then becomes a drama of factionalism, and if the order which replaces the colonisers is an oppressive one, it can become a new drama of resistance, as happens in Indonesia, Korea and China.

Second, modern Asian theatre is inherently and perpetually inter-cultural. Without reducing the exchange to a simple binary, readers may observe very specific moments, individuals and texts that have a profound shaping influence across Asia. Ibsen and *A Doll's House* are as important in Asian theatre history as they are in Western theatre history. Samuel Beckett sparked a global absurdist movement that went far beyond Europe to shape an entire generation of theatre artists throughout Asia. In times of censorship or oppression, just as in Eastern Europe under communism, absurdist theatre and allegorical theatre provided a form of critique and satire otherwise unavailable.

Early scholarship into modern Asian performance and drama followed a 'west-and-the-rest' approach, focusing on the relationship between the nations of Asia and the West. More recently, inter-Asian exchanges have grown in prevalence, both in practice and in the scholarly materials about them. Readers might note in these pages Japan's influence on China and Korea in the first half of the twentieth century. Western theatre was filtered through Japan before arriving in China and Korea, and thus the Western theatre those nations received was framed by the Japanese understanding of it.

More recently, globalisation has made Asia a primary market for Asian theatre. As noted in Chapter 2, the BeSeTo Festival (Beijing, Seoul and Tokyo) regularly brings the theatres of the three named cultures (and many others besides) to the eponymous cities where the festival is held. Singapore has had festivals, as has Jakarta, Kuala Lumpur, New Delhi, Calcutta, Mumbai and many other urban centres. Tours of Asian theatre companies to other Asian nations forges further chains of intercultural connection, as do collaborations, as discussed in Chapters 2, 5, 6 and 9. Expatriates, immigrants and touring artists have brought modern Asian theatre to every corner of the globe. Gao Xingjian lives in Paris. Okada Toshiki collaborated with Pig Iron Theatre Company in Philadelphia in the United States in 2012 to create *Zero Cost House*, his first English-language world premiere. Noda Hideki, after working several times in the United Kingdom, presenting several of his plays in translation, co-wrote *The Bee* with Colin Teevan in 2006 and *The Diver* in 2008. Lest we think this is a recent development, let us remember, however, that and other pioneers of modern Chinese theatre studied at Columbia, Harvard, and Carnegie in the second and third decades of the twentieth century, Osanai Kaoru went to Paris, Berlin and Moscow, and Rabindranath Tagore told W. B. Yeats that Ireland, with its history of British colonialism, was 'a part of Asia'. The twentieth century has begun and ended with Asian artists as a presence around the world.

Translations of modern Asian plays have been published in English and other Western languages. Whereas audiences can see the 'original' on tour, Western artists are able to mount Japanese, Indian, Chinese, Korean, Indonesian, Singaporean and indeed all modern Asian drama in their own nations. Modern Asian drama is being produced, especially by Asian-American and Asian diasporan artists in Europe, all over the world, especially in universities.

Another major theme of this book has been the role of the university, then and now. Universities were often the first site of modern drama; witness the importance of Waseda Daigaku in developing texts and actors for the early shingeki movement. Witness the importance of Waseda Daigaku in the 1960s, when students seeking both political and theatrical revolutions centred their work on their universities, and in one case even naming their theatre company after the school: Waseda Little Theatre. Witness the importance of Waseda Daigaku at the present moment, not only in training the next generation of theatre artists and the next generation of audiences, but also as an archive of historic theatre materials. In other nations, the university is the site where artists are trained, where young theatre makers with a sense of idealism and social justice develop pieces to take into the community, or even make with the community. Universities have been the cradles, incubators, shelters and spiritual and literal homes of the modern theatres of Asia.

Lastly, we might note the increasing influence of other media. From early hybrids with kabuki in Japan and jingju in China to recent multimedia pieces and televised performances of plays, as noted in Chapter 9, one of the greatest challenges to modern Asian theatre is the competition from globalised popular culture and entertainment and indigenous popular media. Film, television and increasingly the internet pay artists better, reach a greater audience and provide stepping stones to a larger career than the theatre. For audiences, film, television and the internet offer inexpensive entertainment, compared to theatre-going, which tends to be more expensive, urban-located and aimed at an educated, elite audience. This is not to suggest that there is no audience for modern Asian drama in the twenty-first century, merely that it is increasingly self-selective.

We are wary of framing the journey of twentieth-century modern Asian theatre, drama and performance as one long teleological voyage. We began this conclusion by also warning of the artificial nature of calendric markers. Now as we conclude the conclusion, we encourage the reader to see the end of this volume not as journey's end but the first step on a much longer exploration of the modern drama of Asia, itself a multiplicity of living theatres. The twenty-first century holds a great deal of promise. There will be continuity with what has come before. But what is past is also prologue. Gao Xingjian, Suzuki Tadaski, O Tae-Sŏk and other theatre-makers from the 1960s, 1970s and 1980s have continued their work, but standing on their shoulders are new generations of theatre makers, whose work only now is beginning to register on the global radar. All theatre is local, but all theatre also has the potential to be global. The 'shrinking globe' will continue to bring more modern Asian theatre into the perceptive realm of the West and intercultural exchange will continue, both as it always has, and in new exciting ways.

# NOTES

## Introduction

1. See Liu, Siyuan, *Performing Hybridity in Colonial-Modern China*. New York: Palgrave Macmillan, 2013, pp.6–7.
2. Kano, Ayako, *Acting Like a Woman in Modern Japan: Theatre, Gender and Nationalism*. New York: Palgrave Macmillan, 2001.
3. These were the revival of *The Seagull* (1898), *Uncle Vanya* (written 1897, performed 1899), *The Three Sisters* (1901) and *The Cherry Orchard* (1904).
4. Liu, p.6.
5. Morinaga, Maki Isaka, 'Osanai Kaoru's Dilemma: "Amateurism by Professionals"' in Modern Japanese Theatre'. *The Drama Review*. Vol. 49, No. 1 (2005), p.121.
6. Ibid.
7. Yamanashi, Mikiki, *Takarazuka Revue Since 1914: Modernity, Girl's Culture, Japan Pop*. Leiden: Global Oriental, 2012, pp.12–16.

## Chapter 1

1. Rimer, J. Thomas, *Toward a Modern Japanese Theatre: Kishida Kunio*. Princeton: Princeton University Press, 1974, p.5.
2. Kano, Ayako, *Acting Like a Woman in Modern Japan: Theater, Gender, and Nationalism*. New York: Palgrave, 2001, p.158.
3. Goodman, David G., 'Modern Japan' in James R. Brandon (ed.), *The Cambridge Guide to Asian Theatre*, Cambridge: Cambridge University Press, 1993, pp.153–60, 170.
4. Boyd, Mari, *The Aesthetics of Quietude: Ota Shōgo and the Theatre of Divestiture*. Tokyo: Sophia University Press, 2006, p.48.
5. Ōyama Isao, *Kindai Nihon Giyoku Shi*, Vol. I, p.8, quoted in Keene, Donald. *Dawn to the West: Japanese Literature of the Modern Era: Volume 4: Poetry, Drama, Criticism*. New York: Columbia University Press, 1999, p.399.
6. Quoted in Toita Kōji, 'Early Meiji Kabuki' in Komiya Toyotaka (ed.), *Japanese Music and Drama in the Meiji Era*, trans. by Donald Keene, Tokyo: Toyo Bunko, 1956, pp.191–2.
7. Leiter, Samuel, *Kabuki Encyclopedia*. Westport, CT: Greenwood Press, 2009, p.218.
8. Poulton, M. Cody, *A Beggar's Art: Scripting Modernity in Japanese Drama, 1900–1930*. Honolulu: University of Hawai'i Press, 2010, p.21.

9. Ibid., p.xi.
10. Ibid.
11. Boyd, p.20.
12. Kano, p.184.
13. Keene, p.439. Although a better translation of *Bokashi no Ie* might be 'A Vicar's House', as Nakamura was intentionally echoing Ibsen's *A Doll House*.
14. See Kano.
15. Kubo Sakae, *Land of Volcanic Ash*, trans. by David G. Goodman. Ithaca: Cornell University East Asia Center, 1993.
16. Jortner, David J., 'SCAP's "Problem Child"': American Aesthetics, the Shingeki Stage, and the Occupation of Japan' in Samuel L. Leiter (ed.), *Rising from the Flames: The Rebirth of Theatre in Occupied Japan, 1945–1952*, Lanham, MD: Lexington, 2009, p.260.
17. Powell, Brian, *Japan's Modern Theatre: A Century of Continuity and Change*. London: Japan Library, 2002, p.150.

# Chapter 2

1. Goodman, David G., 'Modern Japan' in James R. Brandon (ed.), *The Cambridge Guide to Asian Theatre*, Cambridge: Cambridge University Press, 1993, pp.153.
2. Laurence Kominz, 'Introduction' in Laurence Kominz, (ed.), *Mishima on Stage: The Black Lizard and Other Plays*, Ann Arbor: University of Michigan Center for Japanese Studies, 2007, p.1.
3. Senda Akihiko, *The Voyage of Contemporary Japanese Theatre*, trans. by J. Thomas Rimer. Honolulu: University of Hawaii Press, 1997, p.1.
4. Ibid., p.2.
5. Goodman, p.157.
6. Sorgenfrei, Carol Fisher, *Unspeakable Acts: The Avant-Garde Theatre of Terayama Shūji and Postwar Japan*. Honolulu: University of Hawai'i Press, 2005, pp.85–6.
7. Uchino Tadashi, 'Images of Armageddon: Japan's 1980s Theatre Culture', *The Drama Review*, Vol. 44, No. 1 (2000), pp.85, 88.
8. Uchino, pp.85–6.
9. Salz, Jonah, 'Super-kyogen: Radically Traditional Urban Comedies' in David J. Jortner, Keiko McDonald and Kevin J. Wetmore, Jr. (eds), *Modern Japanese Theatre and Performance*, Lanham, MD: Lexington, 2006, pp.123–48.

# Chapter 3

1. Liang Qichao, 'Popular Literature in Relation to the Masses', trans. by Faye Chunfang Fei, in Faye Chunfang Fei (ed.), *Chinese Theories of Theater and Performance from Confucius to the Present*, Ann Arbor: University of Michigan Press, 1999, pp.109–11.

2. Hu Shi, 'The Main Event in Life', trans. by Edward M. Gunn, in Xiaomei Chen (ed.), *The Columbia Anthology of Modern Chinese Drama*, New York: Columbia University Press, 2010, p.65.
3. Zhang Wentian and Wang Fuquan, 'Wang'erde jieshao' (Introduction to Wilde), in *De Profundis* (*Yu zhong ji*). Shanghai: Shangwu yinshuguan, 1932 (1922), pp.30–1.
4. Ouyang Yuqian, 'P'an Chin-lien', trans. by Catherine Swatek, in Edward M. Gunn (ed.), *Twentieth-Century Chinese Drama: An Anthology*, Bloomington: Indiana University Press, 1983, p.73.
5. Bai Wei, *Linli*. Shanghai: Shangwu yinshuguan, 1925, pp.143–4.
6. Ibid., pp.141–2.
7. Hong Shen, 'Xiju Xieshe pianduan' (A Fragment on the Drama Association), in Tian Han et al. (eds), *Zhongguo huaju yundong wushinian shiliaoji* (Collected Materials of Fifty Years of Chinese Spoken Drama), Vol. 1, Beijing: Zhongguo xiju chubanshe, 1958, p.108.
8. Ibid., p.109.
9. Ayako Kano, *Acting Like a Woman in Modern Japan: Theater, Gender, and Nationalism.* New York: Palgrave, 2001, p.225.
10. Xia Yan, 'Under Shanghai Eaves', trans. by George Hayden, in Xiaomei Chen (ed.), *The Columbia Anthology of Modern Chinese Drama*, New York: Columbia University Press, 2010, p.447.
11. Tian Han, *Tian Han quanji* (Collected Works of Tian Han), Vol. 15, Beijing: Wenhua yishu chubanshe, 2000, p.163.

# Chapter 4

1. For an introduction of reform of traditional theatre in 1950s, see Siyuan Liu, 'Theatre Reform as Censorship-Censoring Traditional Theatre in China in the Early 1950s', *Theatre Journal*, Vol. 61, No. 3 (2009), pp.387–404.
2. For more information on the background of the play, see Yomi Braester, *Painting the City Red: Chinese Cinema and the Urban Contract*. Durham: Duke University Press, 2010.
3. Zhang Guangnian, 'Tan dumuju' (On One-Act Plays), *Juben* (*Play Script*), No. 5 (1954), pp.10–14.
4. Li, Hong, 'Di sizhong juben' (The Fourth Type of Play). *Nanjing ribao* (*Nanjing Daily*), 11 June 1957.
5. The quote is from Brecht, Bertolt, 'Life of Galileo', 2007, http://buehnenkunst.ohost. de/auditions_coming_up_files/Life%20of%20Galileo%20by%20Brecht.pdf (accessed 15 May 2013). The incident is described by Lin Kehuan, a dramaturge and later Artistic Director of the Central Youth Theatre, in Shi Yan, 'Xiju de xungen zui chedi–Lin Kehuan fangtan' (Theatre's Search for Root was the Most Thorough – Interview with Lin Kehuan). *Nanfang zhoumo* (*Southern Weekend*), 11 December 2008.
6. W and M are the initial letters of the Chinese characters 'wo' and 'men', which form the first person plural 'we' or 'us'.

7. He Jiping, 'The World's Top Restaurant', trans. Edward M. Gunn, in Xiaomei Chen (ed.), *Reading the Right Text: An Anthology of Contemporary Chinese Drama*, Honolulu: University of Hawai'i Press, 2003, pp.134–222.

## Chapter 5

1. In order to be consistent with the convention of romanising Chinese names in the previous two chapters, the names in the Taiwan section also follow the *pinyin* system. In cases where I know there is a preferred spelling of an artist's name, I include it in parentheses. However, because of bilingual and Cantonese conventions in Hong Kong, naming convention in the Hong Kong section follows customary usage, with *pinyin* in parentheses.
2. Diamond, Catherine, 'Reflected and Refracted: Metatheatrics in Taiwan', *Journal of Dramatic Theory and Criticism*, Vol. 9, No. 2 (1995), p.94.
3. Chan, Joanna, 'Crown Ourselves with Roses' in Xiaomei Chen (ed.), *The Columbia Anthology of Modern Chinese Drama*, New York: Columbia University Press, 2010, p.1073.

## Chapter 6

1. Clark, Donald N., *Korea in World History*. Ann Arbor: Association for Asian Studies, 2012, p.1.
2. Parquet, Darcy, *New Korean Cinema*. New York and London: Wallflower, 2009, p.32.
3. Robinson, Michael, 'Contemporary Cultural Production in South Korea: Vanishing Meta-Narratives of Nation' in Chi-yun Shin and Julian Stringer (eds), *New Korean Cinema*, New York: New York University Press, 2005, p.19.
4. Clark, p.59.
5. Nichols, Richard, 'Introduction' in Richard Nichols (ed.), Modern Korean Drama, New York: Columbia University Press, 2009, p.1.
6. Yi Tu-hyŏn, 'Ancient-1945: A History of Korean Drama' in *Korean Performing Arts: Drama, Dance and Music Theater*, Seoul: Jipmoondang Publishing Company, 2001, p.23.
7. The English name for the country comes from Koryŏ, the name of the kingdom from 918 to 1392.
8. Jang Won-Jae, *Irish Influences on Korean Theatre During the 1920s and 1930s*. Gerrards Cross: Colin Smythe Limited, 2002.
9. Nichols, p.6.
10. Ibid., p.7.
11. Ibid., p.8.
12. Clark, p.58.

13. Yoon, Min-Kyung, 'North Korean Art Works: Historical Paintings and the Cult of Personality', *Korean Histories*, Vol. 3, No. 1 (2012), p.54.

14. Oh-con Cho, 'Korea' in James Brandon (ed.), *The Cambridge Guide to Asian Theatre*, Cambridge: Cambridge University Press, 1993, p.185.

15. Kim, Suk-Young, *Illusive Utopia: Theater, Film and Everyday Performance in North Korea*. Ann Arbor: University of Michigan Press, 2010.

## Chapter 7

1. Mehta, Kumudini Arvind, *English Drama on the Bombay Stage in the Late Eighteenth Century and in the Nineteenth Century*. Bombay: University of Bombay, 1960, p.33.

2. Ibid., p.46.

3. Ibid., p.47.

4. Ibid., pp.125–6.

5. See Karnad, Girish, 'The Arts and Social Change in India', in *Indian Culture in Motion*. Amsterdam: Royal Tropical Institute, 1998.

6. Ibid.

7. Quoted Gokhale, Shanta, *Playwright at the Centre: Marathi Drama from 1843 to the Present*. Calcutta: Seagull Books, 2000, p.11.

8. This phrase has been used by a number of people to describe text-based theatre. I first encountered it in an article titled 'Manipuri Playwrights: An Overview' by Arambam Somorendra. *STQ* 14/15, pp.178–82.

9. Gargi, Balwant, *Folk Theatre of India*. Calcutta: Rupa and Co, 1991 [1966], p.18.

10. Gokhale, p.10; Mehta, pp.126, 184.

11. Ibid., p.12.

12. Quoted in Gokhale, p.13.

13. Gokhale, p.14.

14. Ibid., p.18.

15. Quoted in Bhatia, Nandia, *Staging a Change: Modern Indian Drama and the Colonial Encounter*. PhD diss., University of Texas, Austin, 1996, p.79.

16. Bhatia, pp.41–2.

17. Ibid., p.42.

18. Ibid., p.41.

19. Ibid., p.249.

20. See Bhatia, p.93.

21. See Bhatia, pp.140–5. Interestingly, the Dramatic Performances Control Act has remained in effect in many parts of India, providing an excuse to ban several plays by Tendulkar, a play by Thopil Bhasi called *You Made Me A Communist* (1954) and several productions by Utpal Dutt.

22. Quoted in Gokhale, p.16.

23. Ibid., p.16.

24. Gokhale, pp.63–4.

25. Ibid., p.61.

# Notes

26. Ibid., p.70.
27. Mukherjee, Sushil, *The Story of the Calcutta Theatres 1753–1980*. Calcutta: K.P. Bagchi & Company, 1982, p.7.
28. Rangacharya, Adya, *The Indian Theatre*. New Delhi: National Book Trust, 1971, p.94.
29. Mukherjee, p.13.
30. Rangacharya, p.97.
31. See Mukherjee, p.21 and Bannerjee, Sumanta, *The Parlour and the Streets: Elite and Popular Culture in Nineteenth Century Calcutta*. Calcutta: Seagull Books, 1989, p.163.
32. Banerjee, p.1.
33. Ibid., p.1.
34. Ibid., p.72.
35. Ibid., p.153.
36. Quoted in Banerjee, p.159.
37. Ibid.
38. Ibid., pp.202–3.
39. Quoted in Chatterjee, Sudipto, *The Colonial Stage(d)*. PhD diss., New York University, 1998, p.145.
40. Ibid., pp.166–7.
41. Ibid., p.171.
42. Quoted in Chatterjee, p.188.
43. Ibid., pp.140 and 203.
44. Guha-Thakurta, p.2.
45. Ibid., p.127.
46. Ibid., p.127.
47. Ibid., p.146.
48. Quoted in Lal, Ananda (ed.), *The Oxford Companion to Indian Theatre*. Delhi: Oxford University Press, 2004, p.462.
49. Ibid., p.463.
50. In Pradhan, Sudhir, *Marxist Cultural Movements in India: Chronicles and Documents: 1936–47*. Calcutta: National Book Agency, 1979, p.129.
51. See Bhatia, p.433. See also Bannerji, Hemani, 'Language and Liberation: A Study of Political Theatre in Bengal', *Ariel* 15, 131–44, pp.132–3. See also Battacharya, Malini, 'The IPTA in Bengal', *Journal of Arts and Ideas*, 5–22 January-March, p.7.
52. Bhatia, Nandi, 'Staging Resistance: The Indian People's Theatre Association' in Lisa Lowe and David Lloyd (eds), *Politics of Culture in the Shadow of Capital*, Durham: Duke University Press, 1997.
53. See Mee, Erin B., *Theatre of Roots: Redirecting the Modern Indian Stage*. Kolkata: Seagull Books, 2009.
54. Sangeet Natak Akademi, Annual Report. Delhi: Sangeet Natak Akademi, 1986/87, p.39.
55. Awasthi, Suresh, '"Theatre of Roots": Encounter with Tradition', *TDR* 33, 4:48–69, 1989, p.67.
56. Roy, Amitava, 'Folk Is What Sells Well' in *RASA, The Indian Performing Arts in the Last Twenty-Five Years,* Calcutta: Anamika Kala Sangam Trust, 1995, p.12.
57. Hashmi, p.90.

58. Quoted in van Erven, Eugene. *The Playful Revolution: Theatre and Liberation in Asia*. Bloomington: Indiana University Press, 1992, p.141.
59. Hashmi, Safdar, *The Right to Perform*. Delhi: Samat, 1989, pp.11–2.
60. Jain, Kirti, 'In Search of a Narrative: Women Theatre Directors of the Northern Belt' in Subramanyam, Lakshmi (ed.), *Muffled Voices: Women in Modern Indian Theatre*, New Delhi: Shakti, 2002, pp.151–2.
61. Kapur, Anuradha, 'Reassembling the Modern: An Indian Theatre Map Since Independence'. In the Program for the South Asian Women's Theatre Festival, NSD, 2010, p.6.
62. Ibid., p.7.
63. Erin B. Mee, interview with Amal Allana, Delhi, 28 July 2010.
64. Kapur, 'Reassembling', p.10.
65. Ibid., p.11.
66. Ibid.
67. Zuleikha Chaudhari, programme note, Bharat Rang Mahotsav, *On Seeing*, 2009, pp.40–1.
68. Personal interview.
69. Zuleikha Chaudhari, programme note, Bharat Rang Mahotsav, *On Seeing*, 2009, p.40.

# Chapter 8

1. Panikkar, Kavalam Narayana, *Karimkutty* and *The Lone Tusker*. Calcutta: Seagull Books. 1992, p.41.
2. G. Venu, in *Production of a Play in Kutiyattam*, defines nirvahanam thus:

   It is not the original text as it is, that is presented in Kutiyattam. One act of the original drama is selected and adding numerous details not entirely irrelevant, but drawing from a fertile imagination, the presentation of that single act is lengthened for days and days! This lengthening device is called "Nirvahanam." In terms of this technique one character of the drama describes in detail the biodata of his own or that of another important character in the story. As all the characters of Kutiyattam are puranic ones, details of their lives given in other puranas than the one used by the dramatist are garnered and included in Nirvahanam. All the verses used for the Nirvahanam are recited by the Nangiar. The actor enact[s] the roles of various characters during the Nirvahanam. (*Production of a Play in Kutiyattam*, Trissur: Natana Kairali, 1989, pp.100–1)

3. 'The attaprakaram is concerned with the roles of the individual actors; it prescribes the ways in which each actor should perform his part and the important points that he has to remember while acting his part' (Venu, pp.24). The attaprakaram also details the gestures to be used, and discusses the 'various modes of acting such as *vachyarttha* (denoted sense), *vyangyarttha* (connoted sense), [and] *slesharttha* (wordplay)' (Nambiar, P. K., 'Rhythm and Music', *Sangeet Natak*, nd, p.102). There

are also staging manuals, known as *kramadipika*, which lay out 'the method of production of the play concerned, giving close attention to minor details' such as make-up and costume, and the mode of entrances and exits (Venu 1989, p.24; and Nambiar n.d., p.102). For a complete attaprakaram and kramadipika of the first act of Bhasa's *Abhishekanatakam*, known as *Balivadham* when performed in kutiyattam, see G. Venu's book *Production of a Play in Kutiyattam* (1989).

4. Panikkar 1992.
5. Panikkar, Kavalam Narayana. Unpublished interview with Suresh Awasthi Nd, p.12.
6. Venu, p.97.
7. Ibid., p.104.
8. Panikkar 1992, p.40.
9. Gupt, Bharat. *Dramatic Concepts Greek and Indian*. Delhi: D.K. Printworld, 1994, p.181.
10. Panikkar nd, p.4.
11. Panikkar 1992, p.40.
12. Venu, p.98.
13. Panikkar 1992, pp.45–6.
14. Panikkar, Kavalam Narayana, Interviews with author. Thiruvananthapuram, Kerala, July 1999.
15. Panikkar 1992, p.46.
16. Ibid., p.46.
17. In Sangeet Natak Akademi, 'Round-Table on the Relevance of Traditional Theatre', *Sangeet Natak*. Special Issue. Delhi: Sangeet Natak Akademi, 1971, pp.5 and 29.
18. Awasthi, p.48.
19. Kaushal, J. N., 'Last Month in Delhi: *Hayavadan*'. *Enact* 63. Np.
20. Karnad, Girish, *Three Plays*. Delhi: Oxford University Press, 1994, p.81.
21. Courtwright, Paul, *Ganesha: Lord of Obstacles, Lord of Beginnings*. New York: Oxford University Press, 1985, p.98.
22. Karnad 1994, p.74.
23. Ibid., p.119.
24. Ibid., p.120.
25. Ibid., p.82.
26. Karanth, K. Shivaram, *Yakshagana*. New Delhi: Abhinav Publications, 1997, pp.50–1.
27. Karnad 1992, pp.78–9.
28. Ashton, Martha Bush, *Yakshagana: A Dance Drama of India*. Delhi: Abhinav 1977, p.37.
29. Ibid., pp.75, 79.
30. Gargi, p.79.
31. Karnad 1994, pp.87–9.
32. Ibid., pp.84.
33. Van Erven, p.141.
34. Karnad 1994, pp.101–2.
35. Ibid., p.81.
36. Ibid., p.136.
37. Ibid., p.14.

38. Narasimhan, Sakuntala, *Sati: A Study of Widow Burning in India*. Delhi: Penguin, 1990, pp.11–2.
39. Karanth, pp.38, 87.
40. Gargi, pp.159–60.
41. Karnad 1994, p.125.
42. For a very brief history of partition, see Chapters 1 and 2 of *India After Gandhi* by Ramachandra Guha. New York: Harper Collins, 2007. For a brief overview of the integration of the Princely States into the Indian nation, see Chapter 3.
43. Anand, Uma, 'Emergence of a National Theatre in India', *Indian and Foreign Review*, Vol. 11, No. 17 (1974), p.16.
44. Sangeet Natak Akademi, *Annual Report*. Delhi: Sangeet Natak Akademi, 1986/1987, p.39.
45. The officially recognised languages of India, listed roughly in order of the number of people who speak them, are: Hindi, Bengali, Telugu, Marathi, Tamil, Urdu, Gujarati, Kannada, Malayalam, Oriya, Punjabi, Assamese, Kashmiri, Sindhi, Konkani, Nepali, Meiteilon (Manipuri) and Sanskrit. As of 1992 English is no longer an official language of India, although it is still an important bridge language used by people who do not speak the same Indian language.
46. Dharwadker, Aparna, *Theatres of Independence: Drama, Theory, and Urban Performance in India Since 1947*. Iowa City: University of Iowa Press, 2005, p.24.

# Chapter 9

1. Much information for this chapter came from the essays and entries in the major reference books in English about Asian theatre: Brandon, James R., *Brandon's Guide to Theater in Asia*. Honolulu: University of Hawai'i Press, 1976, Brandon, James R. (ed.), *The Cambridge Guide to Asian Theatre*. Cambridge: Cambridge University Press, 1993, Leiter, Samuel (ed.), *Encyclopedia of Asian Theatre*. Westport, CT: Greenwood, 2007, Rubin, Don, Chua Soo Pong, Ravi Chaturvedi, Ramendu Majumdar, Minoru Tanokura and Katharine Brisbane (eds), *The World Encyclopedia of Contemporary Theatre: Asia/Pacific*. London: Routledge, 1998, as well as numerous individual texts, book chapters and essays on the individual nations, companies and artists. Of all the modern theatres in this book, Southeast Asian in the most underrepresented in English, although scholars such as Catharine Diamond, Nancy Nanney, Evan Darwin Winet, James Brandon, William Peterson, Krishen Jit, Kathy Foley and others have increased the amount material available in English. One positive effect of globalisation has been the increased availability of playtexts and scripts from Asia, as well as the rest of the world.
2. Wetmore, Jr., Kevin J., '*Samritechak* and Intercultural Shakespeare in Cambodia' in Alexander C. Y. Huang and Charles S. Ross (eds), *Shakespeare in Hollywood, Asia and Cyberspace*, West Lafayette, IN: Purdue University Press, 2009, pp.166–71.
3. Diamond, Catherine, *Communities of Imagination: Contemporary Southeast Asian Theatres*. Honolulu: University of Hawai'i Press, 2012, p.32.

# Notes

4. See Durand, Maurice M. and Nguyen Tran Huan, *An Introduction to Vietnamese Literature*, trans. by D. M. Hawke, New York: Columbia University Press, 1985, pp.120–4. for the role of drama in modern Vietnamese literature.

5. This announcement and attitude resulted in many other independence movements in French colonies all over the world, such as Algeria.

6. Obermeyer, Ziad, Christopher J. L. Murray and Emmanuela Gakidou, 'Fifty Years of Violent War Deaths from Vietnam to Bosnia: Analysis of Data from the World Health Survey Programme', *British Medical Journal*, Vol. 336 (2008), p.1482.

7. Nguyen, Khai Thu, 'Marking the Nation from Outside: Vietnamese Americans as Abject in the Vietnamese Play *Dạ Cổ Hoài Lang*' in Kevin J. Wetmore, Jr. (ed.), *Portrayals of Americans on the World Stage: Critical Essays*, Jefferson, NC: McFarland, 2009, pp.163–76.

8. See Diamond, pp.82–6 for detailed information on *Sân khấu nhỏ* and 5B.

9. Winet, Evan Darwin, *Indonesian Postcolonial Theatre: Spectral Genealogies and Absent Faces*. London: Palgrave, 2010, p.1.

10. Ibid., pp.134–7.

11. Ibid., pp.160–4.

12. Winet, Evan Darwin, 'The Critical Absence of Indonesia in W.S. Rendra's Village' in Kiki Gounaridou (ed.), *Staging Nationalism: Essays on Theatre and National Identity*, Jefferson, NC: McFarland and Company, 2005, p.143.

13. Winet, Evan Darwin, 'Modern Indonesian Theatre' in Samuel L. Leiter (ed.), *Encyclopedia of Asian Theatre*, Westport CT: Greenwood, 2007, p.271.

14. Bodden, Michael H., *Resistance on the National Stage: Theatre and Politics in Late New Order Indonesia*. Athens, OH: Ohio University Press, 2010, p.310.

15. For a full history of Kee Thuan Chye and summaries and analyses of the plays listed here, see Susan Philip, 'Kee Thuan Chye's Political Plays: An Analysis', *Asian Theatre Journal*, Vol. 29, No. 2 (2012), pp.355–578. Information on Kee and his work is from this article.

16. Krishen Jit, 'Kuo Pao Kun – The Man of the Future in Singapore Theatre' in Kuo Pao Kun (ed.), *The Coffin is Too Big for the Hole and Other Plays*, Singapore: Times Books, 1990, p.12.

17. Jit, p.9.

18. Diamond, p.309.

# GLOSSARY

**Aharya** (Indian) – make-up and costuming.

**Aimeiju** (Chinese) – Transliteration of 'amateur drama', another name for modern drama.

**Angika** (Indian) – physical expression.

**Angura** (Japanese) – A transliteration of the word 'underground', refers to avant-garde theatre of the 1960s and 1970s.

**Ankoku Butō** (Japanese) – 'Dance of utter darkness' – A dance form developed in the wake of the Second World War that employs a variety of diverse techniques to explore and celebrate the grotesque and the taboo.

**Anukramam** (Indian) – flashback in kutiyattam.

**Attakkatha** (Indian) – script for a kathakali play.

**Attaprakaram** (Indian) – acting manuals passed from teacher to student in kutiyattam training. 'The attaprakaram is concerned with the roles of the individual actors; it prescribes the ways in which each actor should perform his part and the important points that he has to remember while acting his part' (Venu 1989:24). The attaprakaram also details the gestures to be used, and discusses the 'various modes of acting such as vachyarttha (denoted sense), vyangyarttha (connoted sense), [and] slesharttha (wordplay) (P. K. Nambiar n.d.:102). There are also staging manuals, known as kramadipika, which lay out 'the method of production of the play concerned, giving close attention to minor details' such as makeup and costume, and the mode of entrances and exits (Venu 1989:24; and Nambiar n.d.:102).

**Baihuaju** (Chinese) – 'Vernacular drama' – Early Chinese name for spoken drama in the western mode, eventually shortened to 'huaju'.

**Batavani** (Indian) – Jokes that satirised a current event or person in power.

**Bhagavata** (Indian) – A character in yakshagana who functions as the narrator and 'organiser' of the theatrical event, similar to the sutradhar of Sanskrit drama.

**Bharud** (Indian) – Dramatic songs distinguished by their humorous double entendres.

**Bhavai** (Indian) – Open-air Gujarati community theatre honouring the goddess Amba.

**Bhoopali** (Indian) – A type of music.

**Brahmin** (India) – One of the castes.

**Burrakatha** (Indian) – Dramatic ballad singing popular in Andhra Pradesh.

**Chakyar** (Indian) – The caste name for those who traditionally have both the right and responsibility for performing kutiyattam in Kerala temples and stages.

**Ch'anggǔk** (Korean) – 'Singing drama' – A modern form of the traditional theatre form P'ansori, using a group of singers rather than a solo artist.

**Dadra** (Indian) – A type of music.

**Dasavata** (Indian) – A genre of performance in which mime, pageantry, music and dance together tell the story of any one of Vishnu's 10 incarnations, proceeding episodically.

**Diya** (Indian) – Hand-held oil lamp.

**Drama modern** (Malay) – Modern spoken drama in Malaysia.

**Drama sebabak** (Brunei) – Modern drama promoting Islam.

**Drishya Kavya** (Indian) – A Sanskrit term that literally means 'visual poetry'.

**Gaijin** (Japanese) – Literally 'outside person'. A Japanese work meaning 'foreigner' or 'non-Japanese'.

**Geeta** (Indian) – Vocal music.

**Ghazal** (Indian) – A type of music.

**Hanamichi** (Japanese) – The bridge through the audience that serves as the entry way for the main character in kabuki.

**Hanpozenshinshugi/hanposhugi** (Japanese) – Sawada Shōjirō's 'half-step principle': when seeking to move theatre forward and a full step will alienate the audience or leave them behind, the theatre must take a half-step.

**Huaju** (Chinese) – The modern theatre of China, meaning 'spoken drama', that developed in Shanghai in the beginning of the twentieth century.

**Jatra** (Indian) – Outdoor theatre popular in both urban and rural areas of Bengal, Bihar and Orissa.

**Jingju** (Chinese) – Known in the west as 'Beijing Opera' this is the traditional theatre of China.

**Kalappurattu natakkuka** (Indian) – A special movement pattern in kutiyattam used to indicate that the character is travelling from one place to another.

**Kathak** (Indian) – Classical north-Indian dance developed as court entertainment

**Kathakali** (Indian) – Genre of dance-drama from Kerala, South India.

**Katsureki mono** (Japanese) – 'Living history plays' were an early experiment in modernising the kabuki, written primarily by Kawatake Mokuami.

**Keertan** (Indian) – Type of music with specific rhythm.

**Kettatuka** (Indian) When an actor hears something spoken by an unseen character from offstage . . . he feigns to hear it by suitable movements of the head, hands or the mudras. . . . The actor not only enacts hearing the words of the unseen speaker but also brings out fully the meaning of the speech that he has heard by imitating exactly the facial expressions of the unseen speaker and enacts with mudras the meaning of his words (Venu 1989:98).

**Khyal** (Indian) – Musical plays performed by troupes in Rajasthan in the late eighteenth- and nineteenth-centuries.

**Kịch nói** (Vietnamese) – The modern theatre of Vietnam, literally 'spoken plays'.

**Kindaigeki** (Japanese) – A generic term for modern drama.

**Kindai gikyoku** (Japanese) – Another term for modern drama.

**Kokumin engeki** (Japanese) – During the Second World War, 'national drama' was patriotic theatre that supported the war effort.

**Kutiyattam** (Indian) – A particular way of performing Sanskrit drama in Kerala, South India.

**Kuttampalam** (Indian) – The building where kutiyattam is traditionally performed.

**Kuzithalam** (Indian) – Pair of cymbals used in kutiyattam.

**Lakhon chiet** (Cambodian) – 'National drama' written by Hang Tun Hak in the 1950s.

**Lakhon niyeay** (Cambodian) – Modern spoken drama.

**Lakhon vao** (Laotian) – 'Spoken drama' - the modern spoken drama of Laos.

**Lakon phut samai mhai** (Thai) – Modern spoken drama of Thailand.

**Lalit** (Indian) – Devotional entertainment performed as part of several festivals, usually incorporating some kind of social critique.

**Lavani** (Indian) – Sung poetic narratives with a specific metric form.

**Likay** (Thai) – Hybrid, modern, commercial form in Thailand which mixes classical dance, modern music, contemporary western and classical Thai costume, and melodramatic stories.

***Mahabharata*** (Indian) – One of the great epics of India.

**Maichou** (Indian) – Scholar, wise man in Manipur.

**Mudras** (Indian) – Codified full-body gestures, used in most genres of classical dance and dance-drama in India.

**Mukhabhinaya** (Indian) – Facial acting, or facial gesture, in kutiyattam.

**Musumeyaku** (Japanese) – Female performers of female roles in the Takarazuka.

**Muwaixi** (Chinese) – 'Out of curtain scenes' – Practice in Beijing Opera of performing transitional scenes in front of a curtain to hide set changes.

**Nangiyar** (Indian) – Female performer who accompanies the chakyar on stage, she performs female roles and when the chakyar performs keeps the rhythm on a pair of cymbals (kuzhithalam).

**Natya** (Indian) – Drama.

**Natyasastra** (Indian) – Literally 'the science of drama', a Sanskrit treatise on aesthetics attributed to Bharata, The Natyasastra divides acting into four main components: vachika, vocal expression; angika, physical expression through the body; satvika, emotional expression through the face; and aharya, makeup and costuming.

**Nautanki** (Indian) – A genre of performance named after the heroine of its most popular stories.

**Netrabhinaya** (Indian) – Eye acting, or eye gestures in kutiyattam.

**Nirvahanam** (Indian) – Elaboration. G. Venu, in Production of a Play in Kutiyattam, defines nirvahanam: It is not the original text as it is, that is presented in Kutiyattam. One act of the original drama is selected and adding numerous details not entirely irrelevant, but drawing from a fertile imagination, the presentation of that single act is lengthened for days and days! This lengthening device is called 'Nirvahanam'. In terms of this technique one character of the drama describes in detail the biodata of his own or that of another important character in the story. As all the characters of Kutiyattam are puranic ones, details of their lives given in other puranas than the one used by the dramatist are garnered and included in Nirvahanam. All the verses used for the Nirvahanam are recited by the Nangiar. The actor enact[s] the roles of various characters during the Nirvahanam (1989:100–01).

**Nritta** (Indian) – Dance.

**Oddolaga** (Indian) – The introductory or 'entrance' dance of important characters in yakshagana, in which the character appears little by little from behind a hand-held curtain, an elaboration that can last for as long as 30 minutes.

**Onnagata** (Japanese) – Male performers in kabuki theatre that specialise in female roles.

**Otokoyaku** (Japanese) – Female performers of male roles in the Takarazuka.

**Ovi** (Indian) – A type of music.

**Pandvani** (Indian) – A genre of musical storytelling that originated in the Chhattisgarh region.

**Pativrata** (Indian) – Loyalty to one's husband in the form of taking on his experiences as one's own.

**Post-shingeki** (Japanese) – Modern drama after 1960, reacting against the western influence in shingeki.

**Puja** (Indian) – Sacred offerings to the deities.

**Pya zat** (Burmese) – 'New plays'– the modern theatre of Myanmar/Burma.

*Ramayana* (Indian) – One of the great epics of India.

**Rishi** (Indian) – Sage, wise person.

**Robam kbach boraan** (Cambodian) – Classical court dance of Cambodia.

**Rōen** (Japanse) – The abbreviated title of Workers Theatre Association (Kinrōsha Engeki Kyōkai), which provided discount theatre tickets to its members.

**Sandae gǔk** (Korean) – 'Mountainside Ritual Drama' - a traditional Korean masked theatre form, performed outdoors.

**Sandiwara** (Brunei) – Hybrid form of spoken drama.

**Sangeetnatak** (Indian) - 'Music drama' in nineteenth century India, described either as opera or musical theatre.

**Sân khấu nhỏ** (Vietnamese) – Experimental little theatre.

**Sati** (Indian) – When a widow joins her husband on his funeral pyre both the act and the victim are referred to as sati. The word 'sati' comes from the Sanskrit sat, meaning truth. It originally referred to a woman who was 'true to her ideals' – in other words, a virtuous or pious woman. Because pativrata, or loyalty to one's husband in the form of taking on his experiences as one's own, has become an ideal for women, sati came to be seen by some as the ultimate act of loyalty and fidelity, bringing honour to both the sacrificed widow and her husband's family (Narasimhan 1990:11–12). However, sati is both illegal and widely condemned.

**Satvika** (Indian) – Emotional expression in and through the face.

**Seigeki** (Japanese) – Kawakami Otojiro referred to his theatre as 'seigeki', meaning 'true drama', which he felt reflected reality better than the more stylised kabuki.

**Seiyō kabuki** (Japanese) – 'Western kabuki', the name Meiji Japanese gave to western theatre.

**Shimpa** (Japanese and Korean) – 'New school drama', an early hybrid form of modern drama that was highly melodramatic.

**Shingeki** (Japanese) – 'New theatre' – shingeki is the modern theatre of Japan based on naturalistic models from the west.

**Shingǔk** (Korean) – The Korean version of shingeki, imposed on Korea by the Japanese – A modern, naturalistic theatre based on western models.

**Shinkokugeki** (Japanese) – 'New National Theatre,' a type of hybrid modern theatre developed by Sawada Shōjirō for urban audiences, believing shingeki too elite and kabuki too lowbrow. It was well known for its swordplay.

**Shizuka na engeki** (Japanese) – 'Quiet theatre movement' – a trend in the 1980s that depicted the lives of quiet desperation of the middle class.

**Shōgekijō-undō** (Japanese) – 'Little Theatre Movement', another name for the avant-garde theatre movement that began in the 1960s and continues through the end of the century.

**Sutradhar** (Indian) – The producer and narrator of a Sanskrit drama. Many Sanskrit plays begin with a 'curtain speech' by the sutradhara, announcing the title of the play to be performed, and outlining its plot. The sutradhara brings the audience into the play, linking their world outside the theatre with the world of the play.

**Taehangno** (Korean) – 'University Avenue' – the district of Seoul where many theatres are located.

**Takarazuka** (Japanese) – All female theatre company established in 1912 and continuing to the present specialising in musicals and revues.

**Tamasha** (Indian) – A theatrical genre popular in Western India that developed in the 1600s as a court entertainment for the Peshwa rulers and an entertainment and inspiration for Maratha soldiers.

**Thanathunatakavedi** (Indian) – Literally 'one's own theatre', a term used for a genre of modern theatre in Kerala that is inspired by and incorporates aspects of 'indigenous' genres of performance such as kathakali, kutiyattam and kalarippayattu, a martial art practiced in Kerala, South India and used widely to train actors and dancers.

**Thang-ta** (Indian) – A martial art practiced in Manipur, and used widely for theatre and dance training.

**Thouryathrikam** (Indian) – The combination of geetha (vocal music), nritta (dance) and vadya (instrumental music) to create multisensory and multidimensional moments in performance.

**Thumri** (Indian) – A type of music.

**Tōsō geki** (Japanese) – 'Struggle plays' – Early works by Shimizu Kunio directed by Ninagawa Yukio that depicted the struggles modern human feel in repressive societies in the 1960s.

**Vachika** (Indian) – Vocal expression.

**Vadya** (Indian) – Instrumental music.

**Vag** (Indian) – Plot-based scenario in tamasha.

**Vattattil catinatakkuka** (Indian) – A circular movement pattern in kutiyattam used to indicate that the character is travelling to a distant place.

**Vedas** (Indian) – Religious texts.

**Vidushaka** (Indian) – A clown figure in kutiyattam, his job is to translate the Sanskrit text of the play into Malayalam (the language spoken in Kerala) and to make political and social analogies between events in the play and events in the real world.

**Vivek** (Indian) – A figure in jatra who functions as the conscience of a given character by singing about the character's inner moral conflicts.

**Wenhuaju** (Chinese) – 'Cultural drama' – Early modern spoken drama in China, performed by 'culture societies.'

**Wenmingxi** (Chinese) – Another early name for modern drama in the first two decades of the twentieth century in China, meaning 'civilised drama'.

**Xinju** (Chinese) – 'New Drama', the name given to modern theatre in China in the 1910s to distinguish it from jiuju ('old drama').

**Xin wenhua yundong** (Chinese) – 'New Cultural Movement' – Early twentieth-century movement in China to upend traditional culture, including the theatre.

**Yakshagana** (Indian) – Genre of dance-drama from Karnataka, South India.

**Zangirimono** (Japanese) – Literally 'crop-hair plays', a form of modern drama for the kabuki featuring characters without samurai topknots (and hence, modern), written primarily by Kawatake Mokuami.

# BIBLIOGRAPHY

## General Asian Theatre

Bowers, Faubion, *Theatre in the East: A Survey of Asian Dance and Drama.* New York: Grove, 1956.

Brandon, James R., *Brandon's Guide to Theater in Asia.* Honolulu: University of Hawai'i Press, 1976.

—(ed.), *The Cambridge Guide to Asian Theatre.* Cambridge: Cambridge University Press, 1993.

Leiter, Samuel (ed.), *Encyclopedia of Asian Theatre.* Westport, CT: Greenwood, 2007.

Rubin, Don, Chua Soo Pong, Ravi Chaturvedi, Ramendu Majumdar, Minoru Tanokura and Katharine Brisbane (eds), *The World Encyclopedia of Contemporary Theatre: Asia/Pacific.* London: Routledge, 1998.

Scott, A. C., *The Theatre in Asia.* London: Weidenfeld and Nicolson, 1972.

## Japanese Theatre

Boyd, Mari, *The Aesthetics of Quietude: Ōta Shōgo and the Theatre of Investiture.* Tokyo: Sophia University Press, 2006.

Cavaye, Ronald, Paul Griffith and Akihiko Senda. *A Guide to the Japanese Stage: From Traditional to Cutting Edge.* Tokyo: Kodansha, 2004.

Downer, Lesley, *Madame Sadayakko: The Geisha who Bewitched the West.* New York: Gotham Books, 2003.

Eckersall, Peter, *Theorizing the Angura Space: Avant-garde Performance and Politics in Japan, 1960–2000.* Leiden: Brill, 2006.

Fukushima, Yoshiko, *Manga Discourse in Japanese Theatre.* London: Keegan Paul, 2003.

Goodman, David G. (ed.), *After Apocalypse: Four Japanese Plays of Hiroshima and Nagasaki.* New York: Columbia University Press, 1986.

—, *Japanese Drama and Culture in the 1960s: The Return of the Gods.* Armonk, NY: M.E. Sharpe, 1988.

Hane Mikiso and Louis G. Perez, *Modern Japan: A Historical Survey.* 5th ed. Boulder, CO: Westview, 2013.

Havens, Thomas R. H., *Artist and Patron in Postwar Japan: Dance, Music, Theatre and the Visual Arts, 1955–1980.* Princeton: Princeton University Press, 1982.

Jortner, David, Keiko McDonald, and Kevin J. Wetmore, Jr., (eds), *Modern Japanese Theatre and Performance.* Lanham, MD: Lexington, 2006.

Kano, Ayako, *Acting Like a Woman in Modern Japan: Theater, Gender, and Nationalism.* New York: Palgrave, 2001.

Kawamura Takeshi, *Nippon Wars and Other Plays*. London: Seagull, 2011.

Keene, Donald, *Dawn to the West: Volume 4: Poetry, Drama and Criticism*. New York: Columbia University Press, 1999.

Kikuchi Kan, *History and Trends of Modern Japanese Literature*. Trans. S. Sakabe. Tokyo: Kokusai Bunka Shinkokai, 1936.

Kominz, Laurence (ed.), *Mishima on Stage: The Black Lizard and Other Plays*. Ann Arbor, MI: University of Michigan Center for Japanese Studies, 2007.

Kubo Sakae, *Land of Volcanic Ash*. Trans. David G. Goodman. Ithaca: Cornell East Asia Center, 1993.

Leiter, Samuel L. (ed.), *Rising from the Flames: The Rebirth of Theater in Occupied Japan, 1945–1952*. Lanham, MD: Lexington Books, 2009.

Miller, J. Scott, *Historical Dictionary of Modern Japanese Literature and Theatre*. Lanham, MD: Scarecrow Press, 2009.

Mishima, Yukio, *Five Modern No Plays*. Trans. Donald Keene. Tokyo: Charles Tuttle, 1957.

—, *My Friend Hitler and Other Plays of Yukio Mishima*. New York: Columbia University Press, 2002.

Morinaga Maki Isaka, 'Osanai Kaoru's Dilemma: "Amateurism by Professionals" in Modern Japanese Theatre', *The Drama Review*, Vol. 49, no. 1 (2005), pp.119–33.

Ōyama Isao, *Kindai Nihon Giyoku Shi*, Vol. I, Yamagata: Kindai Nihon Gikyoku Shi Kankō Kai, 1969.

Poulton, M. Cody, *Spirits of Another Sort: The Plays of Izumi Kyōka*. Ann Arbor: University of Michigan, Center for Japanese Studies, 2001.

—, *A Beggar's Art: Scripting Modernity in Japanese Drama, 1900–1930*. Honolulu: University of Hawai'i Press, 2010.

Powell, Brian, *Kabuki in Modern Japan: Mayama Seika and His Plays*. New York: St. Martin's Press, 1990.

—, *Japan's Modern Theatre: A Century of Continuity and Change*. London: Japan Library, 2002.

Ridgely, Steven C., *Japanese Counterculture: The Antiestablishment Art of Terayama Shūji*. Minneapolis: University of Minnesota Press, 2010.

Rimer, J. Thomas, *Toward a Modern Japanese Theatre: Kishida Kunio*. Princeton: Princeton University Press, 1974.

Robertson, Jennifer, *Takarazuka: Sexual Politics and Popular Culture in Modern Japan*. Berkeley: University of California Press, 1998.

Rolf, Robert T. and John K. Gillespie (eds), *Alternative Japanese Drama*. Honolulu: University of Hawaii Press, 1992.

Senda Akihiko, 'Performing Arts Now in Japan: Trends in Contemporary Japanese Theatre'. New York: Japan Foundation, n.d.

—, *The Voyage of Contemporary Japanese Theatre*. Trans. J. Thomas Rimer. Honolulu: University of Hawaii Press, 1997.

Shields, Nancy K., *Fake Fish: The Theater of Kobo Abe*. New York: Weatherhill, 1996.

Sorgenfrei, Carol Fisher, *Unspeakable Acts: The Avant-Garde Theatre of Terayama Shūji and Postwar Japan*. Honolulu: University of Hawai'i Press, 2005.

Takaya, Ted T., *Modern Japanese Drama: An Anthology*. New York: Columbia University Press, 1979.

Bibliography

# Bibliography

Toita Kōji, 'Early Meiji Kabuki' in Komiya Toyotaka (ed.), *Japanese Music and Drama in the Meiji Era*. Trans. Donald Keene, Tokyo: Toyo Bunko, 1956.

Uchino Tadashi, 'Images of Armageddon: Japan's 1980s' Theatre Culture'. *TDR,* Vol. 44, No. 1 (2000), pp.85–96.

Yamanashi, Makiko, *A History of the Takarazuka Revue Since 1914*. Leiden: Global Oriental, 2012.

# Chinese Theatre

Braester, Yomi, *Painting the City Red: Chinese Cinema and the Urban Contract*. Durham: Duke University Press, 2010.

Brecht, Bertolt, 'Life of Galileo', 2007, http://buehnenkunst.ohost.de/auditions_coming_up_files/Life of Galileo by Brecht.pdf (accessed 15 May 2013).

Chen, Baichen and Dong Jian (eds), *Zhongguo xiandai xiju shigao* (*A Draft History of Modern Chinese Drama*). 2nd ed. Beijing: Zhongguo xiju chubanshe, 2008.

Chen, Xiaomei, *Acting the Right Part: Political Theater and Popular Drama in Contemporary China*. Honolulu: University of Hawai'i Press, 2002.

—(ed.), *Reading the Right Text: An Anthology of Contemporary Chinese Drama*. Honolulu: University of Hawai'i Press, 2003.

—(ed.), *The Columbia Anthology of Modern Chinese Drama*. New York: Columbia University Press, 2010.

Chen Yun, 'Nianqing de yidai' (The Young Generation), *Juben*, No. 8 (1963), pp.42–68.

Chen Zidu, Yang Jian, and Zhu Xiaoping, 'Sangshuping jishi' (Sangshuping Chronicles), *Juben*, No. 4 (1988), pp.4–28.

Cheung, Martha P. Y. and Jane C. C. Lai (eds), *An Oxford Anthology of Contemporary Chinese Drama*. New York: Oxford University Press, 1997.

Conceison, Claire, *Significant Other: Staging the American in China*. Honolulu: University of Hawai'i Press, 2004.

Cong Shen, 'Zhuni jiankang' (To Your Health), *Juben,* No. 11 (1963), pp.2–43.

Cui Dezhi, 'Baochunhua' (Winter Jasmine), *Juben*, No. 2 (1979), pp.2–40.

—, 'Liu Lianying', *Renmin wenxue*, No. 4 (1955), pp.65–81.

Cui Dezhi, et al., *Saturday Afternoon at the Mill and Other One-Act Plays*. Beijing: Foreign Languages Press, 1957.

Diamond, Catherine, 'Reflected and Refracted: Metatheatrics in Taiwan', *Journal of Dramatic Theory and Criticism*, Vol. 9, No. 2 (1995), pp.85–96.

Dong Jian and Hu Xingliang, *Zhongguo dangdai xiju shigao, 1949–2000* (*A Draft History of Contemporary Chinese Drama*). Beijing: Zhongguo xiju chubanshe, 2008.

Duan Chengbin, 'Bei yiwangle de shiqing' (Something Forgotten), *Juben*, No. 1 (1957), pp.3–15.

Ebon, Martin (ed.), *Five Chinese Communist Plays*. New York: John Day Co, 1975.

Fang Zixun and Tian Benxiang (eds), *Xianggang huaju xuan* (*Selected Spoken Drama Plays of Hong Kong*). Beijing: Wenhua yishu chubanshe, 1994.

Fei, Faye Chunfang (trans. and ed.) *Chinese Theories of Theater and Performance from Confucius to the Present*. Ann Arbor: University of Michigan Press, 1999.

Ferrari, Rossella, *Pop Goes the Avant-Garde: Experimental Theater in Contemporary China*. Calcutta: Seagull Books, 2013.

Gao Xingjian, *Gao Xingjian xiju ji (Collected Plays by Gao Xingjian)*. Beijing: Qunzhong chubanshe, 1985.

—, *The Other Shore: Plays by Gao Xingjian*. Trans. Gilbert Fong. Hong Kong: Chinese University Press, 2000.

Gunn, Edward M. (ed.), *Twentieth-Century Chinese Drama: An Anthology*. Bloomington: Indiana University Press, 1983.

Guo Moruo, *Selected Works of Guo Moruo: Five Historical Plays*. Beijing: Foreign Language Press, 1984.

Hai Mo, 'Dongxiao hengchui' (The Vertical Flute is Played Horizontally), *Juben*, No. 11 (1956), pp.3–46.

He Qiu, 'Xin juzhang laidao zhiqian' (Before the New Director Arrives), *Juben*, No. 4 (1955), pp.29–45.

Hong Shen, 'Xiju Xieshe pianduan' (A Fragment on the Drama Association) in Tian Han et al. (eds), *Zhongguo huaju yundong wushinian shiliaoji* (Collected Materials of Fifty Years of Chinese Spoken Drama), Vol. 1, Beijing: Zhongguo xiju chubanshe, 1958, pp.107–11.

Huang, Alexander C. Y., *Chinese Shakespeares: Two Centuries of Cultural Exchange*. New York: Columbia University Press, 2009.

Jin Jian, 'Zhao Xiaolan', *Juben*, No. 1 (1953), pp.5–24.

Jin Zhenjia and Wang Jingyu, 'Fengye hongle de shihou' (When the Maple Leaves Turned Red), *Renmin xiju*, No. 4 (1977), pp.22–50.

Jinyun, 'Gou'erye niepan' (Uncle Doggie's Nirvana), *Juben*, No. 6 (1986), pp.4–30.

Kenley, David, *Modern Chinese History*. Ann Arbor: Association for Asian Studies, 2012.

Lan Cheng, 'Fengshou zhihou' (After the Harvest), *Juben*, No. 2 (1964), pp.6–39.

Leiter, Samuel L. and Daniel Yang, 'The Hong Kong Repertory Theatre: An Interview with Daniel Yang', *Asian Theatre Journal*, Vol. 10, No. 2 (1993), pp.191–201.

Li Hong, 'Di sizhong juben' (The Fourth Type of Play), *Nanjing ribao (Nanjing Daily)*, 11 June 1957.

Li Longyu, 'Xiaojing hutong' (Small Well Lane), No. 5 (1981), pp.36–76.

Li Ruru, *Shashibiya: Staging Shakespeare in China*. Hong Kong: Hong Kong University Press, 2003.

—, *The Soul of Beijing Opera: Theatrical Creativity and Continuity in the Changing World*. Hong Kong: Hong Kong University Press, 2010.

Li Zhun, Zhao Jishen, and Yang Lanchun, 'Li Shuangshuang', *Juben*, No. 7 (1963), pp.2–31.

Liley, Rozanna, *Staging Hong Kong: Gender and Performance in Transition*. Hawaii: University of Hawaii Press, 1999.

Liu Chun, 'Zouxiang ziyou–Mou Sen he tade xiju' (Toward Freedom–Mou Sen and His Theatre), *Huanghe*, No. 12 (1997), pp.156–75.

Liu Shugang, 'Yige sizhe dui shengzhe de fangwen' (The Dead Visiting the Living), *Juben*, No. 5 (1985), pp.8–37.

Liu, Siyuan, '"A Mixed-Blooded Child, Neither Western Nor Eastern"–Sinicization of Western-Style Theatre in Rural China in the 1930s', *Asian Theatre Journal*, Vol. 25, No. 2 (2008), pp.272–97.

# Bibliography

—, *Performing Hybridity in Colonial-Modern China*. New York: Palgrave Macmillan, 2013.

—, 'Theatre Reform as Censorship-Censoring Traditional Theatre in China in the Early 1950s', *Theatre Journal*, Vol. 61, No. 3 (2009), pp.387–404.

Lu Yanzhou, 'Guilai' (The Return), *Juben*, No. 4 (1956), pp.57–68.

Luk, Yun Tong, 'Post-Colonialism and Contemporary Hong Kong Theatre: Two Case Studies', *New Theatre Quarterly*, Vol. 14, No. 56 (1998), pp.366–72.

Ma Sen, *Xichao xia de Zhongguo xiandai xiju* (*Modern Chinese Drama Under Western Waves*). Taipei: Shulin, 1994.

Ma Zhongjun, Jia Hongyuan, and Qu Xinhua, 'Wuwai you reliu' (Hot Currents Outside the House), *Juben*, No. 6 (1980), pp.55–65.

MacKenzie, Clayton G, 'Questions of Identity in Contemporary Hong Kong Theater', *Comparative Drama*, Vol. 29, No. 2 (1995), pp.203–15.

McDougall, Bonnie S., and Paul Clark (eds), *Popular Chinese Literature and Performing Arts in the People's Republic of China, 1949–1979*. Berkeley: University of California Press, 1984.

Meng Jinghui, *Meng Jinghui xianfeng xiju dang'an* (*Meng Jinghui Avant-Garde Theater Dossier*). Beijing: Xinxing chubanshe, 2010.

Meserve, Walter J. and Ruth I. Meserve (eds), *Modern Drama from Communist China*. New York: New York University Press, 1970.

Miller, Arthur, *Salesman in Beijing*. New York: Viking Press, 1984.

Quah, Sy Ren., *Gao Xingjian and Transcultural Chinese Theater*. Honolulu: University of Hawai'i Press, 2004.

Sha Yexin, 'Chen Yi shizhang' (Mayor Chen Yi), *Juben*, No. 5 (1980), pp.2–39.

—, *Sha Yexin juzuoxuan* (*Selected Plays of Sha Yexin*). Nanchang: Jiangxi renmin chubanshe, 1986.

—, *Yesu, Kongzi, Pitoushi Lienong* (*Jesus Christ, Confucius, and John Lennon*). Shanghai: Shanghai wenyi chubanshe, 1989.

Shen Ximeng, 'Nihong dengxia de shaobing' (Guards under the Neon Light), *Juben*, No. 3 (1963), pp.2–41.

Shi Yan, 'Xiju de xungen zui chedi–Lin Kehuan fangtan' (Theatre's Search for Root was the Most Thorough–Interview with Lin Kehuan), *Nanfang zhoumo* (*Southern Weekend*), 11 December 2008.

Snow, Lois Wheeler, *China on Stage: an American Actress in the People's Republic*. New York: Random House, 1972.

Sun Huizhu and Zhang Mali, 'Guazai qiangshang de Lao B' (Old B on the Wall), *Juben*, No. 3 (1985), pp.31–41.

Sun Yu, 'Funü daibiao' (The Women's Representative), *Juben*, No. 3 (1953), pp.13–34.

—, 'Funü daibiao de xiezuo jingguo' (The Writing Process of 'The Women's Representative'), *Juben*, No. 3 (1953), pp.83–97.

Tian Benxiang and Fang Zixun (eds), *Xianggang huaju shigao* (*A Draft History of Hong Kong Spoken Drama*). Shenyang: Liaoning jiaoyu chubanshe, 2009.

Tian Han, 'Guan Hanqing', *Juben*, No. 5 (1958), pp.2–29.

—, *Tian Han quanji* (Collected Works of Tian Han), Vol. 15, Beijing: Wenhua yishu chubanshe, 2000.

Tian Qinxin, *Tian Qinxin de xi ju ben* (*Tian Qinxin's Play Scripts*). Beijing: Beijing daxue chubanshe, 2010.

Tung, Constantine and Colin Mackerras (eds), *Drama in the People's Republic of China*. Albany: State University of New York Press, 1987.

Wagner, Rudolf G., *The Contemporary Chinese Historical Drama*. Berkeley: University of California Press, 1990.

Wang Jifang, *Ershi siji zuihou de langman: Beijing ziyou yishujia shenghuo shilu* (*Last Romance of the Twentieth Century: Documents of Freelance Artists in Beijing*). Beijing: Beifang wenyi chubanshe, 1999.

Wang Peigong, 'WM (Women)', *Juben*, No. 5 (1985), pp.6–23.

Wang Shaoyan, 'Putao lanle' (The Grapes Are Rotten), *Juben*, No. 3 (1955), pp.107–23.

Wei Min, Meng Bing, and Lin Lang, 'Hongbai xishi' (Weddings and Funerals), *Juben*, No. 5 (1984), pp.1–40.

Weinstein, John B., 'Ding Xilin and Chen Baichen: Building a Modern Theater through Comedy', *Modern Chinese Literature and Culture*, Vol. 20, No. 2 (2008), pp.92–130.

—, 'Multilingual Theater in Contemporary Taiwan', *Modern Chinese Literature and Culture*, Vol. 17, No. 2 (2000), pp.269–83.

Xing Ye, 'Kaihui' (The Meeting), *Juben*, No. 3 (1953), pp.58–67.

Yan, Haiping, 'Modern Chinese Drama and Its Western Models: A Critical Reconstruction of Chinese Subjectivity', *Modern Drama*, No. 35 (1992), pp.54–64.

—(ed.), *Theater and Society: An Anthology of Contemporary Chinese Drama*. Armonk, NY: M.E. Sharpe, 1998.

Yang, Daniel S. P., 'King Lear in Beijing and Hong Kong', *Asian Theatre Journal*, Vol. 28, No. 1 (2011), pp.184–98.

Yang Lüfang, 'Buguniao you jiaole' (The Cuckoo Sings Again), *Juben*, No. 1 (1957), pp.34–69.

Ying Ruocheng and Claire Conceison, *Voices Carry: Behind Bars and Backstage During China's Revolution and Reform*. Lanham, MD: Rowman & Littlefield, 2008.

Yu Jian, 'Xiju zuowei dongci, yu aizi youguan' (Theatre as Verb, Related to AIDS), *Huacheng*, No. 8 (1996), pp.117–26.

Yue Ye, 'Tonggan gongku' (Through Thick and Thin), *Juben*, No. 10 (1956), pp.3–50.

Zhang Guangnian, 'Tan dumuju' (On One-Act Plays), *Juben*, No. 5 (1954), pp.10–14.

Zhang Wentian and Wang Fuquan, 'Wang'erde jieshao' (Introduction to Wilde), in Wenxu yanjiuhui (ed.), *De Profundis* (*Yu zhong ji*), Shanghai: Shangwu yinshuguan, 1932 (1922), pp.1–66.

Zhao Huan, 'Nanhai changcheng' (Great Wall of the South China Sea), *Juben*, No. 4 (1964), pp.5–37.

Zhao, Yiheng, *Towards a Modern Zen Theatre: Gao Xingjian and Chinese Theatre Experimentalism*. London: School of Oriental and African Studies, University of London, 2000.

Zong Fuxian, 'Yu wu sheng chu' (In the Land of Silence), *Renmin wenxue*, No. 6 (1978), pp.49–76.

Zuni Icosahedron, 'Zuni Icosahedron', http://www.zuni.org.hk/ (accessed 20 May 2013).

—, 'Zuni Icosahedron YouTube Channel', http://www.youtube.com/user/zuniicosahedron (accessed 20 May 2013).

# Korean Theatre

Clark, Donald N., *Korea in World History*. Ann Arbor: Association for Asian Studies, 2012.

Jang Won-Jae, *Irish Influences on Korean Theatre During the 1920s and 1930s*. Gerrards Cross: Colin Smythe Limited, 2002.

Kardoss, John, *An Outline History of Korean Drama*. Greenvale, NY: Long Island University Press, 1966.

Kim Joungwon (ed.), *Korean Cultural Heritage Volume III: Performing Arts*. Seoul: The Korea Foundation, 1997.

Kim Suk-Young, *Illusive Utopia: Theatre Film and Everyday Performance in North Korea*. Ann Arbor: University of Michigan Press, 2010.

Kim Yun-Cheol and Kim Miy-he (eds), *Contemporary Korean Theatre: Playwrights, Directors, Stage-Designers*. Seoul: Theatre and Mann Press, 2000.

Korean National Commission for UNESCO, *Korean Dance, Theater and Cinema*. Seoul: The Si-sa-yong-o-sa Publishers, 1983.

Lee Kang-baek, *Allegory of Survival: The Theatre of Kang-baek Lee*. Trans. Alyssa Kim and Hyung-jin Lee. Youngstown, NY: Cambria Press, 2007.

Lee Yun-Taek, *Four Contemporary Korean Plays*. Trans. Dongwook Kim and Richard Nichols. Lanham, MD: University Press of America, 2007.

Nichols, Richard (ed.), *Modern Korean Drama: An Anthology*. New York: Columbia University Press, 2009.

Oh T'ae-Sŏk, *The Metacultural Theater of Oh T'ae-Sŏk*. Trans. Ah-jeong Kim and R. B. Graves. Honolulu: University of Hawai'i Press, 1999.

Parquet, Darcy, *New Korean Cinema: Breaking the Waves*. London: Wallflower, 2009.

Robinson, Michael, 'Contemporary Cultural Production in South Korea: Vanishing Meta-Narratives of Nation' in Chi-Yun Shin and Julian Stringer (eds), *New Korean Cinema*, New York: New York University Press, 2005, pp.15–31.

Yang Hye-suk (ed.), *Korean Performing Arts: Drama, Dance & Music Theatre*. Seoul: Jipmoondang Publishing Company, 1997.

Yoon Min-Kyung, 'North Korean Art Works: Historical Paintings and the Cult of Personality', *Korean Histories*, Vol. 3, no. 1 (2012), pp.53–72.

Yu Ch'ijin and Ch'ae Man-sik, *Korean Drama under Japanese Occupation*. Trans. Jinhee Kim. Paramus, NJ: Homa & Sekey Books, 2004.

Yuh Ji Hyon Kayla, 'The Great White Way Revived in Seoul' in Kevin J. Wetmore, Jr. (ed.), *Portrayals of Americans on the World Stage: Critical Essays*, Jefferson, NC: McFarland, 2009, pp.214–24.

# Indian Theatre

Anand, Uma, 'Emergence of a National Theatre in India', *Indian and Foreign Review*, Vol. 11, No. 17 (1974), pp.16–17.

Awasthi, Suresh, '"Theatre of Roots": Encounter with Tradition', *TDR*, Vol. 33, No. 4 (1989), pp.48–69.

Banerjee, Sumanta, *The Parlour and the Streets: Elite and Popular Culture in Nineteenth Century Calcutta*. Kolkata: Seagull Books, 1989.

Bannerji, Hemani, 'Language and Liberation: A Study of Political Theatre in Bengal', *Ariel*, Vol. 15 (1984), pp.131–44.

Bhabha, Homi, *The Location of Culture*. London: Routledge, 1994.

Bharucha, Rustom, *Rehearsals of Revolution: The Political Theatre of Bengal*. Honolulu: University of Hawai'i Press, 1983.

Bhatia, Nandi, *Staging a Change: Modern Indian Drama and the Colonial Encounter*. PhD diss., University of Texas, Austin, 1996.

—, 'Staging Resistance: The Indian People's Theatre Association' in Lisa Lowe and David Lloyd (eds), *The Politics of Culture in the Shadow of Capital*, Durham: Duke University Press, 1997.

—, 'Staging the 1857 Mutiny as "The Great Rebellion": Colonial History and Post-Colonial Interventions in Utpal Dutt's *Mahavidroh*', *Theatre Journal*, Vol. 51 (1999), pp.167–84.

—, *Acts of Authority/Acts of Resistance: Theater and Politics in Colonial and Postcolonial India*. Ann Arbor: University of Michigan Press, 2004.

Bhattacharya, Malini, 'The IPTA in Bengal', *Journal of Arts and Ideas*, No. 2 (January-March 1983), pp.5–22.

Bhattacharya, P. K. *Shadow Over Stage*. Kolkata: Barnali, 1989.

Chatterjee, Sudipto. *The Colonial Stage(d)*. PhD diss., New York University. 1998.

Courtwright, Paul, *Ganesha: Lord of Obstacles, Lord of Beginnings*. New York: Oxford University Press, 1985.

Dattani, Mahesh, *Collected Plays*. New Delhi: Penguin, 2000.

—, Email to the author, 26 November 2003.

Deshpande, G. P. (ed.), *Modern Indian Drama: An Anthology*. Delhi: Sahitya Akademi, 2000.

Dharwadker, Aparna, *Theatres of Independence: Drama, Theory, and Urban Performance in India Since 1947*. Iowa City: University of Iowa Press, 2005.

Gargi, Balwant, *Theatre in India*. New York: Theatre Arts Books, 1962.

—, *Folk Theatre of India*. Calcutta: Rupa and Co, 1991 [1966].

Gokhale, Shanta, *Playwright at the Centre: Marathi Drama from 1843 to the Present*. Calcutta: Seagull Books, 2000.

Gupt, Bharat, *Dramatic Concepts Greek and Indian*. Delhi: D.K. Printworld, 1994.

Hashmi, Safdar, *The Right to Perform*. Delhi: Samat, 1989.

Jacob, Paul (ed.), *Contemporary Indian Theatre: Interviews with Playwrights and Directors*. Delhi: Sangeet Natak Akademi, 1989.

Jain, Kirti, 'In Search of a Narrative: Women Theatre Directors of the Northern Belt' in Subramanyam, Lakshmi (ed.), *Muffled Voices: Women in Modern Indian Theatre*, New Delhi: Shakti, 2002.

Kambar, Chandrasekhar (ed.), *Modern Indian Plays (Vols 1 and 2)*. Delhi: National School of Drama, 2000.

Karanth, K. S., *Yakshagana*. Delhi: Abhinav Publications, 1997 [1975].

Karnad, Girish, 'The Arts and Social Change in India' in Karel Werdler, Girish Karnad, Felix van Lamsveerde and Urvashi Butaliam (eds), *Indian Culture in Motion*, Amsterdam: Royal Tropical Institute, 1998.

—, *The Fire and The Rain*. Delhi: Oxford University Press, 1998.

—, *Naga-Mandala, Play With a Cobra*. Delhi: Oxford University Press, 1990.

—, *Tale-Danda*. Delhi: Ravi Dayal, 1993.

—, *Three Plays*. Delhi: Oxford University Press, 1994.

Kaushal, J. N., 'Last Month in Delhi: *Hayavadan*', *Enact*, Vol. 63 (1972), np.

Kumar, Sheila, 'What to do with Baby Corn', *The Sunday Review*, 21 June 1998.

Lal, Ananda (ed.), *The Oxford Companion to Indian Theatre*. Delhi: Oxford University Press, 2004.

Mangai, A., 'Cultural Intervention through Theatre: Case Study of a Play on Female Infanticide/Foeticide', *Economic and Political Weekly*, Vol. 33, No. 44 (1998), pp.70–2.

Mangai, A, S., Raja Samuel and Mina Swaminathan, 'Confronting Discrimination: Some Approaches to the Issue of Female Infanticide', *Search Bulletin*, July-September 1998, pp.64–74.

Mee, Erin B., 'Contemporary Indian Theatre, Three Voices', *Performing Arts Journal*, Vol. 19, No. 1 (1997), pp.1–26.

—, *Theatre of Roots: Redirecting the Modern Indian Stage*. Kolkata: Seagull, 2009.

—(ed.), *Drama Contemporary: India*. Baltimore: Johns Hopkins University Press, 2001.

Mee, Erin and Helene Foley (eds), *Antigone on the Contemporary World Stage*. Oxford: Oxford University Press, 2011.

Mehta, Kumudini Arvind, *English Drama on the Bombay Stage in the Late Eighteenth Century and in the Nineteenth Century*. Bombay: University of Bombay, 1960.

Mukherjee, Sushil, *The Story of the Calcutta Theatres 1753–1980*. Calcutta: K. P. Bagchi & Company, 1982.

National School of Drama, Brochure for the Bharat Rang Mahotsav, 2002.

—, Brochure for the Bharat Rang Mahotsav, 2003.

—, Brochure for the Bharat Rang Mahotsav, 2007.

Panikkar, Kavalam Narayana, *The Right To Rule and Domain of the Sun*. Kolkata: Seagull Books, 1989.

—, *Karimkutty and The Lone Tusker*. Kolkata: Seagull Books, 1992.

—, '*Karimkutty*: From Written Script to Action Text', *Seagull Theatre Quarterly*, Vol. 7 (1995), pp.62–4.

—, 'Contemporary Indian Theatre, Three Voices', *Performing Arts Journal*, Vol. 19, No. 1 (1997), pp.1–26.

Pradhan, Sudhir, *Marxist Cultural Movements in India: Chronicles and Documents: 1936–47*. Calcutta: National Book Agency, 1979.

Rangacharya, Adya, *The Indian Theatre*. New Delhi: National Book Trust. 1971.

Roy, Amitava, 'Folk Is What Sells Well' in Bimal Mukerjee and Sunil Kothari (eds), *RASA, The Indian Performing Arts in the Last Twenty-Five Years*, Calcutta: Anamika Kala Sangam Trust, 1995.

Sangeet Natak Akademi (SNA), *On Indian Drama and Theatre*. Seminar proceedings. Delhi: Sangeet Natak Akademi. 1956.

—, 'Round-Table on the Contemporary Relevance of Traditional Theatre', *Sangeet Natak*. Special issue. Delhi: Sangeet Natak Akademi. 1971.

—, 'Traditional Idiom in Contemporary Theatre', *Sangeet Natak*. Special issue. Delhi: Sangeet Natak Akademi, 1985.

—, *Annual Report*. Delhi: Sangeet Natak Akademi, 1986–7.

—, *Contemporary Indian Theatre: Interviews with Playwrights and Directors*. Delhi: Sangeet Natak Akademi, 1989.

Sharma, Tripurari, 'Playwright, Director, Activist: An Interview with Tripurari Sharma', *Seagull Theatre Quarterly*, Vol. 20/21 (1999), pp.99–132.

Solomon, Rakesh, 'Culture, Imperialism, and Nationalist Resistance: Performance in Colonial India', *Theatre Journal*, Vol. 46 (1994), pp.323–47.

Subramanyam, Lakshmi (ed.), *Muffled Voices: Women in Modern Indian Theatre*. Delhi: Shakti Books, 2002.

van Erven, Eugene, *The Playful Revolution: Theatre and Liberation in Asia*. Bloomington: Indiana University Press, 1992.

Venu, G., *Production of a Play in Kutiyattam*. Trissur: Natana Kairali, 1989.

## Southeast Asian Theatre

Bodden, Michael H., *Resistance on the National Stage: Theatre and Politics in Late New Order Indonesia*. Athens, OH: Ohio University Press, 2010.

Brandon, James, *Theatre in Southeast Asia*. Cambridge: Harvard University Press, 1967.

Cohen, Matthew Isaac, *Performing Otherness: Java and Bali on International Stages, 1905–1952*. London: Palgrave McMillan, 2010.

Diamond, Catherine, 'Parallel Streams: Two Currents of Difference in Kuala Lumpur's Contemporary Theatre', *TDR*, Vol. 46, No. 2 (2002), pp.7–46.

—, 'Dreaming our own Dreams: Singapore Monodrama and the Individual Talent', *New Theatre Quarterly*, Vol. 24, No. 2 (2008), pp.170–88.

—, *Communities of Imagination: Contemporary Southeast Asian Theatres*. Honolulu: University of Hawai'i Press, 2012.

Durand, Maurice M. and Nguyen Tran Huan, *An Introduction to Vietnamese Literature*. Trans. D. M. Hawke. New York: Columbia University Press, 1985.

Hatley, Barbara, *Javanese Performance on an Indonesian Stage: Contesting Culture, Embracing Change*. Honolulu: University of Hawai'i Press, 2008.

Kee Thuan Chye, *The Big Purge*. Singapore: Times Editions, 2004.

—, *1984 Here and Now*. Singapore: Times Editions, 2004.

Kuo Pao Kun, *The Coffin is Too Big for the Hole and Other Plays*. Singapore: Times Books, 1990.

Nanney, Nancy, 'Malaysian Theatre Resources', *Asian Theatre Journal*, Vol. 29, No. 2 (2012), pp.402–18.

Nguyen, Khai Thu, 'Marking the Nation from the Outside: Vietnamese Americans as Abject in the Vietnamese Play *Dạ Cổ Hoài Lang*' in Kevin J. Wetmore, Jr. (ed.), *Portrayals of Americans on the World Stage*, Jefferson, NC: McFarland & Company, 2009, pp.163–78.

Obermeyer, Ziad, Christopher J. L. Murray and Emmanuela Gakidou, 'Fifty Years of Violent War Deaths from Vietnam to Bosnia: Analysis of Data from the World Health Survey Programme', *British Medical Journal*, Vol. 336 (2008), pp.1482–86.

Philip, Susan, 'Kee Thuan Chye's Political Plays: An Analysis', *Asian Theatre Journal,* Vol. 29, No. 2 (2012), pp.355–478.

Wetmore, Jr., Kevin J., '*Samritechak* and Intercultural Shakespeare in Cambodia' in Alexander C. Y. Huang and Charles S. Ross. (eds), *Shakespeare in Hollywood, Asia and Cyberspace,* West Lafayette, IN: Purdue University Press, 2009, pp.166–71.

Winet, Evan Darwin, 'The Critical Absence of Indonesia in W.S. Rendra's Village' in Kiki Gounaridou (ed.), *Staging Nationalism: Essays on Theatre and National Identity,* Jefferson, NC: McFarland and Company, 2005, pp.141–67.

—, *Indonesian Postcolonial Theatre: Spectral Genealogies and Absent Forces.* London: Palgrave McMillan, 2010.

# For Additional Drama in English see the Following Bibliographies:

## Chinese Drama:
Liu Siyuan and Kevin J. Wetmore, Jr, 'Modern Chinese Drama in English: A Selective Bibliography', *Asian Theatre Journal,* Vol. 26, No.2 (2009), pp.320–51.

## Japanese Drama:
Wetmore, Jr., Kevin J., 'Modern Japanese Drama in English', *Asian Theatre Journal,* Vol. 23, No. 1 (2006), pp.177–203.

## Korean Drama:
Nichols, Richard (ed.), *Modern Korean Drama: An Anthology.* New York: Columbia University Press, 2009, pp.319–25.

# INDEX